The Dressing Drink

A Memoir

An orphan's legacy intertwines triumph and tragedy, revealing the truth behind the glamour—sip carefully, one unforgettable page at a time.

Thomas King Flagg

Dressing Drink – n. A ritualistic or habitual alcoholic beverage consumed while getting dressed, often before an event, night out, or performance. It can symbolize anticipation, confidence-building, or a moment of personal indulgence before stepping into a public role. For some, it's a solitary pause of reflection; for others, a social cue signaling the beginning of the evening's transformation.

ISBN: 979-8-9996442-5-1 (Flagg Publishing LLC)

The Dressing Drink © 2025 by Thomas King Flagg

All rights reserved:

This literary work is a work of fiction based in part on family stories and recollections. The author has exercised creative license in crafting the narrative, characters, and events portrayed herein. While inspired by family history, this work does not purport to be an accurate or factual account of actual events or persons. The author has taken creative liberties in adapting, embellishing, and reimagining family stories and recollections for literary purposes. This work is not intended to be, and should not be construed as, an accurate historical or biographical account. Readers should not rely on this work as a source of factual information about the author's family history or any real persons or events.

All names, characters, places, and incidents in this work are either products of the author's imagination or are used fictitiously. Any resemblance to actual persons, living or dead, or actual events is coincidental, except where clearly stated otherwise.

All trademarks appearing in this book are the property of their respective owners. This book may not be re-sold or given away to other people. If you'd like to share this book with another person, please purchase an additional copy for each person you share it with.

The Dressing Drink © 2025 Flagg Publishing LLC. All rights are reserved, including the right to reproduce this book or portions thereof. No part of this book may be reproduced in any form without the author's express written permission.

Life is, in fact, a battle, evil is insolent and strong; beauty enchanting but rare; goodness very apt to be weak; folly very apt to be defiant; wickedness to carry the day; imbeciles to be in great places, people of sense in small, and mankind generally unhappy. But the world as it stands is no illusion, no phantasm, no evil dream of a night; we wake up to it again for ever and ever; we can neither forget it nor deny it nor dispense with it.

—*Henry James*

Thomas King Flagg
2024

1

Dear Reader,

You'll find no gaudy bunting outside this tent, no barker crying, "Step right up, step right up, ladies and gentlemen." No fire eaters. No Fat Lady taking damp paper tickets, no midgets who hold an arcane knowledge of the sordid in their sly smiles. Only me: the major attraction of this very private, quite exclusive Side Show.

I am sometimes billed as:

The Boy with the Amazing Invisible Father, or

The Boy with the Amazing High-Flying Mother, but usually I appear as the Boy with the Missing Pieces.

In my act I shuffle scrapbooks, study blurry photos, and paste together explanations of Who They Were. I work alone, accompanied only by my typewriter. But this tent is filled with memories. Some are real. Some are imaginary. Don't be shy. Don't be embarrassed for me. Come on in. See the show.

My act begins with Mother. She was never called Mom, or Mama, or Mammy. Only Mother. Her unique act with dogs, young son, and cocktail shaker was also a solo. A "dressing drink" provided the necessary charger to get through dinner. Or the three-martini lunch. She worked high above the center ring of Philadelphia society, and she had a class act. Her name was Dorothy Mary Flagg. People still remember. She never used a safety net.

Dorothy Mary Flagg
(The Mother of Thomas King Flagg)

2

Radnor, Pennsylvania
"Denbigh"
March 1932

Discouraged, Dorothy Mary reached beneath her horse's belly, undid the girth, and slid off the saddle. As she stored it in the tack room and rubbed the chestnut, Tzar, down, Dorothy Mary thought about the rescue mission with her friends. No luck today. They hadn't found the Lindbergh baby. Not even another clue. Not a strange footprint in the woods and fields surrounding Denbigh, her family's estate. No, the FCL Jr.s hadn't had any luck today at all.

Dorothy Mary, Allison Simpson, and Maggie Clothier had formed their secret society, the FCL Jr. (which stood for Find Charles Lindbergh Jr.), after Dorothy Mary had found a muddied blue baby's cap in the woods behind Denbigh House. Twenty-month-old Charles Lindbergh had just been taken from his crib in Hopewell, New Jersey. The radio and newspapers blazed with news of the kidnapping. Dorothy Mary knew that none of the servants had an infant, and there were no babies in her family. In addition, New Jersey wasn't too far away. It seemed inescapable logic to the sixth grader that the kidnapper—a tall, foreign man with a knife in his hand and the baby tucked beneath an arm—had hidden the child somewhere around Denbigh. The purpose of the FCL Jr.s was to rescue the baby before he died of hunger.

Each FCL Jr. member had a special responsibility. Maggie Clothier listened to the radio each night and gathered the latest kidnapping news. Allison Simpson was in charge of keeping the baby warm once they found him. She brought a red rubber hot water bottle and an extra sweater every day. Dorothy Mary was in charge of feeding the baby.

She brought a doll bottle filled with cream and kept it warm and ready for little Charles Lindbergh by carrying it beneath her undershirt, next to her skin.

Every day after their classes at Miss Shipley's were over, the FCL Jr.s gathered at Denbigh's stable to comb the woods and fields on horseback. They looked for footprints and listened for a baby's whimpering; but so far, they heard nothing and discovered no other clues.

Dorothy Mary with her horses

Dorothy Mary gave Tzar a final pat goodnight, closed his stall and left the stable. There was an hour before she would have to be dressed for dinner—just enough time to see if the radio was on in the library. Maybe Miss Trendall, her nurse, would let her listen, or maybe she could sneak in and turn on the radio. Perhaps the baby had been found.

Dorothy Mary didn't want anyone to notice her, so she entered Denbigh House through the side servants' entrance. She and her two older brothers, Griswold and David, were not allowed downstairs unsupervised. They were restricted to their bedrooms and to the third-floor nursery. The cook, butler, and serving maids were at work in the kitchen and pantries, preparing for that evening's dinner party. They were too busy to pay attention to Dorothy Mary as she slipped through the servants' hall to the main staircase. The stairwell door opened onto the foyer. From there she could see if anyone was in the library, music room, or dining room. All of these, as well as her mother's study, were empty. Mother would be upstairs, taking a nap. Perhaps no one would notice if Dorothy Mary turned on the wireless in the library. It was worth a try.

Drawing of Dorothy Mary

The radio, in its arched walnut case, stood on a table next to her father's armchair. She stealthily switched it on and turned down the volume so low that she could barely hear it.

In a metallic voice the announcer said:

"Okay, America. This is Walter Winchell, bringing you your Lucky Strike Hit Parade. And remember, Americans, Luckys are kind to your throat. I know. I've smoked them for eleven years. Lucky's exclusive toasting process forces out harsh irritants, purges and purifies every tobacco leaf, and gives you extra mildness, extra goodness. Luckys are made from the world's choicest tobaccos to give you extra deliciousness. Modern ultraviolet rays make Lucky's tobacco extra mellow. So, for extra mildness, extra goodness, extra deliciousness, and extra mellowness, it's Lucky Strike every time. Remember: It's Toasted.

"And now, before the news, your Lucky Strike Hit Parade. Here's Kate Smith to sing her RCA Victor hit recording of *When the Moon Comes Over the Mountain*."

Shelves of gold-stamped leather volumes around her in the library did not reflect the interests of the Flagg family. Mother and Father had received them as a wedding present from Grandfather King, who liked to collect books. Every room of his house in New York City was filled with books—piles and piles of them. Grizzy, David, and Dorothy Mary were forbidden to touch the volumes in the library. Only Rodgers, the butler who had been trained by Grandfather King to care for these volumes, had permission to handle them. Every three years he took them off the shelves, dusted them, oiled their covers, and carefully replaced them. No one ever read the books. When she was a little girl, Dorothy Mary used to think the books were lonely, but now they seemed more like wallpaper.

Dorothy Mary's gaze wandered to the Chinese Coromandel screen standing in the corner behind her father's chair. Listening to Kate Smith sing, she sat down cross-legged on the floor in front of the screen awaiting news of the Lindbergh baby.

The screen stretched up higher than she could comfortably see, enveloping her in its panels. Dorothy Mary had a ritual that was followed whenever she gazed at the Coromandel screen. She pretended to be a special visitor to the Forbidden City. Dressed in silk robes, with delicate ornaments trembling in her hair, her journey began at the Lion Gate. Two pop-eyed stone lions snarled on either side of a round gate as she boarded a ferry that would take her across the moat surrounding the Emperor's palace. An expressionless, pot-bellied official pushed the ferry off, and her boat was slowly poled along, brushing through the slender, flowering trees dipping their boughs into the still water. The many-colored silken tassels attached to the boat's canopy were tousled by the breeze. A flute player seated in the stern played a thin melody as the boat glided past paddling ducks and under an arched bridge. The courtesans above whispered to each other behind their square fans. They waved and smiled as her boat passed beneath the bridge. She alit at a stairway carved with dragons. A servant carrying a peacock feather fur followed her as she moved among the guests.

A summer party was in progress. Children tossed a ball back and forth. Knots of women chattered and gossiped. A nurse helped one of the Emperor's sons haul a struggling fish from the water. In the central palace, a group of musicians played while a troupe of dancers moved in sharp-edged slow motion. In the distance, a group of hunters aimed curved bows at a stag.

High on a throne, the Emperor was seated with noblemen all around, watching the merrymaking from beneath frowning brows. Unexpectedly his small, black eyes shifted to Dorothy Mary. In a rush of self-doubt, she asked herself what she could say that would please him.

Walter Winchell's staccato, "And now the news," rescued Dorothy Mary from the Emperor's scrutiny. He related the commonplace horrors of the Depression: the percentage of the unemployed was climbing; factories were closing in New York and

Detroit; bank robbers in Chicago had stolen $30,000 in broad daylight and shot two tellers; drought and dust storms had wiped out the spring wheat crop from Texas to Saskatchewan; Franklin Delano Roosevelt would try for the Democratic nomination for president.

None of this meant much to Dorothy Mary. The family rarely went to Philadelphia, so she had never seen breadlines or soup kitchens or men selling apples. The Depression wasn't happening at Denbigh. She did remember that her Father used the same tone to say "Democrats" that he used to say "Catholics." There was no news of the Lindbergh Baby, so Dorothy Mary turned off the radio and went upstairs to Nurse Trendall.

Dorothy Mary Flagg with her brothers,
Grizzy and David, at Denbigh

3

Radnor, Pennsylvania
"Denbigh"
June 1939

The hollow scratching of branches against the roof awakened Dorothy Mary. Rain splashed onto the casement of the open bedroom window. Pulling the window shut and firmly turning the latch, she wiped her hands on the sides of her silk nightgown. The loudness of the thunder indicated that the storm was overhead now. Lightning silhouetted the trees at the far end of the garden and was instantly reflected in the oblong pool that was its focus. Floating pads of water lilies blocked some of the mirrored flash. But the tall, thin girl didn't pay attention to any of the storm's histrionics.

Rain, she thought. *Of all times. God, let it stop by tomorrow.* A furrow between her eyebrows deepened. She stood at the window, watching streams of water rush from either side of the peaked roof of the green and white striped tent. It had been erected on the lawn the previous day by three of her mother's gardeners and a half dozen local boys.

Tomorrow was to be her day.

The guests had been invited, family friends had come from Europe, the band was hired, fifty cases of Clicquot '32 were locked in the wine cellar, ready to be put on ice. The occasion was her eighteenth birthday, the beginning of her year as a debutante—and her introduction to Philadelphia society.

Dorothy Mary snapped on her bathroom light, squinting against the sudden brightness. She checked the security of her pin curls. A few in the back at her hairline were undone. She wound the stragglers around a finger and, opening a bobby pin against her teeth, secured each coil. She added a second bobby pin at right angles to the first—just in case. Without their normal fringe of black mascara, her blue eyes stared blankly from beneath almost-blonde eyelashes and brows. She plucked a stray hair from beneath her left eyebrow. This finished, she opened her mouth wide to check her lower teeth for signs of nicotine stain. Satisfied that there was nothing more to do, she snapped off the light, careful not to damage her long, lacquered fingernails.

Pulling on a robe, she opened her door and walked into the silent house. Her thin shadow silently followed and then preceded her as she passed beneath the glow of each stairwell lamp. *Everyone else in Denbigh must be asleep*, she thought.

Denbigh Manor

On the ground floor, the thunder was muffled into a low grumble. Dorothy Mary walked quickly down the hall past the ticking pendulum of the grandfather clock; into the dining room, where on the mantle the twin silver pheasants flanked the blue and white Ming vases, past the sideboard where the crystal and silver tureens stood empty, polished and ready to be loaded with cashews and mints, into the butler's pantry with its glasses in well-behaved rows, and into Denbigh's kitchen.

The light of the icebox illuminated the room. Dorothy quickly found what she wanted: a half-finished bottle of champagne left over from dinner, and an orange from the fruit bowl. She closed the icebox door and left the kitchen, stopping in the pantry for a highball glass. Dorothy Mary headed for the library. Turning on the lamp, she settled into her mother's armchair, with her feet tucked beneath the cushion and her toes braced against the side of the chair. Pouring a full glass of champagne and placing the empty bottle on the floor, she listened again for the storm. It sounded fainter now. Less thunder. Careful not to spoil her manicure, she began to peel the orange.

Dorothy Mary wished that she could make tomorrow come faster. It would be the first time in a year that she would see her old classmates from Shipley's, and all the Main Line boys she knew.

She sipped her champagne and tried to imagine what they would think of her now. She knew she was different. She felt eons older than the scared rabbit from Miss Shipley's who'd been packed off to a strange finishing school a little more than a year ago. So much had happened in Florence: good things like new friends, Coco Chanel suits, new languages; bad things like the loneliness, like the war in Italy, and like her operation. She cringed at the thought of the bright scar on her abdomen where the Italian quacks had removed her appendix. She remembered the makeshift hospital in Florence: straw mattresses on the floor of a church. Dirty sheets. Denbigh's horses received better care than did the sick of Florence. The woman with half her face blown away, who moaned from the mattress beside her. No running water. Black-robed nuns scrubbed the floors each night. The piney scent of cleaning fluid blended with the smells of the unwashed sick around her. Cockroaches scurried in the shadows. She remembered the kaleidoscopic dreams she'd had under the ether and her own faraway voice screaming, "Mother, Mother." The hands pressing her down onto the operating table. The dizzying pain when she came to in the midst of the operation. The feverish dreams of faces framed in black.

The nuns who nursed her through the fever said it had nearly killed her. But she had survived. They said she should thank God and the Holy Virgin for the miracle. But Dorothy Mary didn't believe in miracles. She knew she had survived because she was special. God had no more to do with it than did the little Emperor carved into the costly Coromandel screen behind her father's chair.

Now she was back in the library at Denbigh. She wasn't a little girl anymore.

Dorothy Mary finished her glass of champagne. Putting the orange peels into her empty glass and carrying the fruit in one hand, she turned off the light and retraced her route up the two flights of stairs, moving from one pool of light to the next. Once back in her bedroom, she unlatched the window, though the rain was still falling lightly. The lightning and thunder had stopped. The surface of the pool was pockmarked, the trees dripped, and beads of water fell from the scalloped border of the tent.

Dorothy Mary took off her robe and settled back into bed. Smiling to herself, she admired her long, red fingernails as they removed the last strands of fiber and loosened a segment of the orange. She placed one end of the slice into her mouth, gently bit through its skin and meditatively sucked on it, worrying about the day to come. From near her dressing table, the hem of her floor-length gold lamé gown for the next evening's dance fluttered in the morning's first breeze, making a soft shushing sound. Dorothy Mary put the rest of the orange onto the glass top of her bedside table, pulled the smooth, linen sheets with the initials *MFK* up over her shoulder and rolled onto her side. Just before she fell asleep, she sighed and tried to convince herself, repeating over and over what Mother had said to her:

"Everything will be just perfect... Everything will be just perfect."

II

Grizzy dreamt of a deep pool in a cold lake, and of a trout hanging in the green water, waiting. The fish's eyes scanned the water ahead, behind, below, above, until it spotted a scuttling crayfish. Claws raised, antennae jerking, the crayfish darted across the sandy bottom. The trout shot downward. Its jaws closed over the newly molted, soft body. The trout resumed its patrol.

The fisherman attached the iridescent Royal Coachman to his line. In one cast, the fly reached the trout's pool. The fisherman let the Coachman settle below the surface and waited for the fish to rise.

The trout saw the movement of the fly as it landed on the pool's white ceiling. Another meal. It watched the fly sink. Its jaws opened wide as it rushed upward. The trout bit—and Grizzy dreamed of the stab of pain as the hook, hidden by the feathered finery of the Coachman, pierced the inside of the fish's cheek. The fish tried to swim downward, but the safety of the pool's bottom taunted him, out of reach. He dashed forward and back, wrestling to free his mouth. But something followed him and tugged at him.

The fisherman reveled in the power of the trout as it arced out of the water, a splashing blur of silver and green landing closer to him. Knowing that the hook would tear free in seconds, Grizzy warily reeled in his line.

The fish knew only one thing: escape. Helpless, it was pulled into the shallow, warmer water. And then, with its tail kicking, was swung into the air.

The fish struggled, trying to swim, but the air offered no resistance. Its gill covers flapped, exposing red, feathery organs. Its mouth parts worked frantically. The fisherman pulled his net from his belt. Holding the line taut, he scooped the fish from the shallows.

Hurrying from the lake's edge, the fisherman studied the trout as it lay against the reeds, its mouth opening and closing on the morning air. He held the trout firmly against the ground. With one motion he pulled his knife from its sheath. Without bothering to stun the trout he inserted the point of his knife into the fish's anus, and slowly ripped forward, slicing cleanly through the fish's belly. Yellow loops of intestine bulged in the wake of the knife. With three fingers he scooped the innards from the bleeding fish and cast them aside. A second cut through bone exposed the trout's heart. He tugged the liver free and flung it carelessly onto the bank.

Asleep in his narrow bed on Denbigh's third floor, Grizzy smiled.

III

Mrs. Stanley Griswold Flagg was too busy for sleep, and only half aware of the thunderstorm. She sat against the pillows of her four-poster bed, rechecking the list of 178 guests who had sent flowers to Dorothy Mary.

She knew it would be a battle, but she'd have to make sure that Dorothy Mary sent her thank you notes promptly. Philadelphia society matrons had long memories. Nothing could be allowed to stand in the way of her plans. Especially now, when the S. Griswold Flaggs were finally, after twenty years of doing the right thing at the right time, on the verge of acceptance by the old families of Philadelphia.

Perhaps it was a mistake to take Dorothy Mary out of Shipley and send her off to finish in Florence. The plain, frizzy-haired girl who had practically lived in her riding clothes, had returned from *L'Institut Mlle. Schmidt* with a French wardrobe, a British accent, and a patina of continental sophistication that was definitely not Main Line. She pronounced her name "Dothrey" now. Her conversation was studded with Italian and French expletives. Bigger than her Main Line britches, Dorothy Mary had a calculating worldliness that made Mrs. Flagg nervous.

Mrs. Flagg was accustomed to managing her children with the same authority she exercised over her household. She made it clear that the children were not to mix with the servants on a regular basis. Until they were in their late teens, the authority of Nurse Trendall and Rodgers, the butler, was absolute. Conversation at each meal had to be carefully orchestrated so that her husband's explosive temper was not ignited. Another rule that Mrs. Flagg understood vividly told her that fast, flashy girls never married well in Philadelphia.

Dorothy Mary's new independence would simply have to be curbed. Dorothy would marry well, or she wouldn't marry at all.

Dorothy King's marriage to Griswold Flagg had evolved into a cool, formal alliance that had lasted for twenty-three years. They moved in separate spheres. His life was centered on the family pipe-fittings factory and his clubs in New York. He was often absent on weekends. He never offered an explanation, and she never questioned him. She knew that he was asleep in the adjoining bedroom and was glad that a locked door protected her. She was thankful that he never knocked on her door at night anymore.

Dorothy Mary, Grizzy, and David with Mr. and Mrs. Griswold Flagg

In addition to their three children—Grizzy, David, and Dorothy Mary—Griswold Flagg had given her Denbigh, and the money to maintain it in style. She had complete autonomy over the estate and had taken care to see that it formed the correct backdrop. Tyrannical with her thirty servants, she made sure that the lawns were immaculate, that something fragrant was always blooming in the formal garden, that the silver and crystal gleamed, that a pitcher of ice water was available in each bathroom, and that the servants behaved properly. Everything at Denbigh was elegant, but restrained, just to the point of boredom.

Her aim was to be a power in Philadelphia's most exclusive society. Grizzy and David were already in demand as wealthy young bachelors, but she gauged her success by Dorothy Mary. After all, it was no problem to marry off a handsome young man. But marrying off an only semi-pretty daughter into one of *the* families took real skill. Mrs. Flagg had begun her crusade early. A month after this last child was born, she had been registered in Caldwell's "Book" in the downtown Philadelphia store. Nearly eighteen years ago, Mrs. Griswold Flagg had reserved tomorrow as Dorothy Mary's day.

She wanted only one thing from her daughter: a marriage with one of the "Philadelphians," as those privileged few families so modestly enjoyed being called. This would ensure Mrs. Flagg's confirmation into the embrace of Philadelphia's elite. Her gaze turned to the list of bachelors who would be attending tomorrow's garden party and dinner dance. The light from the bedside lamp, passing through the hand-knotted net canopy of the bed, threw a webbed shadow onto the high ceiling. She settled back against the pillows and scrutinized the list of pedigrees. Her eyes narrowed, as though she could threaten the very event into submission.

Mrs. Flagg understood her planning, direction and discretion were paramount to the success of the family. She was far more concerned about the outcome of her family's position and future than Dorothy Mary's heartstrings.

This was her success as much as anyone else's.

IV

Intoxicating, she thought.

Dorothy Mary was intoxicated with her reflection in the gilt mirror. Turning sideways, she admired her tiny waist, emphasized by the sash of the aqua tulle dress. Her skin felt deliciously bare beneath the puffy sleeves of the matching jacket. With an old-fashioned bouquet of camellias and lacy baby's breath in her left hand, she greeted imaginary guests. Extending her long-gloved arm, she was suitably demure as she was introduced to the Drexels, to the Cassats, and to old Mrs. Clement. She tilted her head just the slightest bit to display the trailing streamers of the minute confection of a hat that perched atop her upswept curls and sparkled a special smile—a blend of little girl and temptress that always worked with men. She had perfected it on waiters in Florence and knew it would be surefire with the likes of Ridgley Coxe and Stewie Frazer. She practiced looking arch and superior as she greeted her fellow debutantes—those unnecessary irritations who had to be invited. After all, it was the men, not some gaggle of Main Line schoolgirls, who were important.

She whirled as her father emerged unexpectedly from his room at the end of the landing. Hoping that he hadn't seen her preening before the mirror, she donned her most innocent face, and asked breathlessly, "Well, Daddy—How do I look? Isn't my dress divine? Don't you think this hat is adorable? Do you like me in this color?"

Stanley Griswold "Giff" Flagg took stock of the girl pirouetting for his appraisal. She was all angles—bony elbows, abnormally long neck and uneven, protruding teeth. No curves. But her dress hid her nubile figure's defects, and the excitement that powdered her plain face masked those less-than-perfect features. She did have a wonderful, sparkly smile. Realizing that she was waiting for an answer, he replied, "Yes. Yes to all of your questions. You look fine."

Before she could launch herself at him again, he hurried downstairs, calling for Rodgers, the butler. The champagne must be put on ice. The liquor supply needed a last-minute check.

Dorothy Mary watched him race downstairs, turned back to the mirror once more and thought, *He forgot to wish me Happy Birthday*.

Below her father's bellow for Rodgers, Dorothy heard her mother's *sotto voce* call. Lifting her dress so as not to sully it, she glided down the wide staircase and into the leather-paneled study from which her mother directed Denbigh's affairs.

The dark purple orchid pinned to Mrs. Flagg's shoulder competed with the pigeon-blood ruby on her breast as she issued a volley of instructions, requests and commands.

On a silver salver, Rodgers delivered her very dry gin martini and stationed himself behind her chair.

"Dorothy darling, you look simply lovely. Hasn't it turned into a marvelous day for you? Happy Birthday, dear." Mrs. Flagg lifted her cheek to receive a daughterly kiss.

"Turn around and let me look at you. Really child, you must have something to fill in that neckline. It looks too bare. And honestly, Dorothy, those earrings are a little too much. One cannot wear dangling earrings at a garden party. You should know better." Without waiting for a response, she conveyed to Rodgers that a pearl necklace and button earrings be fetched from her jewel case.

Turning back to Dorothy Mary, she continued, "And remember, dear, I want you to be especially nice to Alicia Wiederscheim. Grizzy is quite taken with her, and she has no friends to speak of amongst us. Make sure that people dance with her. I've put her at your table.

"Try to keep an eye on that blonde, Shelby Thayler. I've heard talk that she's overly interested in David. After what happened with that girl in Baltimore, I don't want any more trouble over females in this family. Darling, I realize that you've become quite addicted to cigarettes, but if you *must* smoke—and I wish you wouldn't—don't, for heaven's sake, do it in front of Mrs. Clement. Those Quakers are quite against it, especially for young girls. It really does make you look quite hard. It's most unattractive and I wish you'd give it up, but since you're too old to spank, all I ask is that you be discreet.

"Now, I've chosen the corsage that Chet Liddell sent for you to wear this afternoon. These orchids are really quite unusual and will be stunning with your coloring. Put that bouquet down and let's pin them on. Remember that tonight at the dance, you must show everyone that you appreciate their gifts by changing bouquets and corsages frequently. You mustn't slight anyone. There, don't you think these will be lovely for this afternoon?"

Before Dorothy Mary could reply, the maid arrived with the necklace and earrings. Dorothy submitted to her ministrations.

Mrs. Flagg continued:

"Now darling, don't plan to go anywhere tomorrow. You must send out the thank you notes for all of these wonderful flowers. It's very important. I've organized it all for you. So please, don't let me down.

"Let me see how you look. That's much better. Lovely, really lovely."

Turning to the maid, Mrs. Flagg demanded, "Anna, did anyone ever have a more gorgeous daughter?"

"No, Mother. Mrs. Flagg looks as fine as Skinner silk." Dismissed, she bobbed a curtsey and left the room.

"Dorothy, be a lamb and find your brothers and make them put on their boutonnieres. And don't get your gloves soiled. The guests will be here shortly."

As an afterthought, she added, "And darling, don't be so nervous—smile a little. Remember, it's *your* day."

V

Escaping from her mother's study with the boutonnieres in hand, Dorothy Mary dutifully searched for her brothers. She found them at the pool. David was at the far end, doggedly finishing a lap. Grizzy dozed in the sun at the deep end, dangling one arm in the turquoise water.

"David, Grizzy. Why aren't you two ready? The guests will be here any minute."

Grizzy was apparently deaf.

Dorothy Mary stepped closer and said, "Grizzy, wake up. Mother will have a fit if you're not dressed on time. You'll ruin everything."

Grizzy was also apparently paralyzed.

Dorothy Mary's shadow was over him now. She prodded him with one toe, to which he opened a single eye.

"*Please*, Grizzy. Get up. Look. I've brought your boutonnieres."

Grizzy quickly arced his arm up, scattering water in all directions, but especially in Dorothy Mary's. She screamed and leapt back. "Grizzy, you son of a bitch!"

"So sorry. Hope I didn't get you too wet, Queen Bee, but if you hadn't awakened me so suddenly…" White teeth gleamed in his tan face as he watched her sizzle with rage, shaking water from the front of her dress.

David, who had seen the end of this episode, snapped his towel at Grizzy. "Cut it out. Leave her alone." David helped Dorothy blot a few drops of pool water from the hem of her dress and took the flowers from her.

"Don't worry about your dress. It'll dry."

Leading her toward the house, he murmured, "Don't let Grizzy get the best of you today. That's just the Beast's way of telling you that he thinks you look swell. And you do—look swell, that is."

David called over his shoulder to Grizzy, "Come on, Monster, let's get dressed."

Grizzy yawned, stretched in the sun and trotted after the two as they disappeared beneath the green and white striped tent.

VI

Her face red and agitated, Dorothy Mary hurried to the mirror at one end of the music room. She would get even with Grizzy, somehow. Why did he always have to spoil things? David was right—the water spots were disappearing. Her dress would be okay. She sighed. No matter what Mother said, the double rope of pearls looked dowdy. They'd have to go. As she tried to unclasp them, she studied the orchids from Chester Liddell. She hadn't really looked at them before. The clusters of pale-yellow blossoms with flesh-colored blotches looked bruised and poisonous. How could Mother think they were beautiful?

She's dotty if she thinks I'll wear these, Dorothy Mary thought. *I'll get the camellia bouquet from the study.*

She was unpinning the spindly stems when Aunt Jeanne appeared at the doorway, holding a fan to her heaving bosom, panting, "Dorothy, I've been looking all over for you. It's time. People are here. Come on, child."

Dorothy snatched off the pearl necklace and stuffed it into a cache pot alongside the mirror. She didn't care what Mother thought. There was no time to change flowers now. Fixing her Sparkle Plenty smile, she took her place in the receiving line between Mother and Aunt Jeanne.

The next hour passed quickly. The sound of gravel scrunching beneath the tires of chauffeured cars was regularly punctuated by Rodgers intoning the names of each arriving party. Mrs. Flagg was a gracious grand dame, welcoming each guest and introducing Dorothy Mary. Like her mother, Dorothy Mary had been trained in European manners. The formality of the Germans, the charm of the French, and an organic twinkled eye of the Irish. There was an embedded choreography of style and movement, relaxed yet ridged, demure and dominating, all stirred in a Tiffany punch bowl.

Dorothy Mary still liked to laugh out loud, because she did it well; it was her trump card. Confidence was king. Using variations of the smile she had rehearsed, Dorothy shook hands with each young man long enough to ensure that he knew she was *especially* pleased to see him. Each shook hands with Aunt Jeanne, thinking that Dorothy Mary was really very pretty, vivacious and awfully sweet.

Dorothy Mary dismissed the young women in pastel lawn dresses and picture hats rapidly. She was friendly, but somewhat distracted, as if she'd suddenly thought of something better that she had to do. They seemed to notice how her front teeth pushed against her upper lip, that her continental accent seemed false, and that her Adam's apple bobbed when she spoke. They shook hands with Aunt Jeanne, probably thinking that Dorothy Mary Flagg had returned from Florence overly impressed with herself.

Dorothy Mary greeted her parents' friends demurely. She knew all the right things to say; she belonged to their club now. They shook hands with Aunt Jeanne, thinking that Giff and Dorothy Flagg had a daughter to be proud of.

The stream of guests swirled out of Denbigh's parlor and sitting room, down into the music room, through the sunroom, and out under the tent. Dorothy felt as if she had shaken hands with all of Philadelphia. She was dying for a cigarette.

She made her way through clusters of well-wishers who raised their glasses and gossiped while balancing plates filled with appetizers. Dorothy smiled and waved and promised more than one group that she would be right back. She found a group of clandestine smokers in the far end of the garden, shielded from the other guests by a curving privet hedge. Dorothy Mary had her close "gang," wherein laughter, cigarettes and cocktails were the ritual sacraments, but there were many younger untested debutantes very happy indeed to have been included. This was their first step into the staircase society of which Dorothy Mary now commanded a predatory view.

She wondered whether all of their mothers had told them not to smoke in front of the pillars of Philadelphia society. She wondered what old Mrs. Clement would do if she saw her granddaughter Cynthia with a cigarette dangling out of her mouth.

Sterling Longwood was at the periphery of the group. Dorothy Mary caught his eye and he immediately offered her a cork-tipped Oval.

"May I light you?" he inquired.

"How kind."

Just as she was beginning to enjoy his flattery—he was telling her how different she looked from the last time he had seen her at the Cricket Club—Rodgers informed her that she was wanted in the drawing room. When Dorothy Mary was called, she responded; there was no dillydallying in her family.

"Would you be a darling and please hold this for me?" she asked Sterling. "I'll be back in a second." And she left him waiting for her, keeping the cigarette going until she returned.

Flagg Family photoshoot at the Debutante Party
Mrs. Flagg top center. Dorothy Mary is second from the top right.

VII

Dressed in navy crepe, her lapis and gold-headed walking stick gripped in one white-gloved fist, Old Mrs. Liddell sat erect in the Chippendale ball-and-claw chair. Beneath her veiled hat, she waited for Dorothy Mary, while an overwrought Mrs. Flagg fluttered at her side, like a moth impaled on a pin. She offered refreshments and groped for conversation. Chester Liddell stood behind the old woman's chair, beaming encouragement at Mrs. Flagg through his thick, gold-rimmed glasses. The old lady was the titular and financial head of the Liddell clan. None of her children would receive more than pocket money until after her death.

Mrs. Flagg had, of course, invited the old woman to today's celebration, but she had not been surprised when the invitation was declined. Old Mrs. Liddell never went anywhere these days. Like a falcon spreading its wings over a fresh kill, she guarded her health viciously. This unannounced visit was important, and Mrs. Flagg was trying hard to please.

"Dorothy King Flagg, stop waving that foolish fan about. You're making me nervous as a cat. I haven't come to see *you*. It's your daughter I'm interested in."

Dorothy Mary felt the old woman's eyes appraisingly shift as she entered. Chester Liddell crossed the room and guided her to his grandmother's chair.

"Grandmother, I'd like you to meet Dorothy Mary Flagg. Dorothy, my grandmother, Mrs. Liddell."

Dorothy waited for the old woman to offer her hand, but as the withered figure made no motion, Dorothy curtsied and smiled.

"Well child, at least I can see that you have manners. I'm sorry to have taken you from your guests, but Chester claims you are one of the few girls worth meeting this season. I've come on his recommendation. Now, if you'll excuse us, your mother and I will have a chat."

Chester shut the drawing room door, removed his glasses, and mopped his glistening, balding forehead. Running a finger around the inside of his collar, he fixed myopic eyes on the aqua blur that was Dorothy Mary.

"Thank you for indulging my grandmother. She can be such a bully. We call her the Little General at home. Sometimes I think she went to West Point instead of Vassar." Chester added, "I'm glad you liked my orchids. They're quite unusual hybrids. I pollinated them myself."

Dorothy Mary wanted to ask him if he had enjoyed it, but restricted herself to a polite, "Oh, really."

Chester continued, "They won second prize in the last IPSA competition."

"IPSA?" Dorothy Mary inquired evenly.

"International Phalaenopsis Society of America. I'm Past-President of the Chestnut Hill Branch."

Thinking about it later, after the dinner and toasts and dancing and too much champagne, when everyone had gone home, Dorothy Mary wasn't sure whether she had screamed with laughter or with rage.

4

    While Chester Liddell was boring Dorothy Mary with talk of orchid pollination, the Flaggs and the Liddells reached an understanding behind those closed drawing room doors. Although it was never so boldly stated, the Flaggs would trade Dorothy Mary, whose income would comfortably support Chester and all his hothouses, for the social prestige conferred by an alliance with the Liddell family. Mrs. Flagg instantly recognized the opportunity that had presented itself. The marriage of Dorothy Mary and Chester Liddell would mean immediate acceptance into those proper Philadelphian clubs which had heretofore considered the Flaggs nouveau. She saw her chance at the Philadelphia Club, the Rittenhouse Club, and the Union League. She grabbed with both hands.

    For the Liddells, it meant that Chester could continue to potter about his greenhouses, while managing Dorothy Mary's money. Another generation of Liddells would be spared the necessity of earning a living. After all, no Liddell had been gainfully employed in recent memory. They had always married money. Old Mrs. Liddell meant to keep it that way.

    In years to come, my grandmother, Mrs. Flagg would regret her unhesitating agreement with the old woman. But that would come only after she herself was old, paralyzed, speechless, confined to a wheelchair after a stroke. Like liquid wax running from a candle stump, tears would flow down her sagging face as an acrimonious Dorothy Mary stood over her, railing, accusing, evening the score. Mrs. Flagg would eventually bow her head in mute testimony to her guilt. And in the end, there would be no one to wipe away her tears.

    But that's getting ahead of our story. Mrs. Flagg, my grandmother, is still in control. Although not wise, she is shrewd. Like a sword swallower, she knows just how far to push in the blade before she cuts her own throat.

Dorothy Mary Liddell in bridal gown

5

Radnor, Pennsylvania
Summer, 1939

"*A Brilliant Season.*"

That's what Philadelphia society columnists claimed Dorothy Mary was enjoying. Calling her "Philadelphia's Most Feted Debutante," they breathlessly chronicled her comings and goings. No detail escaped notice. They related the cut, fabric, and decoration of each of the seemingly endless supply of stunning evening dresses. They gossiped about her mannerisms, hairstyles, furs, and companions. Only her jewelry escaped notice—but then during these post-Depression times, robberies were all too common along the Main Line.

Although she publicly deplored the attention of "all these newspaper people," Dorothy Mary was secretly and smugly pleased with her notoriety. Her friends noted that she never refused a reporter or photographer. She always posed obligingly, smiling ever so faintly, and turning her head to the most flattering three-quarter angle.

She dressed all in black for formal afternoons. Her pale skin and light brown hair stood in stark contrast. Her dark red fingernails and mouth provided the only flashes of color. Before long, everyone was copying her. The black-and-white look became the rage. She affected long, black velvet gloves for the cocktail hour. Soon everyone was wearing them.

Dorothy Mary became noted for her enviable poise and rapid repartee. The Dorothy Mary that stared coolly from the society pages was the quintessence of the unspoken Philadelphia maxim: "The best people don't do anything. They just *are*."

Debutante Dorothy Mary

In her room at Denbigh, Dorothy Mary ransacked each day's papers, hunting for her notices, which she neatly clipped and hoarded in a thick scrapbook. She pored over this treasure in private, studying what had been written about her, thinking of ways to improve her elegant image.

In the month after her birthday, party followed party; dress followed dress; days were spent at teas, playing tennis, or riding over the Radnor Hills. She accepted membership into the Junior League and began to cultivate friendships with other debutantes, realizing, somewhat reluctantly, how important these Main Line schoolgirls might be in her future. Although men were still of primary importance to Dorothy Mary, she kept all of them at arm's length—until she met Joe Padrosche.

Like every other girl, Dorothy Mary carried a mental picture of her dream man. But unlike most girls, she didn't want someone tall, dark and handsome. Height was important to her, as she stood nearly six feet in heels, but her first criterion was that he must *not* be addicted to team sports. Dorothy Mary loathed all these Yale and Princeton types who could only talk of football. Rah Rah left her blah blah. So please, no goalies, no tailbacks, no second basemen, no oily South American polo players and *heavens*, no center forwards. Next, he must be a little unpredictable: she didn't want to be able to second-guess him. Would he be rich? Dorothy Mary never thought in those terms. Everyone she met had money. The question never occurred to her.

Debutante Dorothy Mary – center of attention

Unfortunately, Dorothy Mary had known the young men of her set for ages. They had all grown up together, attended the same awful dancing classes in the Cricket Club ballroom and learned to swim on Bailey's Beach in Newport. There were few new male faces. Now and then somebody's older brother would bring a friend home from college, but Dorothy Mary found that the newcomer was invariably cut from the same cloth as all the Main Line boys she knew. Nearly all of them were team players. To make matters worse, most of them were short. She loved being the center of their attention—they were amusing, they were fun to flirt with—but they were just boys. She never gave them more than a friendly kiss on the cheek when saying goodnight.

Dorothy Mary met Joe Padrosche at Shelby Thayler's dinner dance. She'd been enduring a foxtrot with little Stewie Frazer. Stewie's strategy was to determinedly double-time in a straight line across the floor, execute a box turn, and then busily double-time back, like a mole hunting grubs in a tunnel. His hapless partner was rapidly steered backward. Because Stewie was too short to see over Dorothy Mary's shoulder, she had to absorb the impact of collisions with other couples. Of course, everyone was up punishing the parquet, the box step of the foxtrot lending order to what would otherwise be construed as organized cocktail chaos. Men led and ladies followed... as best they could. Stewie would apologize, pause, double-time in place, re-establishing his peculiar rhythm, and then plunge off again. What he lacked in height and imagination, Stewie made up in energy. When a tall man cut in and put Stewie's frenetic propulsion to a halt,

Dorothy sighed discreetly with relief. Stewie introduced Joe Padrosche to Dorothy Mary before bouncing away to join the stag line.

Dorothy Mary commented on Stewie's dancing. She imagined that her new partner would find the woes of a debutante amusing. She thought she was being particularly witty when he interrupted.

"Miss Flagg, I try to teach Shelby's sculpture class at the Art Alliance. She invited me here merely to increase the number of available men. Since you are a debutante of some wide experience, I suppose you also know that your own dancing is not perfect. To begin with, your hand belongs on the top of my shoulder." Imperiously, he moved her left hand to the correct position. "If you keep pulling down on my sleeve, I'll have to send this jacket all the way to London to have it recut."

He gave her right hand a shake.

"And hold my hand firmly. Yours feels like a dead cuttlefish. That's better. Now, pay attention to what we're doing."

They swung into the first of the interlocking circles of a waltz. Dorothy Mary's cheeks turned as red as her lips, which she'd momentarily pursed over gritted teeth.

She had *never* been so rudely criticized by a stranger.

Hoping that no one had overheard, she fixed a bright smile on her lips. The other couples waltzing beneath the Colony Club's pink-shaded chandeliers *must* think that Dorothy Mary Flagg was having a wonderful time. She flashed gleaming teeth to the faces that whirled by, while she prayed for this waltz to be over or for someone to cut in. She tried to anticipate her partner's movements, but their feet collided twice. He did not react. She hoped it had hurt him.

But no one cut in and the band segued into a tango. Things were going better now. What a relief not to be eternally shuffling backward. She saw Shelby Thayler in the arms of Stewie Frazer. He was doing his other dance floor ploy: backbreaking dip and lunge. Even if Padrosche was arrogant, he certainly knew how to dance and show off his partner. After one tricky open figure, in which he spun her in a wide circle and then caught her close, Joe smiled down at Dorothy Mary and said, "You're really quite a good dancer when you put your mind to it."

Matching him smile for smile, Dorothy Mary replied, "And you're the most conceited man I've ever met."

"Coming from you, Miss Flagg, I take that as a compliment."

They were applauding after the tango when Dorothy Mary spotted Stewie Frazer edging toward them across the polished floor. Linking her arm through Joe's and turning her back on Stewie, Dorothy suggested they sit the next one out. He agreed, on one condition: a truce.

Back in her room at Denbigh, Dorothy Mary reflected that the truce was the beginning of it all. Her anger had evaporated. She thought Joe Padrosche was divine.

Still dressed in her pale blue formal with the overskirt of tiny, glittering stars, she kicked off her silver slippers, hummed a waltz, hugged herself and slowly circled the room.

Their truce had been followed by other dances—two-steps, foxtrots, jitterbugs—and by much talk. He told her about Spain. She told him about Florence. There was something about his heavy-lidded eyes that reminded her of the Italian men who had watched her as they lounged in the shadowed doorways along the Piazzale Michelangelo. He made her a little nervous, but he was fascinating.

She told him about her adventures as a debutante, of her aching feet and the miles she had danced. Of how she thought Caldwell's should issue snappy silver lamé track shoes along with those pink printed rosters of names and addresses of debutantes.

He told her about working his way across the Atlantic on an ocean liner as a dance instructor for the first-class passengers. Moving with the music, two fingers of his right hand demonstrated his method of introducing dance steps so that his matronly pupils wouldn't walk all over his feet. Then he took the cigarette from Dorothy Mary's hand and showed her how to dance with him. Their fingers two-stepped across the table littered with half-filled glasses and forgotten place cards. His unexpected touch seemed to run clear through her hand and up to her shoulder. A little confused, she drew her forearm away and changed the subject, pretending that nothing had happened. But he understood.

He told her of the city of Toledo. Of its narrow, labyrinthine streets and of the three civilizations—Roman, Gothic and Moorish—that had built walls around the medieval town. Once he had climbed up into one of the towers of the Alcazar Castle, pried off an iron grating and seen the whole city spread out before him like a jumbled picnic blanket. The narrow streets zigzagged up toward the highest point of the city. They were built in this way so that Toledo could be defended even after her walls were breached. Soldiers could easily jump from roof to roof.

After the last dance, Joe saw Dorothy Mary to her car.

In the moonlight, he said that she was like Toledo, with lots of defenses. He hoped she didn't mind if he tried to scale the Moorish wall. Dorothy Mary recognized this as a very smooth line, but it was wonderful.

The next day she called Shelby Thayler. After the obligatory thank yous and subsidiary gossip, she began to ask questions about Shelby's Spanish sculpture teacher.

II

Mrs. Griswold Flagg stood in the gravel path of Denbigh's rose garden, a black

Chinese kitchen shear in one hand. She was snipping spent blossoms and pruning the potted rose bushes that were trained to grow into stiff topiary balls. None of her gardeners were allowed to touch these plants that stood in a fragrant double file along the path. They were her special chore. As she worked, she kept watch for the Japanese beetles that had been shredding the leaves of her treasured plants.

Mrs. Flagg in the gardens.

She thought about Dorothy Mary and Chester Liddell. Mrs. Flagg was biding her time. She was certain that a frontal assault on Dorothy Mary would fail. If confronted with her mother's plan to marry her to Chester Liddell, Dorothy Mary would flatly refuse. After all, Chester paled in comparison to Dorothy Mary's other friends. He was a sweet boy, but hardly exciting. His prematurely balding head and blubbery body made him seem rather like an embryo chicken: big forehead, big belly. One could only hope his appearance would improve with age.

At present, Mrs. Flagg was content to allow Dorothy Mary the illusion of freedom. She would slowly put her plan into action. She would begin in Newport that summer by calling in old debts, asking friends to arrange parties and dinners for Dorothy Mary. She would make sure that Chester Liddell was included in each guest list. Perhaps if the two saw enough of each other, a romance would naturally evolve.

Mrs. Flagg wore a black carpenter's apron over her dress. Into one of its commodious pockets, she stuffed clippings and faded flowers. The small bottle of kerosene in another apron pocket bumped softly against her thigh as she patrolled from plant to plant. A few Japanese beetles were wriggling in the oily liquid. It took them a long time to die.

A pair of Japanese beetles was mating on the next plant. Their bright green heads and ruddy wing covers gleamed metallically as the male hunched over the female, prodding her with his abdomen. Mrs. Flagg took the bottle from her apron pocket and unscrewed it. Plucking the insects from the flower between forefinger and thumb, she dropped them into the kerosene and replaced the lid. Quickly rubbing her hand against her apron, she wiped away the unpleasant sensation of the tiny, hooked legs gripping her fingers. She watched as the pair frantically spun and bobbed.

She wondered whether they would still be coupled together the next morning when they were dead and thrown upon the compost heap.

III

Dorothy Mary was frantic.

She had nothing to wear. The floor and twin beds of her room were covered with frothy dresses that had been tried and discarded. She had spilled face powder down the front of the pale-yellow crepe that she'd planned to wear. The pink tulle with the heart-shaped neckline was too juvenile. She'd just worn the blue with the silver stars. Black was impossible for Lucinda's party—everyone would wear pastels. White looked too much like a bride. She wanted to look *just right*. It was so important. *Joe* was going to be there.

The seafoam green with ivory satin panels would have been fine, but there were half-moon perspiration stains beneath the arms. It would never do.

She settled on the peach satin with the gold brocade inserts. Struggling into the snug tapered sleeves, Dorothy Mary discovered that it was impossible for her to fasten any of the tiny buttons that traveled down the spine of the dress. She thought of ringing for Bridgette, but then remembered that it was her day off. Mother and Father had already left. The car for her and David would be here soon. There was no time to spare. Dorothy fumbled on all fours in the bottom of her closet for the peach satin shoes that matched the dress. Grabbing her mother-of-pearl sequin handbag and gloves, she rushed downstairs, calling her brother David. She knew he'd be waiting in the bar of the library.

"David, please put down that drink and fasten me up. I can't reach these buttons and the car will be here any minute!"

David smiled at his sister's state. Why was she so agitated? They both knew that it was just another party, like all the others that season. It would be a pleasant affair, but it was hardly worth getting upset over. He rather dreaded it—the same faces, the same conversations.

As David's fingers got the hang of fastening the tiny peach-covered buttons into their minute satin loops, he felt his sister's shoulders relax.

"What's got you so upset? You're usually so calm about these affairs."

"Oh, David, I don't know. I just couldn't find anything that looked right. I spilled powder on my yellow dress, and it's ruined. Nothing but this looked any good. And I want to look nice."

"For your new friend, Padrosche?"

Dorothy Mary was caught off guard. She hadn't told David anything about Joe. She looked at her brother over her shoulder.

"How do you know him?"

David's head was intently bent over the buttons. He looked up.

"We met in the stag line at Shelby's dance. Seems like a nice enough guy. I saw that he monopolized you all evening, and you seemed to be having a pretty good time. Even Stewie Frazer noticed. He complained that he couldn't get near you. I suppose that's lucky for you."

Dorothy flushed and smiled. "I guess you're right."

David hooked the last button. "There, you're all done up. I've got your wrap. We have to go."

Sitting in the shadows in his mother's study, Grizzy had overheard this conversation. He was sure that Mamma didn't know about Baby Sister and Joe Padrosche. He wondered what it would be worth to her.

IV

With the ebony and mother-of-pearl inlaid backgammon board on the table between them, Grizzy and Mrs. Flagg sat in the screened gazebo. The ornate wooden structure was one of Mrs. Flagg's "finds." She had bought it from the owners of Minnewaska when that Catskill hotel had fallen on hard times. Her workmen had disassembled it and removed it from its lakeside perch. Framed by rhododendrons and mountain laurel, it sat on a bank of ferns near one of the streams that ran through Denbigh's woods.

The insistent whirring of a June bug's wings against the screen and the rattling of the dice in their leather cup were the only sounds on this warm, still afternoon. Mrs. Flagg was playing with the white pips. Grizzy had chosen the red. He was losing.

It was Mrs. Flagg's move. Grizzy thought she was sufficiently engrossed in their game to introduce a new topic of conversation.

"Mamma," Grizzy accented the last syllable, "what will happen to Denbigh when you and Father go?"

Mrs. Flagg threw the dice and studied the board.

"I suppose we'll close the house as we generally do in the summer and leave Rodgers to look after things."

"No, Mamma, I mean, when you and Father are dead—not just gone for the summer."

Mrs. Flagg knocked out one of Grizzy's pips and moved one of hers off the board. Pleased with her luck, she looked at her son.

"Well, everything will be divided among the three of you, and the servants will be given pensions."

Grizzy shook the dice. "Who will get the house?"

"Grizzy, by that time none of you will want this big place. It's too expensive to run. Good servants are hard to find and nearly impossible to keep. With the unions offering a minimum wage now, no one wants to work for fifteen dollars a week, plus room and board."

Grizzy needed a four to get his pip back on the board. He rolled the dice; double sixes. He cursed his luck.

"Well, how will the things be divided? The paintings, for example. Who will get Grandfather King's Holbeins?" Mrs. Flagg rolled the dice and moved two more of her pips off the board.

"You mean those in the dining room?"

Grizzy rolled another pair of double sixes. Disgusted with his luck he brushed the dice with his sleeve, and called "Cocked Dice." He rolled again, and this time got a four and a six.

Mrs. Flagg regarded her son, refusing to acknowledge his thinly disguised cheating.

"I rather thought those would go to Dorothy Mary. Your grandfather promised them to her when she was a little girl."

"How much do you think they're worth?" Grizzy asked.

"What an appalling question," Mrs. Flagg exclaimed, straightening her back. "I have no idea. The paintings were all appraised years ago. The records are in my study. Why are you so interested in them?"

"Oh, I wondered how much Dorothy might get when she has to sell them."

"Why on *earth* would your sister ever have to sell those paintings? She would never do such a thing—they've been in my family for generations."

"Well, a sculpture instructor doesn't make very much, and I figure that Father will cut her off without a cent when he finds out that she's planning to marry a Catholic."

"Grizzy, stop talking nonsense. Dorothy Mary isn't going to marry a Catholic. She doesn't even know any."

"Mamma, you haven't seen her with Joe Padrosche, her new beau. I think it might be serious."

"Grizzy, it's sweet of you to be worried about your little sister. But it's really none of your affair. Let's finish our game. Now, whose turn is it?"

V

Mrs. Flagg was listening for Dorothy Mary's return from tennis. Seated at her writing desk, her back to the door, she entered unpaid bills into her household ledger. Years ago she had found that the wide silver frame around her mother's portrait, on the left corner of the desk, gave a distorted, but nevertheless recognizable view of activities in the hallway behind her.

She had made this discovery when the boys were small and their nurse was off for the day. The reflection of a swift motion in the silver frame had caught her eye and she'd turned to see three-year-old Grizzy smash a metal fire truck into baby David's skull. Blood was everywhere. Grizzy ran into another room, the fire engine still in his hands. After this, she'd formed the habit of spying on people in the hallway as she sat at her desk. She filed her observations away for future use.

A car door slammed and Mrs. Flagg called to her daughter as the front door closed. She watched for Dorothy Mary's reflection in the silver mirror.

"How was your game, dear? Who was at the club?"

"Oh, no one special," Dorothy Mary said dismissively. "The place was fairly deserted. We had the courts to ourselves. I guess people are going away already. Anyway, we lost."

"With whom were you playing?"

"Shelby Thayler and Stewie Frazer. We had a grand time. Stewie does this imitation of Helen Keller and Mrs. Roosevelt that is a *scream*. Every time I started to serve, Stewie would pretend to be blind, using his racquet for a cane. Like this." Dorothy pantomimed with her racquet. "I know it's terrible, but he was so funny. Anyway, most of my serves were out and we lost."

Mrs. Flagg watched Dorothy's face in the silver frame. "Who was your partner, dear?"

A dreamy, unfamiliar look came over Dorothy's mirrored features. "Shelby's sculpture instructor at the Art Alliance. I don't think you know him. His name is Joe Padrosche."

"Padrosche—What kind of name is that?"

"I don't know, but he's Spanish. Shelby thinks he's an extremely talented sculptor. I hope you don't mind, but I've invited him to dinner next Sunday. Oh, Mother, he's such an interesting person."

"Well, dear, I'm awfully sorry, but that's impossible now. It will have to wait until the fall. That's what I wanted to tell you. I've decided that we'll go to Daisy Lawn earlier than considered. The weather has turned so hot and muggy, and Aunt Jeanne has planned several lovely parties for you up in Newport. So, I'll need your help if we're to get off on time. We've got to pack and close up this house. I'm sending some of the staff to Daisy Lawn tomorrow morning. We'll drive up the following day."

"But, Mother, what about Lizzy Newbold's party?"

"Dorothy dear, I hate to have you miss it, but you know the doctor insisted that I cannot take these Philadelphia summers. I've already sent our regrets to Mrs. Newbold. Lizzy will understand when you explain it to her. We'll have Aunt Jeanne include her in one of your parties." With a bright smile, Mrs. Flagg turned toward her daughter, closed the black ledger, and added, "I know you're disappointed about your new friend, but he'll keep 'til fall, don't you think?"

Dorothy Mary leaned against the carved wooden doorframe, her white socks and shoes stained with orange dust from the tennis courts. She slowly bounced her racquet against one bent knee and watched the blood rise to the surface in crosshatched angry red lines.

"Mother, I'm not going to Newport with you."

Mrs. Flagg gathered her bills and straightened them into a neat pile.

"Dorothy, don't be stubborn. We're all going the day after tomorrow. I've too much to do right now to cope with one of your moods."

"But Mother—"

Mrs. Flagg interrupted, "Dorothy Mary, don't whine. You can't always have things your own way. I ask very little of you, and the one time that I do ask for a little cooperation, all I get is a long face."

She turned back to her desk and continued, "Whether you like it or not, you *are* going to Daisy Lawn, and that is that. Now run along. I have so much to get organized."

Mrs. Flagg pulled the checkbook from a desk drawer and, with a sidelong glance, watched Dorothy Mary's reflection disappear from the silver frame.

VI
"Daisy Lawn"
Newport, Rhode Island
Summer 1939

Dorothy Mary sat alone on the steps of the porch that curved around Daisy Lawn. Behind her she could hear the band and imagined Meyer Davis smiling behind his glasses and bouncing to the rhythm.

Her mother was giving a party, and Dorothy Mary and Liz Newbold were the guests of honor. But Dorothy Mary didn't want to be a guest of honor. She didn't want to be anything. Most of all, she didn't want to be in Newport.

It was a cool evening. The breeze had just begun to blow in from the sea. From where she sat she could see the light of Sakonnet Point, flashing in a widening circle, fanning the pale houses along the cliffs and swinging out to sea. Closer to her, fireflies had begun to spangle the darkness with brief points of green light. Dorothy Mary remembered how she and David used to catch fireflies, pull off their tails and run around in the dark with the phosphorescent bits glowing on their shirts. Once David had dabbed firefly juice on her finger to make a special fairy ring for her.

It had been a month since she'd seen Joe and she missed him terribly. She had written to him—long letters on her blue writing paper in her round script. She'd invited him to spend the Fourth of July at Daisy Lawn, but Independence Day had passed without his reply.

She hadn't realized that she would miss Joe with a physical ache. All the words of the love songs seemed so true—written just for her. Somehow, she hadn't bargained for this kind of loss. In the first weeks at Daisy Lawn she'd hovered around the telephone, convinced the next call would be from him, and she knew exactly what she would say. First, she'd lecture him because he had ignored her for so long. Then she would relent and establish their old intimacy.

But his call never came.

She reviewed their times together and their conversations, trying to discover what she could have done wrong. What could she have said? But there was no satisfactory answer. He had simply dropped out of her life.

A feminine voice called, "Come outside. It's much cooler out here."

The Dressing Drink

She recognized Shelby Thayler and Ernie Liddell at the screen door, but not feeling sociable, Dorothy Mary moved closer to the shadows. She hoped they wouldn't see her so she could slip away into the darkness and re-enter the house from a different direction.

Shelby strolled to the porch railing and looked at the sky, exclaiming over the stars. The reassuring creaking of the chain of the wooden swing told her that Ernie was swinging back and forth. Dorothy Mary was about to leave when she heard Shelby make some reference to Padrosche. She listened carefully.

Shelby had been talking about getting her work together for presentation to the Art Students League in New York. She continued, "…but it's been complicated. I need a reference from Padrosche, my sculpture teacher, and he's left the Alliance. They have no forwarding address yet. They seem to think he's gone back to Spain. Come to think of it, he always said he wanted to help with the war there."

Ernie Liddell put in, "Padrosche… Wasn't he the one who was seeing so much of Dorothy Mary? She must be pretty broken up."

Shelby laughed, and said, "Oh no, not Dorothy Mary. I know her better than that. She's a cool one. She was just having fun with him. He was a pleasant diversion, but he's really not in her league, if you know what I mean." The door opened again and others came out onto the porch. Keeping to the shadows, Dorothy Mary snuck away toward the beach, the stars giving her just enough light to guide her to the whitened path leading to the lighthouse.

As she walked, she bit her lip and tried to keep from screaming.

Gone to Spain.

Without even saying goodbye. How could he? It was unfair. She had wanted to be with him, and it pained her that he'd just been feeding her a line after all. She'd meant *nothing* to him. He'd been laughing at her all along and she'd thought that he had cared about her. She had even wanted to bring him to Denbigh.

She wiped her hand hard against her mouth, trying to rub away the memory of his tongue parting her lips. He'd given Dorothy Mary her first real kiss. She'd been alarmed and tried to pull away, but his arms held her. She dug her nails hard into her thumbs. One thing was certain… she wouldn't let him make her cry. She'd never cry.

The saw-toothed grass rasped her legs and snagged the hem of her dress as Dorothy Mary made her way toward the ocean. She wanted to sit on the rocks and watch the tide surge and ebb below her. She had nearly reached the base of the lighthouse when she blundered into the colony of terns that nested below the light. The sky was instantly filled with alarm cries and the flapping of hundreds of white wings as the birds rose from their nests. Scissor tails spread wide, red beaks gaping, they hovered in the intermittent flashes of light and hoarsely screamed. They seemed to fly in slow motion against the black sky. Dorothy Mary knew that the birds were blinded by the light. Since they couldn't see her, they would not attack.

Then something gave beneath her foot, as if she'd stepped on a rotten floorboard in an abandoned house. Crouching, she saw a tern chick fluttering against the grass. Her breath caught, she hoped it wasn't hurt, but its head rolled limply over the side of her hand as she picked it up. The tiny, rubbery beak hung open.

She had crushed it.

Dorothy Mary blew crumbs of sand from its moist open eye and pressed the downy body against her cheek. It smelled like sunshine on salt grass. Amidst the racket of birds above and the whirring of the revolving beacon, she didn't hear herself crooning, "I'm sorry, I'm sorry," as her tears wet its warm, tiny feathers.

VII

Grizzy was having a wonderful time. He watched the bubbles rising and bursting at the top of his champagne glass.

He loved being away from Denbigh. He loved the long, lazy afternoons lying on the beach and the freedom of this sprawling summer house. His room was at the top, conveniently away from the rest of the family. He had privacy, and he had Annette, a local girl who was employed at Daisy Lawn as a live-in maid. He had spotted her the first day and had marked her for his own.

Grizzy made his move slowly, carefully, so as not to alarm her. First a little flattery. Then asking her to spread lotion on his sunburned back. Ploys so trite no intelligent girl would have fallen for them—but he knew that intelligence wasn't Annette's long suit. Then a light touch on the back of her neck. Giving her the special smile. He played upon how dazzled she was by the family's money. Soon enough, he had her coming to visit him in his room. He affected interest in the narrow life that she lived in this summer town, and she fancied that he was in love with her. It wasn't long before he had her starched, pink cotton uniform unbuttoned and her bra off. Of course, she'd protest, but he knew that tonight or tomorrow night, the pleasures of still afternoons and warm evenings stretched invitingly before him. He could afford to wait. She was his pigeon.

His thoughts trailed off as he watched the guests scattered around Daisy Lawn's big living room. His mother was certainly sparing nothing for Baby Sister tonight—champagne, Meyer Davis' band, golden caviar appetizers, dinner for forty. Perhaps Mamma was trying to salve her conscience for dismissing the heart throb, Padrosche.

When Mamma had first confronted him with the task of getting rid of Padrosche, Grizzy was surprised. He knew that his mother was a force to be reckoned with, but hadn't realized she would go to such extremes to protect Dorothy Mary. It was clear that Mamma had something special in mind when she called him into her study and closed the door. That was odd, because it was a hot afternoon.

Dorothy Mary had been in her own little world ever since she had come out, Mamma told him.

Once he'd formed a plan, it had been surprisingly easy. He remembered Padrosche's cluttered studio under the eaves of the Art Alliance. It was late afternoon and classes were over. Padrosche was covering lumps of gray clay with damp rags.

Grizzy rolled crumbs of clay against a paint-splotched work table and came to the point. "Joe, my problem is this. I have a check from anonymous donors on the Main Line. People who are spending a lot of money to help fight fascism in Europe. Our damn government isn't doing anything, so they want to step in. But the problem is, how do I get this money to the people who can use it to buy arms, or dynamite, or food, or whatever?" He waited for Padrosche to rise to the bait.

Padrosche stopped shrouding his students' work and volunteered, "I could give you names of Loyalists who are still fighting Franco. The news here says the war is over in Spain, but I know they're still fighting in the hills. These people will never surrender."

"But this is a check, a cashier's check. How will we get it to them? The censors will find it in the mail."

"There is only one way." Grizzy watched Joe's Adam's apple bob, the light spark in his eyes. "Let me be the one to take it to them."

Triumph.

"We'll pay your passage. When can you leave?"

"I have to pack and make my goodbyes, then I'll catch the first boat. I must tell your charming sister what you and your friends are doing for my country."

"Joe, let's not tell Dorothy Mary. You know how women talk. The less said about this the better. Give me a letter for her. You can explain when you come back."

Grizzy had accompanied Padrosche to New York the next day and waved him out of sight. On the train home he read Padrosche's letter to Dorothy Mary, ripped it to bits and flushed it down the men's john.

The next day, Mamma's will had been changed to give him the Holbeins, and Grizzy had been her fair-haired boy ever since. Mamma would look the other way about Annette, too. After all, Mamma was his pigeon now, just like Annette.

Yes, everything was just peachy. Draining his glass, Grizzy delighted in the wine running down his throat. His thoughts returned to Annette.

Maybe tonight.

VIII

The Chinese musicians seated against one wall of the lantern-festooned teahouse were given their cue when dusk fell. As their thin melody mushroomed into the twilight, the male guests lined the carved stairway of the teahouse to watch the arrival of their female dinner partners. The procession of debutantes was led by a serious, kimono-clad eight-year-old who struck metallic glissandos on bronze chimes. Next came a pair of boys who braced long poles against their waists. Candle-lit lanterns were suspended from these poles. Dorothy Mary was washed in the orange glow of the first pair of lanterns. She gave a nervous pat to the ornaments that trembled in her upswept hair and followed her lantern bearers.

How clever of Aunt Jeanne to have produced this original party, she thought. When her aunt had suggested that it might be unusual to have an Oriental party, Dorothy Mary agreed. Aunt Jeanne and Uncle Maurice had spent years in Shanghai, and she knew that Orientalia was one of her aunt's passions—but she had no idea that anything this elaborate would occur. Twenty debutantes had been invited to the deRham's for lunch. Later in the afternoon, accompanied by excited laughter and chatter, they had been outfitted in a rainbow of embroidered Chinese robes and slippers, with matching silk pants. Dorothy Mary wore a sapphire robe with pink and white lotus blossoms cascading from her shoulders to the tip of each wide sleeve. Other intricate designs spilled down the front of the robe. Dorothy Mary recognized the scrolls of clouds but wasn't sure what the designs represented. She'd have to ask Aunt Jeanne to explain them.

The final touch had been the arrival of a hairdresser who pulled each girl's hair into a chignon and anchored a delicate Chinese bridesmaid's headdress atop it. From a distance it looked as if a benign spider has caught iridescent feathers and raindrops in its web and then spread it over Dorothy Mary's hair.

Dinner was to be served in the teahouse beyond the gardens, near the seawall. Aunt Jeanne had brought her Chinese chef and a platoon of Chinese waiters from New York. For two days they worked tirelessly, to devise a meal of subtly balanced colors, tastes and textures. Later there would be fireworks, dancing, a magician, and a fortune teller.

A pair of lantern bearers preceded each girl. In the muted light the debutantes' costumes glowed like jasper, tourmaline, moonstone. Interspersed throughout the line were boys tooting whistles, banging drums, clashing cymbals. Aunt Jeanne said that these young musicians would frighten off lurking evil spirits. Chaperones trailed the procession as it wound through the gardens of the estate. From the teahouse it could be seen slowly approaching, like a glittering, undulating serpent.

The Dressing Drink

Dorothy Mary with her mother and Aunt Jeanne deRhan

Chester Liddell waited on the carved stairs with the other young men in evening clothes and tried to calm himself. He had decided. He would ask Dorothy Mary tonight. He didn't know just *how* he would do it yet, but it would happen. He felt in his jacket pocket for the ring his grandmother had given him when he left Philadelphia. A month ago, he had come to Newport to pursue Dorothy Mary. He left the orchid houses in the gardeners' hands and knew he'd have to return soon.

At first Chester had no success with Dorothy Mary. She was reclusive and refused his offers of afternoon drives and picnics. She'd stayed at Daisy Lawn most of the time. He'd visited her there and they'd played endless games of Monopoly. He always chose the old shoe for his counter, and Dorothy Mary always chose the little dog. She had attended the dance at the casino with him on the Fourth, but not even the fireworks display had brightened her spirits. And Dorothy Mary *loved* fireworks. Lately she seemed to be emerging from her melancholia, becoming more the persona he had known on the Main Line. It had been arranged that Chester was to be her escort at dinner tonight.

As the procession reached the teahouse, Aunt Jeanne beckoned to Chester. Dorothy Mary took his arm and he led her to their places at a low table where the other debutantes and men were similarly paired and seated. The lantern bearers fitted their poles into standards so that a halo of lantern light enclosed the teahouse, and the boys, released from their duties, ran noisily across the dark lawn. In the kitchen Aunt Jeanne's staff was preparing the boys' wages for scaring away the unfriendly spirits: hot fudge sundaes.

Dinner was served by borrowed waiters donning Chinese hats and sporting long, drooping mustaches. Chester demonstrated the correct use of chopsticks for Dorothy Mary. She remembered the electric thrill that Joe's touch had sent up her arm. Nothing like that occurred when Chester's hand closed over hers. Dorothy Mary was relieved. She smiled into his genial blue eyes behind their thick lenses and felt safe.

Over the last weeks Dorothy Mary had changed her opinion of Chester. Back on the Main Line she had thought him something of a buffoon. After all, he did spend most of his time in greenhouses and droned on about the intricacies of orchid propagation. She'd once characterized him to Sterling Longwood as being "mossy behind the ears." Chester was definitely not with it, and he didn't at all match her image of a dream man, but in the last weeks she had seen other sides of Chester and had grown to like the stolid, balding fellow. He never pushed himself on her. He knew how to share a silence companionably. He seemed content to squire her to various social functions, without making any physical demands. He was as comforting as a familiar armchair on a rainy evening. More than anything else, Dorothy wanted to be protected, sheltered, and cherished. Chester did all these things. He was a nice man. Apart from David, he was the nicest man she knew.

The meal finished, Aunt Jeanne requested that the guests move from the teahouse to chairs near the seawall. The fireworks display that would follow shortly would allow the staff to clear away the dinner paraphernalia and prepare for entertainment and dancing.

"She's certainly not missing a trick tonight," Dorothy Mary mused as she and Chester walked toward the seawall in the shadows beyond the corona of lantern light. Snatches of laughter and talk from other strolling couples drifted back to them as they strolled arm in arm. Quite nonchalantly, Chester stopped and drew Dorothy Mary toward him. Looking into her eyes, he kissed her lightly, first on her lips and then on her smooth forehead. Dorothy gasped in surprise that his lips felt cool and soft against hers. She rested her head on his shoulder for a moment, enjoying the closeness of his embrace. Then, remembering her fragile headdress, she drew back with a smile. A smudge of powder remained on his jacket, which she quickly brushed off. They continued walking, this time with his arm around her shoulder and hers around his waist.

Later in the evening, after the fireworks had drawn oohs and aahs from the assemblage as they burst into giant shimmering dandelions and whistling showers of radiant sparks, after the magician had pulled silver coins from the air and released a cloud of azure butterflies from an empty silk bag, while they were dancing, Chester took the ring from his pocket and awkwardly fitted it onto the third finger of Dorothy Mary's left hand. Dark sapphires glinted on either side of the rose-cut diamond as she admired it.

She said nothing.

When the music stopped, Chester asked Dorothy Mary, rather stiffly, if she would marry him.

Dorothy Mary looked at the ring, and then she looked at Chester's earnest, eager face. Not knowing what else to say and not wanting to disappoint him, she suggested, half joking, that they should consult the fortune teller seated in one corner of the teahouse. She would abide by whatever he said.

Chester explained what they wanted to know to the wizened, black-robed figure. Aunt Jeanne related this to the old man, as he understood no English. Placing one hand on Chester's shoulder and the other on Dorothy Mary's shoulder, the old man closed his eyes and lifted his face, chanting in a quivery voice. Aunt Jeanne explained that he was asking the spirits to give him the wisdom to read the oracle bones properly. Then he threw a handful of yellowed bones onto a scarlet cloth that was spread on the floor. He stooped to examine the characters.

"He sees the lotus and the butterfly," Aunt Jeanne translated. The lotus would sustain and support the butterfly. She would enliven his days. He would live long and prosperously.

Then the old man fixed his small black eyes on Dorothy Mary and said something more. Aunt Jeanne translated that he was giving her a blessing so that she would have many felicitous hours and happy children. Then the old man abruptly turned, collected the bones and sat down, staring straight ahead.

Dorothy Mary turned to Chester and said, "I guess that means yes."

They were engaged.

6

Mother and Father separated when I was two years old, and I only met him after she was dead. While she lived, she scrupulously eradicated any trace of him from our lives as surely as she plucked the occasional maverick hair from beneath her arched brows. She nurtured her hatred of him and passed it on to me as a special legacy laced with fear and mingled with mistrust.

Awash in diamonds, swathed in furs, pictured on the cover of Life, *walking her quartet of poodles down Park Avenue, Mother was afraid that Father would kidnap her little darling and land us all smack dab in the middle of the* Herald Tribune's *gossip columns. For my protection, she had one of the servants take me to and from school. I never understood why this was necessary but assumed that children were always shepherded by their maids. It wasn't until I was older that I connected it to my father.*

One night when we were visiting my godmother, so-called Aunt Pat Roebling, I was too scared to sleep alone in a strange room, even with all the lights on. So, Mother had allowed me to sleep in her double bed. The phone rang in the night, and I picked up to answer. After a pause, an unfamiliar voice said, "This is your father speaking."

Mother must have suspected something, because she snatched the phone away. I remember her exact words:

"You son of a bitch. You've got nerve calling. Don't you ever call again, or I'll have the cops after you so fast, it'll make your head spin."

She slammed the phone down and turned to me. "That son of a bitch. Never sent you so much as a penny postcard on your birthday. Now he decides to call? Don't worry. He'll never get his hands on you while I'm around."

The Dressing Drink

As mentioned on the previous page, cover of Life.

My first memory of Father. Of course, I came to hate him, to regard him as a danger, and Mother and I formed a secret society that fed on her bitterness and resentment of this strange man that only one of us knew. It became something special——one of the few things that Mother and I could share.

She always remembered his birthday and, sitting before her dressing table with a Seagram's Seven and Ginger Ale, wearing only her black lacy slip, she would drag on a cigarette and pensively remark, "Wonder whether I could send a bomb via air mail."

She would invariably warn me, "Remember Tommy, if a strange man ever comes to the door, under no circumstances let him in. Slam the door in his face and come and get me."

I would pull myself up to my full seven-year-old height and vow, "Don't worry, Mother, I'll protect you."

Blowing out a blue cloud of smoke, she would respond, "Your father was a very strong man. I don't think you could."

That always bothered me. Here I was, trying my best to protect Mother from this dangerous maniac and she was busy telling me that I was powerless.

Father has been dead for over a decade now. Although I knew him for a year when he was working on Broadway in Hello, Dolly! *We never became friends. This isn't surprising. He was always a bogeyman when I was a child. I had to be constantly on guard—he might appear at any time to hurt Mother or me, and I knew that there was nothing I could do to stop him. And, in a sense, I'm still as powerless against my father as when I was seven. Only now he seems to turn up more often than he did when he was alive.*

At five one morning, still dressed in my dinner jacket and wearing patent leather pumps, I stopped in at the Mudd Club in TriBeCa. If you've heard of it, you know that it was a New Wave club in the 1980s, with live music and dancing. I liked to go there from time to time. It was such a contrast to the stream of ever-so-fashionable East Side cocktail parties, dinners, and benefits I'd been obligated to attend. You might have called it slumming; I didn't.

The Mudd Club had a gigantic movie screen behind the dance floor with old movies running continuously. But the punks on the floor, with their apricot and turquoise tufts of hair, tight-crotched leather jeans and oh-so-casually ripped T-shirts were usually too spaced or too stoned to notice. The movie's soundtrack was submerged in whatever music shrieked and pounded into the darkness.

I'd ordered a drink and turned to survey the scene, when I saw Father.

Up on the screen, two stories high, he was one of six chorus boys dancing behind Fred Astaire in "Swing Time." When they run it on TV, they usually edit the beginning and cut out Father. You probably wouldn't recognize him anyway. But there he was, smiling and tapping, looking so young and hopeful. He even had a full head of hair. I was excited and proud. I wanted to tell someone, "That's my father!" but there was no friendly eye to catch: everyone else was immersed in the pounding music and the darkness. Not even the bartender noticed. Father had performed for an audience of one. Me.

It wasn't always like that. People—lots of them—once did care about Jack Goode, my father. They cared about him because he made them laugh. He had employed five different names: Irwin Whittridge, Jack Ridge, Irwin Ridge, Jack Good and Jack Goode; but no matter what he called himself, he was a comic, a comedian, a dancer, a clown.

And so, ladies and gentlemen, please resume your seats. Our second act is about to begin. It features our funny man... my dad.

Jack Goode (White hat kneeling in the center) with Cary Grant (Police hat kneeling in the center) amongst other actors/dancers.

7

Columbus Ohio
Spring 1923

    Doctor Kampine had said that Ellen Whittridge, Irwin's mother, could go any time now.

    She'd lost consciousness two days before. Irwin and his older sister took turns watching her through the night. The morning sun against the drawn window shades submerged the parlor in a sepia twilight. Irwin couldn't see his mother clearly, but he listened to her breath: irregular raspy sighs that ended with a strangulated gurgle in her chest.

    That sound reminded Irwin of the bat he'd once found trapped in the backyard cistern. He'd dug a shallow hole and buried the squeaking creature beneath shovelfuls of earth. But it wouldn't die. Every time he pressed its grave, he heard it squealing faintly. Finally, its cries had stopped and Irwin remembered being grateful. He now wished that, like the bat, Mama would let herself die. It was awful to sit and watch her struggle and not be able to help.

    His mother had always been sick. She'd had a weak heart—a legacy of the rheumatic fever she'd had as a child. Throughout his childhood, Irwin's mother had sometimes been pretty, but she'd always been pale. Any physical exertion left her panting. She was too frail to do housework. And, because his father refused to pay for what he regarded as but one more of his wife's extravagances, she had to earn money for a succession of black cleaning women. She'd given violin, voice, and organ lessons. Irwin remembered the platoons of pupils who gathered on the porch in warm weather, waiting for their turns in the parlor. The best pupils were anxious; the worst were bored.

The Dressing Drink

She loved them all.

She'd been the best music teacher in Columbus. Every year her forty-odd students gave a recital in the Episcopal Church. It was as important to Mama as Christmas, and Irwin was usually drafted to be Master of Ceremonies. The last recital had been two years ago in 1921, but then even music lessons had become too taxing for her, and one by one, the students were forced to go to less-inspired teachers. Her dusty violin lay on top of the organ in one corner of the darkened parlor. She hadn't played for a long time. The parlor's daybed had become her sick bed. Hazel had given up her secretarial job to take care of Mama full time.

Every night when Irwin arrived home from clerking in the haberdashery department of the Lazarus store in downtown Columbus, his first stop was Mama's bed in the parlor. He would try to demonstrate the tap routines he sold to the Red Mask Theatre Company at Ohio State. Irwin had danced ever since he was a kid. Mama's brother, Uncle Shep, had taught him. Mama had a keen memory for steps and protested that it was immoral for him to sell the same steps again and again to the university boys. He explained that, even though they had college educations, they couldn't learn the steps very quickly. Because they were too dumb to know the difference, why shouldn't he make a profit? Mama never approved, but she said no more. She knew that Irwin and Hazel had to earn their own money. When she'd been stronger, she had intervened between Father and the children, but when her income from the music lessons stopped, she could no longer protect them. Even though Hazel shopped and cooked all the meals, Father thought it was fair to charge both room and board—just as if they were living in a rooming house.

The previous fall Irwin and Hazel had whirled around this little parlor, practicing the dance routine that won first-prize money at the Spring Lakes Ballroom. Mama played the organ and this same room had been filled with her music and laughter. But that time seemed remote, and the organ had been muffled in its oilcloth cover for months. Mama couldn't even sit up, much less play.

Irwin had hoped she might open her eyes and recognize him when he kissed her and said goodbye, but her eyelids were still. Even in the dim light he could see the bluish color of her lips. Irwin hurried onto the porch to get rid of the sweet-sour odor that came from this unconscious woman who didn't seem at all like his mother. He'd have to hustle to catch the trolley that would take him to work on time. But of course, he was always hustling. He hustled with the pressures of show business and his own inner thoughts until they fostered a bleeding ulcer which would ultimately kill him. His intensities grew and grew with his "hustle." The hustle to survive and succeed multiplied, until there was nothing left.

Jess Whittridge, Irwin's tight-fisted father, had a glossy, yellow Pierce Arrow—but even if he were going the same direction, Jess would never give Irwin a lift. Irwin wouldn't ride in his father's car, anyway. Not since the Saturday afternoon he'd seen him driving along High Street with one arm draped around a woman in a cloche hat and fur scarf. Mama had *just* been confined to the daybed. His father had said that he had to entertain clients all day. Now that Irwin knew his father's secret, he never lost an opportunity to needle him with it. Suddenly he had a good excuse for stealing money from Father's wallet whenever he saw it on top of the bureau. Slipping a few singles or a fiver from the fat wad in the brown billfold seemed only right. Now Irwin was evening the score for Mama, as well as for Hazel and himself.

Hazel walked her brother to the front gate and promised to call him at work if anything happened to Mama during the day. Irwin hated to leave Hazel all alone, but his boss, Mr. Stimpson, was very strict: If Irwin were late, he'd probably be fired. And Irwin needed his job. Years ago, he and Hazel had made a pact to leave home when Mama died. Hazel hated Father, too. She waved goodbye and shaded her eyes against the morning sun. Her new engagement ring glinted on her pale hand. Irwin wondered whether Hazel had gotten engaged to Skid Fenmore, that boob, so she'd have someplace to go when Mama died. Irwin would have to do something about that, but so far he hadn't found the right moment to tell her that she was making a mistake. He couldn't let her marry Fenmore.

But right now, he'd have to hurry if he was going to get to the trolley on time.

II

Covering an entire block in the heart of Columbus, the Lazarus Department Store prided itself on innovation. Lazarus was the first store in the nation to install moving escalators. It also had the much-touted Niagara Soda Water Fountain and an aviary of twittering canaries to entertain shoppers as they rested from bargain hunting. Once, a new, but driverless, electric car had careened out of control across High Street and through the store's plate glass windows. A photograph of the carnage graced the front page of the *Dispatch*. After the shards of glass were cleared away, Lazarus kept the newfangled machine, adding a sign that read, "Everything new comes to Lazarus first."

This self-conscious fervor to be first was responsible for the fashion show that would delay Irwin's lunch today. As predictably as a procession of clock figures emerging to mark the hours, the clerks of the men's department trooped through Lazarus's window at noon each Monday. The displays of crockery and female mannequins in fringed dresses and rolled-down stockings were moved back so there was a clear path in the line of windows that paralleled High Street.

The other clerks complained that they would rather do anything—even check inventory, the most tedious job in the haberdashery department—than appear in the fashion shows. Behind Mr. Stimpson's back they moaned that they felt like sissies. They strode as rapidly as possible through the display windows, as if running a gauntlet. But Irwin never complained about the fashion shows, and he was the only one who never got butterflies. Not only did he like wearing the newest clothes, he also loved having an audience. Irwin had become the star of the Lazarus Fashion Show. He didn't simply show the clothes and make a hasty exit; he did pantomimes with the mannequins and used his tap routines. Today he would show a golf outfit, which consisted of patterned hose, baggy plus-fours, a white shirt, a cardigan sweater with a brown and tan Aztec design, a green striped bow tie and a tan golf cap. He surveyed his reflection in the dressing room mirror and thought that whoever dreamt up these clothes had never set foot on a golf green. Like the voluminous Oxford bags he had worn last week, these clothes were laughable. Bobby Jones would never wear them.

Irwin went upstairs to the sporting goods department and borrowed a golf bag, clubs, and a pink rubber ball. Back in haberdashery, he painted the ball with the white shoe polish he had taken from the notions department. *This ought to get a good laugh*, he thought.

Irwin put a raincoat over his outfit and went outside to check the layout of the display windows. He knew Mr. Stimpson wouldn't miss him because sales in the department ceased in the frantic hours before each fashion show. There were seven window displays between the curtain where he entered and the corner window where he exited. If he could throw the ball into the third window, and then putt it between the legs of three mannequins, it would land on an array of sheets that draped onto the floor. Sort of in the rough. Then he would try to chip the shot into the saucepan perched atop a pyramid of iron pots and pans that Lazarus had on special sale this week. Irwin thought he could do it. Or at least he wasn't afraid to try. He'd had to quit Ohio State after one year, but even as a freshman he'd been captain of the golf team.

Mr. Stimpson stood in the corner window to one side of the pots and pans. Stepping up to the microphone—a large rectangular presence in itself that stood taller than the man's head—he adjusted its height and practiced. "Testing, testing. Can you hear me?" The crowd outside nodded affirmatively. Mr. Stimpson cleared his throat and with a "Good afternoon, ladies and gentlemen," began the fashion show. Each clerk was introduced with flourish, the curtain at the entrance to the display window parted, and each marched toward him.

"Here's Wilbur Hotchkiss wearing the three-piece suit that all the sheiks at OSU will be sporting in the coming fall term." He went on to describe Wilbur's suit, tie, vest, and saddle shoes, lingering lovingly over each detail. With long strides, Wilbur tried to hurry through the display windows. Head down, he clumsily obeyed Mr. Stimpson's dictum. "Turn around, Wilbur, unbutton your jacket and show the folks the cut of the suit."

By the time Wilbur reached the corner window his face was scarlet. He parted the curtains and escaped, glad that today's torture was over.

Behind the curtains at the entrance to the windows, Irwin listened to Mr. Stimpson praise the fashions of each clerk with a budding excitement. He was last on today's program. Mr. Stimpson was saying, "And now, ladies and gentlemen, here's Irwin Whittridge wearing another Lazarus first—our exclusive line of Bobby Jones Fashions that have winning ways both on and off the green."

Mr. Stimpson paused, waiting for Irwin to enter the end window. Mr. Stimpson knew enough about being a producer to have saved the best for last. Proud and excited that he now had a real performer and not the wooden sales force that doubled as mannequins, he repeated, "Here's Irwin Whittridge, wearing our line of Bobby Jones Fashions that are equally at home at active sports or leisure."

Irwin hung back, did not appear. Then he rolled the white rubber ball into what he hoped was the third window. Shouldering the golf bag, with one club in hand, he trudged through the curtains and into the first window, pretending to be all tuckered out. With exaggerated gestures, he searched for his ball. Ripples of laughter began to spread through the crowd as he peered down the neckline of the nearest mannequin's dress. No ball there. Then he spied it in the third window. Just where he had wanted it.

The future Jack Goode.

The Dressing Drink

He carefully lined up his shot, getting down on all fours to check the path the ball would take through the legs of the flapper mannequins in their winter coats. He slid his gaze up one papier maché leg and flicked the fringe on the mannequin's skirt. He smiled wickedly to the delighted crowd. Then he took out his putter and made a flamboyant business of crouching over the ball. He waggled his behind and hitched up his pants. He couldn't tell whether the audience was laughing or not because the plate glass display cases were nearly soundproof. He stroked the putt, and the ball rolled slowly between the legs of each mannequin with Irwin running alongside, urging the ball on. In the end he got down and blew at it. It reached the sheets. Irwin took off his cap and wiped his brow, then took a look at the audience. They *were* laughing. Behind the microphone Mr. Stimpson was silent.

Taking the wedge from the golf bag, Irwin sauntered to the pyramid of pots in the corner window to survey his final shot. He picked up the saucepan and pantomimed that this would be difficult. The crowd knew what he wanted to do. The craze for miniature golf had seized Columbus and all of the Midwest the previous year.

Making a show of it, Irwin went through theatrical contortions before taking his shot. The ball arced high toward the pile of pots and pans. It grazed the ceiling and landed in the saucepan. Then it rebounded straight up before it settled back into Irwin's target. He triumphantly walked into the corner window, retrieved the ball and held it up for the crowd. He glowed, watching their faces as they grinned and applauded. Irwin draped the strap of his golf bag over Mr. Stimpson's shoulder, and still holding the white ball aloft, did an energetic buck and wing through the curtains.

That afternoon, the sales in the haberdashery department were enormous. Everyone wanted the Bobby Jones plus-fours, or the cardigans, or the caps. Business subsided around four o'clock. Mr. Stimpson, congratulating Irwin on his triumph, suddenly remembered to tell him, "Irwin, your sister called about an hour ago. We've been so busy, I've forgotten until just now."

But… Hazel said she would only call if something happened to Mother.

The phone at home was busy. Damn that party line! You could never get through on it. Frazzled, Irwin asked Wilbur Hotchkiss to tell Mr. Stimpson that he was leaving early, changed back into his own clothes and left the Bobby Jones exclusives on the dressing room floor.

He caught the first trolley home. As the car made stops at every other corner in the city, Irwin grew enraged at its slow-motion pace. He wanted to yell at the conductor to hurry up.

Damn Stimpson! This is all his fault.

Eventually, the trolley reached the outskirts of Columbus and headed toward Grandview Heights and Orchard Street. Irwin hoped he was in time. He roiled, thinking that he'd probably been clowning for the audience of shoppers while Mama had been dying. He remembered the way his mother had struggled to breathe that morning, the corners of her mouth caked with some white material. He tried to remember her the way she had been when she was healthy, but his head was stuck on that horrid image. If he'd only known, he wouldn't have left this morning. Irwin jumped off the car before it stopped at his corner and raced up the hill toward home, the same hill that he'd so often tap danced down to the trolley line. But practicing steps was the furthest thing from his mind. He just wanted to get home.

At the top of the hill, only a block from his house, he saw the hearse pull away from the curb.

He stopped, paralyzed, to watch it drive slowly past him and down the hill, back the way he had come. The expressionless driver didn't notice him. He couldn't have known that Irwin was the son of the woman he was taking to the funeral parlor.

Irwin turned and trudged home. At the front gate he paused to think. *Mama's gone—everything will change now.*

8

Columbus, Ohio
Spring 1923

    Irwin noticed changes right away and he didn't like any of them. The most visible were made by Father and that old bitch, Father's sister, his Aunt Edna. They said they had to prepare for Mama's funeral—but Irwin knew better.

    Capable, stout, fiftyish Edna had never been one of Irwin's favorite relatives. Long ago they'd tangled at a family gathering—all because Irwin had collected a jarful of red-legged grasshoppers. He remembered lying on his stomach on the floor of his room with two of his cousins, watching the adults in the parlor below through the grating of the hot air register. It was a dull Sunday afternoon and one of the children got the idea to drop the grasshoppers down into the parlor with the grownups. They couldn't have predicted that Aunt Edna and her new Marcel wave would pass below the register just as the insects were descending. They landed in her hair and bounded off her shoulders like animated springs. Worst of all, one ricocheted down into the bodice of her scoop-necked sundress. She screamed, and as the relatives watched and laughed, she brushed wildly to get rid of the grasshoppers. With one hand Edna fished a grasshopper from the front of her dress while ruffling her hair into a rust-colored frazzle with the other. Irwin giggled at what she had done to her hair as she whooped and screamed.

    He noticed that Aunt Edna was laughing, too. She seemed to be having a good time as the center of attention—until she looked up through the register and saw Irwin's six-year-old face laughing down at her.

    She stormed upstairs. It was the only time in his life that Irwin was ever punished by anyone other than his father. Aunt Edna grabbed him by the shoulders and shook him back and forth until he thought his neck would snap off. He never forgot it. Even now, thirteen years later, he could feel her fingers biting into his shoulders, feel his head jolting back and forth, feel the hot lump in his throat as he tried to keep from crying in front of his cousins. She had been so unfair. The others were just as guilty as he. No, Aunt Edna wasn't one of his favorite relatives. Irwin wished Aunt Edna dead, but now that Mama was gone, Father had invited Aunt Edna to the house. She'd become a semi-permanent household fixture.

She arrived with her suitcase the night Mama died and took charge even before she'd unpinned her hat. She made a quick inspection of the house and declared that she wasn't certain she would be able to do everything all by herself. Everyone would have to help with the cleaning and preparations for the funeral lunch. She said, "I know this is a sad time for you, but work might just be the best thing to take your minds off poor Ellen. I know just how it feels to lose a loved one, but remember," she added, looking especially hard at Irwin and Hazel, "nothing, not even our prayers or our tears can bring her back. She's with Jesus now."

Irwin hated to hear Aunt Edna call Mama "Poor Ellen," especially when she wasn't around to defend herself, but there wasn't anything he could do, because right after that Hazel got hysterical again. After Father made her take some of the sleeping tablets the doctor prescribed, Aunt Edna put one of her beefy arms around Hazel's thin shoulders and led her upstairs. When Aunt Edna came back downstairs, she told Irwin and his father that Hazel was finally resting quietly.

Irwin didn't like the way Aunt Edna had taken over the care of Hazel: that was *his* job. He didn't like being ordered to go to bed either, but he obeyed. He fell asleep hoping that Aunt Edna would be gone in the morning.

Irwin was awakened by a quivery soprano voice singing a hymn.
Aunt Edna.

He sat bolt upright, certain that she was in his room. Then he realized that she must be washing the parlor windows that were directly below his bedroom. He listened carefully to her singing and noticed something a bit strange in the way she lilted into the chorus. The words themselves were innocent. He had often sung them in church:

And He walks with me, and He talks with me,
And He tells me I am his own.
And the joy we share as we tarry there,
None other—has ever—known.

But as her voice lingered over the phrase, "And the joy we share as we tarry there," took on a leering quality that bordered on the erotic. It made Irwin squirm to think of

Aunt Edna sharing a secret with Jesus. He flopped back and rolled onto his side, covering his head with the pillow, but the sounds of her housecleaning frenzy seemed to be transmitted and magnified by his iron bedstead. He couldn't completely block them out. He listened to the footsteps and thumpings downstairs and imagined her scrubbing, taking down curtains, washing, dusting, waxing. He heard her speaking with his father and hoped they would leave him alone—that they wouldn't make him help with the housecleaning. He just wanted to be alone. Maybe if he dressed quietly and grabbed some milk from the icebox and then ran out the back door he'd be able to escape. He wanted to see the only person other than Hazel that he could talk to about Mama—Uncle Shep. Irwin got out of bed, dressed and went down into the kitchen as quietly as he could.

Irwin had taken a swig of milk and was putting the bottle back into the icebox when Aunt Edna entered the kitchen, saw what he was doing and said, "We do have glasses, you know." She looked at him suspiciously as if she knew that he was about to run away.

"Good morning, Aunt Edna," said Irwin. He wiped his mouth with the back of his hand, and then wiped his hand on his corduroy knickers.

"Morning?" she said incredulously. "It's nearly noon. This is certainly a houseful of sleepy heads. Your father only got up an hour ago. It's high time *you* were up and at 'em. I've been working since first light. I figured I'd let your sister sleep as long as she likes, but I expected help from *you* hours ago. We've got lots to do today if we're going to get everything ready for the funeral." Aunt Edna sat down heavily in one of the straight-backed chairs around the kitchen table. She wiped her forehead with the hem of her apron and smiled at Irwin.

He tried to smile back but couldn't quite bring it off. As he closed the icebox door, he wished she wouldn't say things like "up and at 'em." She made it sound like they were comrades in the battle against dirt. Irwin didn't want to be in the same county with her, much less have her believe that they were on the same side. He tried not to notice how her flabby upper arms swung back and forth as she raised her arms to tuck wisps of hair beneath her kerchief.

"I'll swan," she exclaimed, suddenly very animated, "I've never seen such dust kitties as those under that daybed. They're the size of German Shepherds." She smiled, indicating that this was meant as a joke, and again, Irwin tried to smile too, but this was one of Aunt Edna's standard comments. Through his childhood he'd heard balls of dust compared with Shetland ponies, heifers, and elephants; it wasn't funny anymore.

He sat at the far end of the oilcloth-covered kitchen table and wondered whether her joke had ever been funny. He saw his reflection in the straight-sided, chrome-plated toaster and put one index finger over a forgotten crumb of toast, feeling its minute, jagged surface.

Aunt Edna didn't seem to notice his silence and continued, "I guess Poor Ellen wasn't herself for a long time. She was always so persnickety about her housekeeping, but from the looks of this place now, you'd never know it. I've never seen such a mess."

There was a silence and then she got a wild look in her eye and in a loud voice she quoted: "First Peter, chapter one, verse twenty-seven: 'For all flesh is as grass, and the glory of man as the flower of grass. The grass withereth and the flower falleth away: but the word of the Lord endureth forever.' Let that be a lesson to you, Irwin Thomas. All flesh is as grass."

Irwin squashed the crumb flat beneath his finger. Its sharp edges bit into his skin and he watched his fingertip go white from the pressure against the tablecloth.

"Well, as soon as you've finished your breakfast, I want you to take the rug beater and try to do something with those Oriental rugs. They're just little bits of things, but they're full of grit. I hung them on the clothesline out back, so everything's ready for you to get to work. I suppose your Mama didn't have much mind for keeping her house these last months, and I know she'd want everything in her house to be just right for her funeral, so you do a good job. For her sake. Won't you?"

Irwin's finger found another crumb and squashed it flat against the oilcloth. His fingertip blanched white again and he said, "Yes, Aunt Edna," in a barely audible voice.

Irwin got the braided, weighted, rattan rug beater from the kitchen closet and went outside into the late morning sunshine. As he rhythmically swatted the first red, orange and black Oriental rug and filled the spring air around him with dust, he noticed Hazel's bedroom curtains blowing out of her window and hoped Hazel was all right. She wouldn't be out of her room today. When Mama died, Hazel had been all alone with her. As soon as Irwin came home, she went crazy with grief. She sobbed herself into hysteria and not even Irwin could soothe her. Doctor Kampine had prescribed sleeping tablets and said that she should rest until the funeral; her nerves were shot. Then last night she'd been upset again by what Aunt Edna said. Poor Hazel. It wasn't her fault.

With a *thwop*, Irwin brought the rug beater whistling down into the undulating carpet, and cursed his father. Why had he been such a cheapskate? *Thwop*. Why hadn't he hired a real nurse for Mama instead of letting Hazel do everything? *Thwop*. Hazel had been too good—that was the problem. *Thwop*. Father had taken advantage of her. She'd done everything while Mama was sick. All the fetching and carrying, all the shopping and cooking, all the cleaning and nursing, changing sheets, emptying bedpans. Of course she was sick now. It would have been too much for anyone. And now that old bitch Aunt Edna—what nerve she had to say that the house was dirty. Who was she cleaning for anyway? *Thwop*. Only relatives would come here after the funeral. *Thwop*. Who cared what they thought? *Thwop*. They were making too much of this lunch after the funeral. *Thwop*. Father and that Aunt Edna.

I hate both of them. I wish they were dead instead of Mama.

With one final, heavy *thwop,* Irwin stopped beating the rug and wiped the sweat from his forehead. He squeezed his eyes shut and tried to remember how Mama looked before she got sick. But the image of the dying woman in the daybed and her smell kept returning to his mind. Sadness wrenching him, he began to beat the second small Oriental rug and tried not to think that Mama was dead.

When Irwin returned to the house he found Aunt Edna and Father in the parlor surveying their handiwork. They had rearranged all the furniture and were pleased with what they'd done.

Father had his sleeves rolled up and was wiping the back of his neck with his handkerchief. He was saying, "Without that organ we sure have a lot more room to maneuver in." Then he noticed his son and said, rather off-handedly, "Morning, Irwin."

Irwin couldn't believe that they'd pushed Mama's organ out into the front hall and shoved it up against the wall. "But Dad," Irwin protested. "What about the organ? Where's it going to go?"

"To Schraeder's Music Store. The truck will be here sometime this afternoon."

"You mean you're going to sell Mama's organ without even letting Hazel and me know? How could you? It was *Mama's.*"

"Well," said Jesse Whittridge, stuffing his handkerchief into a back pocket and putting his hands on his hips, his temper and color rising, "what else do you think will pay for your mother's funeral? These things are expensive. I've just been to the undertakers, and there's the coffin and the grave plot and the preparation of the body and the flowers and the hearse and God—knows—what—else." He ticked off each item on a finger of one big hand. "You seem to think I'm made of money—just like Ellen did. You must have gotten it from her side of the family. They never did understand the value of a dollar. Do you realize that her doctor bills alone will keep me broke for years? Your mother never, *ever* realized just how much she cost me."

Jesse Whittridge must have suddenly heard himself shouting at his son and become embarrassed because he dropped his voice, took a deep breath and squared his shoulders. He took a few hesitant steps toward Irwin and said in a calmer tone, "Besides, son, no one else can play this old thing. With your mother gone we don't need it and we do need the money."

Irwin made no reply; he could only look at the organ, bundled up in its cover. It waited in the hall like an unwelcome guest at a party. Over his shoulder he heard his father add, "I hate to see it go, too, I know how much it meant to your mother, but I'm afraid there's no other way."

Irwin turned and watched the words come out of his father's mouth. He thought that at least the Old Skinflint should have looked a little bit sad. Instead he seemed pleased. Yes, he was visibly pleased to have Mama's organ out of the room. As if he'd finally been able to scratch a place that had itched him for years. Irwin felt the braided handle of the rug beater in his hand and had an impulse to bring it whistling down across his father's face. He wanted to see those florid features, those bushy eyebrows, those heavy cheeks with their red and maroon tracery of broken blood vessels, recoil and bounce back and forth like the Oriental carpets on the clothesline.

Years later when Irwin relived this day, he always thought that he might have actually struck his father then and there if Aunt Edna hadn't bustled in, taken the rug beater from him and filled his arms with boxes to carry to the attic. Over the topmost box Irwin shot his father a venomous look and went upstairs. He threw the boxes onto his bed, slamming the door behind him. As he smashed his fist into his palm over and over he saw one box tip and spill old musical scores and Mama's violin onto the floor.

It made him even angrier to see that Mama's music and her violin had also been evicted from the parlor. Irwin picked up the instrument and felt its cool, polished surface. He saw the darkened place where Mama had always put her chin. He could see her standing in the parlor, her pale features concentrating on the music.

It was the first time since he'd seen the hearse pull away from the curb that Irwin had cried for his Mama. Folding his arms around the violin, he wept silently. *Oh, Mama,* he thought, *why did you have to die? Why? Why?*

Later he heard Aunt Edna calling his name. It seemed to ring an alarm in his mind. He thought, *Those two vultures downstairs aren't wasting any time getting rid of everything that belongs to Mama. If I don't get down there, there's no telling what they'll throw out next.* He dried his eyes and placed the violin carefully on top of his bureau. It would be safe there.

Upon reentering the parlor, he found that Father had made one last change in decor—he'd moved the gramophone from his own bedroom into the place where the organ had been before. The cobalt blue, lily-shaped speaker and bulky mahogany cabinet jutted further into the room than Mama's organ had. The gramophone's brass horn jutted in on Irwin, making him feel claustrophobic.

Aunt Edna had been busy, too. She'd taken all of Mama's delicate china out of the breakfront and covered the dining room table with it, out in the open. All the bone china cups and saucers that were Mama's special passion stood next to all of her best embroidered napkins and tablecloths. The antimacassars that Mama had crocheted for Hazel balanced precariously on the backs and arms of the parlor furniture. Now Aunt

Edna and Father sat side by side at the dining room table. She was dictating a list of things to be done and groceries that were necessary. Father wrote down everything she said, like the obedient younger brother that he was.

Irwin looked around the parlor. With the organ gone and everything rearranged, it wasn't a familiar place anymore. It didn't even smell the same. He felt like a visitor, a stranger in his own home.

Aunt Edna interrupted the list of groceries that she was dictating to ask Irwin to get the broom and sweep the cobwebs from the ceiling and sides of the front porch. She resumed her dictation, "And we'll need about six pounds of ham from the butcher. Nice and lean, with a piece of fat for the top. Irwin can pick it up this afternoon. You'll let him take the car, won't you, Jesse?"

But suddenly Irwin had had enough. Remembering all those times when his father had refused to give him a lift into town, and remembering his father's arm cuddling that strange woman in the cloche hat, Irwin said defiantly, "I won't take *his* car." And as Father and Aunt Edna watched, he walked stiffly over to the gramophone, wrenched the delicate lily-shaped speaker from it, and hurled it out into the hallway. It crashed against the back of Mama's organ and broke into a thousand shards of bright blue-enameled wood. Then he hurried into the hall to pick up the biggest pieces and throw them down again. He wanted to make sure that speaker was smashed beyond repair. Irwin wanted to break the rest of the machine, too, but before he could get back into the parlor to push over the heavy cabinet, his father grabbed him by the shoulder and whirled him around. Jesse Whittridge slapped Irwin hard across the face, yelling, "What the hell do you think you're doing? Have you gone crazy?"

Irwin's hand flew up to his jaw. He could feel the imprint of his father's hand on his cheek and his ears were ringing. Irwin smiled up at his father. He knew he deserved more than a crack across the face for what he'd done, but he didn't intend to stop now. He heard himself yelling, "You killed her! You killed her! I wish *you* were dead, not Mama. You killed her, you cheap bastard." And he felt triumphant, because for once someone had said the truth. Someone stood up for Mama. He didn't see that his father had picked up the rug beater from where Aunt Edna had leaned it against the wall.

But he heard the familiar whistle of rattan as his father brought it down across his face.

Just in time, Irwin put up his arms to block the blow. He concentrated on grabbing the rug beater, trying to twist it out of his father's grasp, but the handle slipped out of his hands. Irwin saw the snarl on his father's face as the rattan cut into his back and shoulders. In the background, Irwin heard Aunt Edna screaming, "Stop it, Jess! Stop it! You'll kill him!"

Irwin rolled himself into a ball in the corner of the hall next to the organ. He couldn't get away. He tried to make himself as small as possible, but kept yelling hoarsely,

"You killed her. You bastard. You killed her." The only thing he could do to defend himself was to kick at his father's ankles as hard as he could. And then he heard Hazel's voice. She was screaming, too. And there was the sound of her sobbing. And then Father stopped hitting him. Irwin looked up to see Hazel hanging onto his father's arm. In her rumpled white nightdress, her face red and awful from crying, Hazel beat against their father's chest. Father dropped the rug beater to the floor.

Irwin stumbled to his feet, trying to ignore the burning places on his shoulders and back. He looked straight into his father's face and spat.

"Mama's dead now. You can kill me if you want to, but it won't change anything and it'll *always* be your fault. And why don't you stop pretending you're sad about it. I only wish you were dead instead of her."

Irwin pushed his way out of the front door, ran down the porch steps, through the backyard and out into the alley while behind him he heard Hazel sobbing and his father's bellowing, "Irwin. Irwin Whittridge, come back here this minute!" But Irwin ignored him. He'd never speak to his father again. Or Aunt Edna, either.

He realized that he had to leave home for good.

Irwin trudged down the cinder-covered alley toward Uncle Shep's house, choking back tears. He didn't want all the neighbors to see him crying, so he straightened up and tried to walk as if it didn't hurt. His cuts and bruises weren't important now. The only important thing now was figuring out where he would go, and with what money.

II

Irwin never apologized, and in the next days he led a double life. On the surface he was the personification of the bereaved son. At the wake, tears for his mama welled in his eyes. He accepted condolences of the relatives that flocked to the house, tried to comfort Hazel, and made sure to steer clear of his father and Aunt Edna. After the incident they made a point of ignoring him. Father was, no doubt, waiting for an apology, but Irwin didn't care. *Father can rot in hell before I'll talk to him again*, thought Irwin.

Although his sorrow over his mother's death was flavored with a generous dollop of self-pity, it was genuine. He'd been his mother's favorite, and he had loved her dearly. But even though the wake and funeral occupied his time, the back of his mind was constantly busy with plans to leave home.

Soon.

Although he nodded sadly while his aunts reminded him what a good woman his mother had been, he was really planning his escape. Uncle Shep had told him of a cheap boarding house in Toledo. He felt certain that things would be better there than at home.

The Dressing Drink

He'd get a job—any kind of job.

He'd be all right.

While the minister droned on about death and the Resurrection, Irwin decided to request a leave of absence from the Lazarus store. He would call Mr. Stimpson and say the family needed him for the next two weeks. Then, if there was no work in Toledo, he could always come back to Columbus, live in a rooming house and go back to the haberdashery department at Lazarus. He had forty-two dollars saved. It would be tight, but he should be able to live in Toledo for two weeks on that, even after he'd gotten his return bus ticket.

Irwin watched the pallbearers close the walnut coffin lid over his mother's face. He was sad, but he felt relieved, too. His mother had suffered so much. It was better that she was out of pain. And besides, the person they were burying wasn't Mama. Mama was the one he remembered playing the organ and singing. But that woman was dead, too, and now he was free to get away from Father and all the relatives.

Hazel went to pieces at the cemetery and had to be pulled from the mound of floral arrangements that shrouded Mama's grave. On the way home Father comforted her in the back seat of the car, while Irwin fingered the edges of the sealed cards that mourners pressed into his hands and slipped into his pockets. There must have been twenty or thirty of them. Irwin wondered how many contained cash.

Back at the house he took the first opportunity to escape from the relatives who loaded their plates with boiled ham, baked beans, fruit salad, and banana bread. Taking a bottle of glue and a thin knife from the kitchen, he locked himself in his bedroom. He slipped the knife beneath the flap of each envelope and removed all the cash. He didn't bother to look at the cards, but made a neat pile of fives and tens on the bed beside him. Then he meticulously re-glued each envelope. All the while he thought, *Father made a hundred and fifty-five bucks on this funeral, and the Old Bastard sold Mama's organ. And he's still got the first dollar he's ever made, as well as all of the rent money from Haze and me. He'll probably never use any of this for Mama's headstone. He'll probably blow it on his girlfriend.*

Irwin finished gluing the envelopes and put the bills into his wallet. Then he lifted the mattress and placed the envelopes beneath it to make sure the glue would dry without puckering. Once they were dry, he could place them on his father's bureau. The Old Man would never suspect that Irwin had taken the funeral money. Then he packed several changes of clothes and his tap shoes and decided that if he needed anything else he could always call Hazel and ask her to send it.

Irwin unlocked his door. There were voices in the front of the house, but the kitchen sounded empty. Most of the relatives had gone home by now, or were in the parlor. He hid the suitcase behind the winter coats in the downstairs hall closet. No one would find it there.

III

Irwin opened the door to Hazel's room and went in. His sister was asleep in her single bed with the white chenille bedspread drawn up to her chin. On the shelf above her head were the dolls she'd played with as a girl. Irwin remembered how he used to kidnap and hide her favorite baby doll. What a little monster he'd been—but that was before they'd become best friends. On the table by her bed was a hinged gilt frame with his graduation photo in one half and a picture of Mama in the other. There was also a framed snapshot of her fiancé, Skid, taken on his last visit here. Irwin sat down on the edge of the bed.

"Haze. Haze. Wake up." He shook her arm.

"Brother. What time is it? I've been having the strangest dreams. All about you running up a wall. Oooh, my head hurts. I've got to get up and help Aunt Edna with the dishes."

"No, Hazel. You're going to stay right here. You know what the doctor said: no one is supposed to bother you. But I've got something important to tell you."

"Did you have another fight with Father? Is something wrong?"

"No, he's still waiting for me to apologize, pretending that I don't exist. That's just fine by me. Anyway, I wanted you to know that I'm leaving in a few minutes."

"Leaving? No." Tears started rolling down her face. "Where are you going? What'll you do? Do you need some money?"

"No, Haze, I've got plenty. You might need money yourself. Listen, before I tell you anything else, you've got to promise not to tell Father. Or Aunt Edna. I don't want to ever see them again, especially Father. He mustn't be able to find me. Okay?"

"Okay. I promise. But, brother, I don't want you to go away."

"Hazel, I've got to. This isn't my home anymore. Now, do you promise not to tell? Cross your heart and hope to die?"

Without missing a beat, Hazel finished, "Stick a needle in my eye."

"Here's my plan. I'm taking the next bus to Toledo. I've got the name of a boarding house there from Uncle Shep and he's the only one who knows what I'm going to do. I'll look for work tomorrow. I figure I can get a job as a clerk, but if I haven't found anything in two weeks, I'll come back. Stimpson thinks you need me at home. He'll hold my job that long."

Irwin looked at her bedside clock. "Look, I've got to get out of here. I'll write you as soon as I have an address. But, remember, this is *our secret*. Just ours. You've promised. Right?"

Hazel sat up and put her arms around Irwin. "Oh, brother, what will I do without you? It seems like I'm losing everyone all at once." Hazel sniffled and Irwin gave her the clean handkerchief from his breast pocket.

"Please write me—real soon. I'll miss you so much."

"I'll write. You make Skid take care of you for me." Irwin hugged his sister hard against him before he stood up.

"Now remember, keep working on our special step."

With an air of confidence he really didn't feel, Irwin fanned the air above his shoulders as if he were waving a straw hat and winked at her as he closed the door. He quickly opened it again to show her their special step, but when he looked in, she was sitting up, her head against her drawn-up knees and her shoulders shaking with sobs she stifled against the bedspread. She looked like a helpless kid.

He noiselessly closed the door and went to his room. He lifted the mattress and took out all the sympathy cards. The glue had dried and they looked as if no one had tampered with them. He evened them into a neat stack and went downstairs.

He put the cards on top of his father's bureau, then picked up his father's wallet, listening for footsteps coming down the hall. He took all the bills there were and stuffed them into his pocket, refolded the wallet and put it back in its place. Then he got his suitcase from the closet and let himself out of the house by the back door.

He hurried across the ragged grass, ducked beneath the clotheslines, passed the hollyhocks drooping on the side of the garage and slipped out through the back gate. Once he'd dropped the iron latch into its slot, he trotted down the alley without a backward glance at the lights in the windows of the house on Orchard Street.

Jack Goode from the movie *Hollywood Party*.

9

Toledo, Ohio
Spring 1923

    Feeling a bit like a fussy old lady, Irwin wiped the lunch counter with a paper napkin before he propped his elbows on it to survey the grease-spotted menu. He was wearing his only summer suit and didn't want to get it dirty. He'd bought this attire last year when Lazarus had its end-of-the-season half-price sale. At the time he'd been pleased with his bargain: a tussah silk jacket with matching vest and two pairs of elegant silk pants for only twenty-three dollars and fifty cents. Today was the first he'd ever worn the suit and found that it soiled easily. He'd carried the morning paper beneath his arm from the newsstand to this drugstore's lunch counter, and it had made a gray smudge on the side of the nubby beige jacket. He'd have to be careful to keep it clean. He needed to make the best impression he could on potential employers. He wanted them to look at him and think, *Here's a Likable Young Man, an Up and Comer, or perhaps a Captain of Industry or maybe even a Man of the World. Certainly Nobody's Fool.* Irwin was ready to impress people today. Not only was he wearing his best suit, but also he had a firm handshake, a steadfast gaze and clean fingernails. He didn't want grease spots on his elbows to ruin his appearance.

    As he crumpled the soiled napkin into a ball and put it in the ashtray, Irwin's eye caught the reflection of his face framed by placards advertising the daily specials of this establishment. Between:

> TUESDAY: Roast Beef and Gravy
> Two Veg and Pot
> Biscuits
> Coffee .45

and

> WEDNESDAY: Chipped Beef on Toast
> Two Veg and Pot
> Biscuits and Gravy
> Coffee .35

Irwin adjusted the knot of his green silk tie and admired the white polka dots. He'd been hurried out of the bathroom this morning by one of the other boarders and, since his room had no mirror, he hadn't had a chance until now to check his appearance. He straightened his shoulders, smoothed his slicked-down brown hair, smiled a suave nineteen-year-old smile and decided he was certainly Man of the World material. Possibly a Diamond in the Rough.

"What's yours, Mac?" The counterman's oily bald head glistened as he bumped a cup of coffee down in front of Irwin so that most of it sloshed over the rim.

Irwin reached for a handful of napkins and ordered two eggs over easy with sausage, buttered toast, and a glass of tomato juice. He mopped the mess from the saucer and wondered how to get coffee spots off of his trousers.

The counterman bawled, "Adam and Eve on a raft, side o' down and three pigs," to the cook in the kitchen.

Irwin put the mess of soggy napkins in the ashtray and made an annoyed face, but the counterman didn't notice. He washed glasses below the opposite counter and gave Irwin an unobstructed view of the rear of his dirty white uniform. Irwin placed a fresh napkin beneath his cup and thought that tomorrow he'd have to find another place for breakfast when the counterman said, "Good morning, Miss Roberts. And how are you this beautiful day?"

There was something in his tone that whistled without actually doing it. Irwin checked his appearance in the mirror to make sure he still looked suave and then glanced coolly in her direction, two stools away, and smiled. But the blonde didn't see him. She was talking with the counterman.

"The usual?"

"Yes, Charlie, and some coffee as soon as you get a chance."

"Scrambled cow," Charlie yelled to the kitchen. He slid Irwin's breakfast onto the counter toward him. Over his shoulder he said, "How's the show, Miss Roberts? How much longer you gonna be in town?" Charlie poured her coffee. Irwin noticed that he put hers down gently, so it didn't slosh over the rim of the cup.

"We close tomorrow, Charlie. You and your wife had better hurry up if you want to use those comps to see us. We'll open in Springfield on Wednesday." She took a sip of coffee and said, "Good coffee this morning, Charlie."

Irwin watched this exchange while pretending to read his paper. He wondered whether you had to be in show business or you only had to be a pretty blonde to get decent service from Charlie. He turned back to the want ads and circled three openings for clerks while he ate. One job was in a men's shop. Maybe he'd have a real chance at that one.

Across the counter, Miss Roberts said, "Charlie, what's a twelve-letter word for Bobby Jones' putter? It begins with the letter C."

Before Charlie could answer, Irwin responded, "Calamity Jane."

Miss Roberts looked at him across the counter. "Calamity Jane—Are you sure?"

Irwin nodded and smiled.

There was a pause while she entered the answer. Then she flashed a thousand-watt smile back at him and continued.

"Now a five-letter word for an enchantress who turned men into swine. Starts with C, too." She looked at Irwin and waited for an answer.

Irwin took a bite of toast and replied, "Circe."

"Hey, you're pretty good at this. We should have breakfast together more often." She said much more, about how she got stuck on specific words and how often it ruined her timing because she was preoccupied with trying to figure out the word, but Irwin wasn't listening. He took another bite of toast and noticed that there was something special about this girl. Yeah, she was pretty. If she'd been in his class at Grandview High, she'd surely have been Homecoming Queen. But this girl was something more than pretty. She had a larger-than-life quality, a sort of glow. She was laughing and saying, "...and between you and me, the show's bad enough without my lousing it up."

Irwin smiled and said, "What show are you with?"

"*Call of the Woods* at the Regency. You wouldn't be an actor, would you? We sure need one."

"I can dance a little," said Irwin, feeling foolish.

"Well, we don't exactly have dancers. That doesn't mean we don't dance, but everybody does a little of everything: acts, sings, dances. You know. By the way," she added conspiratorially, "I've been known to even pull the curtain. But we've got a bad problem now. We've lost an actor. Sort of unexpectedly, shall we say."

Her tone implied that, of course, Irwin understood without further explanation. He knowingly returned her smile as if her meaning were perfectly clear. He couldn't resist glancing at his reflection in the mirror, rolling his eyes and shrugging his shoulders as if to say, *What the hell is she talking about?*

The blonde saw him making faces in the mirror and laughed. "Hey, why don't you come by and see the manager?"

"Who, me?" said Irwin. Then he changed his mind and realized that it might be possible. Grabbing at the chance, he said, "Yeah me. Sure… swell." On the last word his voice cracked, completely undermining his Man of the World demeanor.

Trying not to sound too eager he added, "That would be great, Miss. I hope you don't mind but I overheard our friend Douglas Fairbanks over there call you Miss Roberts. I'm Irwin Whittridge. Pleased to meet you."

She nodded and began to eat the steak and eggs that had arrived. While she ate, she worked on her crossword puzzle. She didn't ask Irwin for any more answers and he returned to the Want Ads, wondering how such a thin girl could manage to eat such a huge breakfast. Their conversation seemed terminated, but he couldn't concentrate on the paper. His thoughts were racing.

A show! It would be great if they'd give me a job. There's probably no real chance, but maybe they'll let me try out. I could do my stuff for them. Everyone says I'm good enough for the Big Time. And the company will be leaving town soon. Then Father will never be able to find me.

Irwin ordered a second cup of coffee, finished his breakfast and waited for Miss Roberts to leave. He paid his bill, thought about leaving two cents for Charlie, but then changed his mind and left a nickel beneath his cup. If he were lucky, he'd never need Charlie's services again.

If he were lucky, he'd be in Show Business.

"Mind if I walk with you to the theatre now, Miss Roberts? I'm new in town, and I don't exactly know where the Regency is."

"Sure, come on, kiddo." Thora Roberts stuffed her puzzle book into her shoulder bag and said, "Bye, Charlie. Thanks for the breakfast. See you tomorrow."

II

Jake Murray looked up from his copy of *Billboard*, eyed the boy Thora Roberts introduced as Irwin Whittridge and thought, *Irwin Whittridge, what a God-awful name. Looks as green as they come. Christ—not another stage-struck, smart aleck, dumb kid.* Thora's short, pleated skirt flirted with him as she flounced backstage. He folded his paper.

"Well, what can I do for you?"

"Miss Roberts said you were looking for an actor."

"Yes, we certainly are. But we need an older man. Can't use you. Sorry." Murray terminated the interview by lighting his cigar, reopening his paper with a practiced flick and resettled himself in the velvet-covered orchestra seat.

Irwin stood there, a bit shell-shocked a moment before he dragged his feet up the aisle of the darkened theatre. He'd imagined that at least he'd dance for Mr. Murray. Now it was all over before he'd even had a chance.

He'd reached the glowing exit sign that led to the lobby before he took a deep breath, squared his shoulders and retraced his steps. He stood in front of Mr. Murray again and waited to be noticed. Murray pretended not to see him. Irwin cleared his throat and in a barely audible voice said, "Excuse me, sir."

Murray lowered his paper and glared at the teenage boy who once again stood in the aisle, humbled, his hands unconsciously turning his straw hat round and round by its brim. "I haven't had much experience—and I know I'm too young to be exactly what you had in mind, but I'd like to try out for this part."

Then he almost unconsciously began spinning and turning his boater faster, until it moved with a life of its own. The straw hat flipped in front of him before rolling up Irwin's arm. It then bounced off his shoulder into free fall. Just before it hit the floor Irwin snatched it up, catching Murray's eye and smiling a winning smile.

"Awe-dish-un." Murray accented each syllable as if speaking to a dim-witted foreigner. "The word is audition." There was a pause and then he said in a resigned voice, "What have you done?"

"Done? You mean on the stage? Well, only amateur theatricals in school."

Murray sighed and flicked his ashes onto the floor.

Irwin continued, "But I can sing and dance pretty well, and if I'm not good enough for your company yet, I can sell tickets or usher, or help backstage. I'm willing to do almost anything."

"Well, kid, I don't think so. This is a small show. Everyone has to double in brass, if you catch my drift. Sorry, but we're not running a school for would-be actors here. We don't have time to train people. You understand."

But Irwin wasn't willing to give up so easily. He fixed Murray with his most straight-from-the-shoulder gaze and said gravely, "But Mr. Murray, I learn real fast. I won't be any trouble. Give me a chance. What have you got to lose?"

Murray considered this argument. It would be painless to give the kid a chance. If he stunk, and he probably would, the cast would have a laugh. On the other hand, if he worked out…

"Okay. It's against my better judgment, but I know you'll never be satisfied until you get your chance. Tell me, ah…"

"Irwin, sir. Irwin Whittridge."

"Err-win?" Murray repeated the name as if it tasted like quinine, "Do you play any sports?"

"Basketball and golf." He wasn't about to ask why Mr. Murray wanted to know.

"Hmm, basketball, golf, and a dancer. That means you're light on your feet. Any good with your fists?"

"I can hold my own."

"How old are you, boy?"

"Twenty," Irwin lied.

Murray thought a moment before saying, "My boy, I was just about to wire East for a new character man, but since I like your attitude, I'll hold off and give you your chance. We'll probably both regret it, but be at rehearsal at noon. You'll take the part of Old Flapjack. It's only eight sides. If you can cut the mustard, the part is yours and you'll start in Springfield. Now understand, you're not right for it, but with a wig and beard to hide that baby face and with lots of padding, you just might pass for a heavy. Go back and ask Jimmy Ardell for a copy of the script."

Irwin started to thank him, but Murray interrupted.

"Don't thank me. You haven't got the part yet. Only an audition. We'll see how it goes. Oh, and if you work out, you'll have other duties, too. But we'll have time to talk about that later. Just ask for Jimmy backstage."

They shook hands and Murray watched Irwin mount the stage and walk hesitantly across the set to the wings at stage left. Murray counted, "One, two, three..." He grinned as the boy reappeared on the count of ten. Murray knew he'd get lost and wouldn't be able to find the corridor behind the backdrop. Irwin looked quizzically out into the orchestra.

"Go right," Murray shouted and chuckled to himself. This audition would be rich. *Yup, just as green as they come*, he thought. *But if this kid works out, it'll save me twenty bucks a week.* He turned to the review of the new George White hit. He imagined the ice that was filling up the box office and sighed. He didn't see Irwin thank him and disappear into the opposite wing.

III

Jimmy Ardell, the juvenile, was two years older than Irwin and everything Irwin wanted to be: good-looking, well-dressed, with the jaunty assurance of a Young Man About Town. Irwin liked him immediately. For his part, Jimmy was glad to see a potential replacement for the character actor. Jimmy explained that, as the hero of *Call of the Woods*, he was the only one who had no scenes with Old Flapjack. So, he was forced to do double duty and he'd been performing both roles ever since the character man left the show.

The Dressing Drink

"And let me tell you, it's hot enough on stage without racing into the wings to change costumes ten times a night."

Jimmy led Irwin up a circular staircase to his third-floor dressing room. "I'll give you a guided tour later. Now's not a good time. Most everybody's done in." At the third floor landing he opened his door with a flourish, and led the way inside. "It ain't The Palace, but it's better than lots I've seen, and it's the best we'll have 'til we hit New Orleans in six months. Take a seat."

Jimmy swept a pair of pants from the tattered upholstered chair and motioned for Irwin to sit down. It was Irwin's first visit to a dressing room. He'd expected spangles, glamour—not the peeling plaster and dank smell of this cramped room that looked like a rummage sale in progress. Clothing of all description spilled from a black trunk lettered "J. Ardell—Theatre."

Jimmy picked a worn copy of the script from his messy makeup table, and straddled the chair that stood in front of it. "If you get the part, that'll be good for both of us. I can help you, but I've gotta know what I'm working with. So, you've gotta level with me. Okay?"

Irwin nodded.

"You've never worked with a tab show before, have you?"

"What's a tab show?" Irwin asked and grinned.

"Jesus. Have you ever been on stage before?"

"Couple of times in high school."

"Christ. Alright, Irwin." Jimmy thought for a moment and then explained, talking a mile a minute as if he could force Irwin to understand everything if he talked fast enough.

"First of all, you shouldn't think that this is any great stuff. Tab shows are strictly fourth rate—they're the lowest form of show business. It works like this: Murray takes a Broadway show and cuts it to the bone. Murray's a genius for doing that. He can take a musical or an operetta that's been killing 'em on Broadway and turn it into a surefire fifty-minute disaster."

"But I thought the show lasted two and a half hours?"

"It does, but it's the olios that stretch it out."

At the word *olios* Irwin's eyebrows furrowed.

"You know, olios are acts between scenes. Done before the olio curtain, the one with all the advertisements on it. Specialty acts, okay?"

"Yeah."

"Anyway, Murray's no dodo. He makes a bundle on these shows because his costs are low and he doesn't pay any royalties because we do the shows under phony names. *Call of the Woods* appeared on Broadway as *Rose Marie*, but except for Indian Love Call, you'd never know it. Compared with the Broadway originals, I guess our shows are pretty awful. But most of the audiences have never seen a New York show, and besides they like the olios and sometimes they even like the whole shebang. All in all, it's not a bad way to make a living. Lot of traveling. Get to see a lot of this country. And it's a way to get into the business and a sure paycheck 'til something better comes along. Now, here's the script."

Irwin looked at the dog-eared copy. It seemed like Old Flapjack had a lot of lines. *Oh shit*. He'd never be able to learn all that in an hour and a half.

He glanced at the tawdry dressing room and remembered how large the theatre had seemed, and how shabby the scenery was close up. More than anything, he wanted to get out of this dressing room and out of this theatre. He'd been an idiot to ever think he could be an actor. What the hell was he doing here, anyway?

He started to get up from the chair and to say that he'd made a mistake, that he'd decided to forget the whole thing, when Thora appeared at the dressing room door, gave Jimmy a kiss on the cheek and said to Irwin, "Congratulations. I never thought you'd get this far. Murray doesn't give auditions to everyone who walks in off the street." Turning to Jimmy she said, "Do you think you can teach him the part?"

"Sure, sweetheart. I can teach this part to a trained seal. I can do anything to get out of those goddam costume changes."

So, during the next hour Irwin got a crash course in the part of Old Flapjack. He learned that he was on stage only five times:

1. In the opening number, in which he introduces himself to the audience;
2. In a scene with the Indian Chief, in which they plot the kidnap of the heroine, played by Thora Roberts;
3. In the capture of the heroine;
4. In the barroom scene, where he overhears that the heroine, who is being used to lure the Mounties away from the fort so that the Indians can steal the supply of rifles and ammunition, is his long-lost daughter, and;
5. In the final scene, in which he rescues his daughter from her captors. Old Flapjack is then killed by an Indian arrow, but the girl frees the hero. They escape to the fort, save the rifles and the day.

Together Jimmy and Irwin read and reread the lines. After only a few readings Irwin was able to get through them without glancing at the typed script. Jimmy told him what to expect at the rehearsal. He should not overact, but should copy the mannerisms of the others and appear to be saving his energy for the evening's performance. After an hour Jimmy stopped their rehearsal.

"Well, Irwin, that's about all I can do. The rest is up to you. You know the lines pretty well now—just deliver them. With any luck, you'll be fine." He got up to leave, but stopped at the door to ask, "By the way, did Murray ask you if you played any sports?"

"Yeah, he did. How did you know?"

"He always asks that. He likes to surround himself with ex-basketball players especially. Things can get a little rough for us, especially in the Blue Ridge and further south. The audiences there can sometimes be strange—can turn on you. Murray had one bad experience there and now he likes to have some strong arms to help out once in a while. Before the previous character actor started in the business, he played a lot of football."

"Why did he quit the show?"

"Got TB. Couldn't take the pressure. See you in fifteen minutes."

Alone in Jimmy's dressing room, Irwin glanced at his watch and thought, *I'll go downstairs in five minutes. Then only ten more minutes and it'll be all over. I'll probably be laughed out of the place and make a complete ass of myself. Jesus Christ, why did I ever start this? Why didn't I get out of here while I could?* The taste of the sausage he'd eaten for breakfast kept rising to the back of his mouth and he felt sick to his stomach.

Irwin reread his opening lines once more. Jimmy said that they were delivered facing the footlights. Trying not to feel ridiculous, Irwin stood up, shouldered an imaginary musket and recited to the cracked plaster over the rusted porcelain sink:

"I'm Jules Le Bloc, the trapper. The gal Hilda is my child. I search for the fur of the savage beast, deep in the forest wild. And if my name is hard to say, why simply put it back, And where'er I be, remember me, simply as Old Flapjack."

With the script in his pocket and his hat in his hand, Irwin went down the circular staircase to wait for the cast to gather onstage.

IV

The rehearsal and his audition went better than Irwin could have imagined. Once he was onstage and actually saying his lines, he no longer felt sick or scared. In fact, he even enjoyed himself. It was just like being in the windows at Lazarus, only it wasn't as confined. He remembered most of the lines, except for one place where he got stuck when he was helping the Indian Chief tie Thora to a stake. But Thora prompted him, and it went smoothly from there to when Old Flapjack died. He decided that Thora was a terrific girl. She was better than any Homecoming Queen. At Grandview High she would have definitely been Queen of the Senior Prom.

Between his scenes he read along with the others, amazed that they said their lines with so little expression. They hurried through them and it sounded like they were talking in their sleep. He was surprised that without their makeup and costumes, the actors and actresses looked very much like ordinary people—the kind who went to the Methodist Church in Columbus. He would later learn that they were exhausted from two months of one and two-night stands across the West, giving two performances a day. Their two weeks in Toledo were considered a sort of rest stop. Only Jimmy and Thora were bouncy and resilient. The three others—an aging prima donna, who still had traces of what must have been great beauty; a middle-aged, comfortable-looking character actress; and the handsome, but flabby male lead—all seemed bored with this rehearsal and eager to get it over with.

After the last lines had been spoken, Murray said, "Curtain. That's it. No notes." The cast disappeared backstage. Irwin was disappointed that none of the actors stayed to congratulate or meet him. But Mr. Murray was impressed. He shook Irwin's hand and welcomed him to the cast, and praised his quick study. Murray said that he'd never expected Irwin to be up in the part in only two hours. In addition to character parts, Irwin was to assist Bill McKinley, the stage carpenter. He was to do whatever Bill said and make himself generally useful. Irwin would earn fifteen dollars a week. Then Murray said something that Irwin would live with all his life.

"No offense, boy, but Errr-win Whitt-ter-ridge isn't right for the stage. Too long. Tell me, what do your friends call you?"

"Brother." At Mr. Murray's pained look, Irwin explained, "My sister Hazel always called me Brother, and it caught on." He smiled ingenuously.

"Brother Whittridge, Brother Whittridge. No, that's no good either. Sounds too much like a preacher. Okay. Let's just shorten what you've got to Ridge. How about Jack Ridge? Sounds better. Short, quick. More our style. From now on, as long as you're with J. Murray and Company, you'll appear as Jack Ridge."

Within an hour Jack had barreled back upstairs into Jimmy's dressing room to dredge a costume for the night's performance from Jimmy's trunk. While Jack tried to concentrate through his excitement, Jimmy taught him about beards and makeup and padding, and Jack practiced his lines until Jimmy told him to quit or he'd stuff that black beard down his throat. But Jack didn't mind at all. He had a new name, a new profession, and two new friends.

10

This early phase of my father's—Jack's—career reminds me of a story I read about a farmer in New England who ended up with an abandoned elephant. The farmer had let a traveling circus use his field, and when their manager absconded with the profits, the stranded performers fled, leaving the elephant behind.

The farmer saw his chance to make a few bucks and he advertised the presence of the elephant on view in his barn for a small admission fee. This was in the early 1800s before zoos were commonplace. An elephant was then a fabulous storybook creature, worthy of the attention of gawkers. For a while the farmer made a profit. Neighbors flocked in and plunked down their nickels to wonder at the animal's great size, huge ears, tiny eyes, and sinuous trunk. But, soon enough, the curiosity of the local villagers was exhausted. The crowds dwindled. In the meantime, the elephant consumed its weight in hay each day, and the farmer was losing money. So, he decided to turn showman and hit the road with his elephant. But there were two problems. First, he didn't want anyone to see the elephant free of charge, and second, they'd have to walk from town to town over stony, unpaved roads. To hide the elephant, he made a canvas cape that completely covered its body. To further maintain secrecy, he decided to travel only at night. To protect the beast's feet, he had the local blacksmith construct four bucket-sized leather shoes—the equivalent of Mary Janes for a pachyderm.

So, I have this image of the farmer who was trying to make a buck, trudging along lonely New England roads by starlight, leading an elephant draped in canvas. He would hear behind him the heavy step of its leather slippers as they walked through the sleeping countryside.

Somehow it reminds me of Father.

Jack Goode with Actress Ethel Merman in a scene from the Broadway production of the Musical *Hello, Dolly!* (New York).

11

1926

    Six months after his debut in Springfield, Ohio, Jack was still trouping with J. Murray & Company. At first he was flattered to be recognized as "one of those show folk," an exotic species to towns like Vandalia, Piquia, Cottondale and Taladega. He liked seeing his smiling photograph and the name JACK RIDGE in large letters on the sandwich board outside the theatre. The stars that surrounded his name and picture were only made of gold pasteboard, but in bright sunlight they glittered like the real thing.

    It had been a busy six months and he'd learned a lot. His apprenticeship with Bill McKinley, the stage carpenter, taught him the fundamentals of stagecraft. He knew how to construct flats and drops, how to paint trees and cabins so they looked three-dimensional, and how to make doors and windows that not only opened on cue, but also didn't maim or injure anyone in the process. From Mr. Murray he had learned how to find his light, to project his voice, to move so that his sight lines weren't blocked by another performer, bits of business to occupy his hands. In addition, Rodger Hawkins, the male lead, gave Jack his first lessons in the art of scene stealing.

    For Hawkins, all the world was a stage, and he made sure to never be far from the limelight. His idol was David Belasco and he made a fetish of wearing black felt hats and a sweeping cape to enhance his on-and-offstage entrances. He always sported a diamond stickpin in his silk cravat and a matching ring on his pinkie. "Badges of the profession," he called them. Although they worked together every day, Hawkins kept Jack at a cool professional distance. He considered the boy a rank amateur and demanded to be always addressed as "Mr. Hawkins." It was plain to everyone that he was jealous of Jack's natural gifts and that he resented his easy success.

A few weeks after Murray hired him, Jack had learned where all his laughs were in *Call of the Woods* and he looked forward to them at each performance. When a matinee audience in Cincinnati didn't respond as expected, he was puzzled. He'd done everything the same and yet they didn't laugh at all at a joke that had always gotten big hoots. After the performance he asked Thora about it.

"What happened this afternoon while I was doing the 'We'll roast her. We'll toast her' bit? Why didn't they laugh? Did I do something wrong?"

"No, you were fine. It's Rodger."

"But he fed me the lines, same as ever."

"Sure he did. But how long are you going to let him play with that diamond ring of his? He flashes it to the audience like a semaphore. I'm surprised you got any laughs at all."

"What should I do?"

"That's up to you. And while we're on the subject, watch out for Maude. Her favorite trick is to wave her handkerchief during someone else's lines. If you don't do something, it'll get worse. When I started with the company, she did it to me. Night after night, she'd play drop the hankie. It drove me crazy. Then one night I grabbed it away from her onstage. As she dropped the hankie, I crossed, swept it up with my upstage hand, gingerly stepped on her foot with my downstage leg. She winced with pain, and I mimed dabbing tears from my eyes and minced off. Fixed her wagon. Never happened again."

At that evening's performance Jack kept one eye on Hawkins' hand.

Thora was right!

Whenever Jack had a line, Rodger moved the fingers of his hand ever so slightly. Once, he patted his hair. Another time he toyed with the fringe on his buckskin costume, but the result was always the same; the audience watched that sparkly ring. Jack sacrificed two scenes to Rodger's trick and then decided he'd had enough. In the capture scene, just before Jack got to the 'We'll roast her. We'll toast her' bit, he suddenly grabbed Hawkins' wrist. With a crafty look on his face, and keeping in character as Old Flapjack, he ad-libbed:

"Where'd you get this pretty trinket, Red Hand?" He flashed the ring at the audience so they saw it and continued, "Steal it from some cavalry officer you bushwhacked? Looks too good for the likes of a sneak thief like you."

Jack snatched the ring from Rodger's hand, tossed it into the air, caught it, and, with one of Old Flapjack's cackles, stuffed it into his pocket.

"Until I've got the furs you've promised for my part of our bargain, I'll keep it safe, right here." He patted the pocket and leaned on his musket, his eyes on Hawkins' startled face, daring him to object.

"Let's just call it Old Flapjack's personal insurance policy. It'll keep you honest.

The Dressing Drink

Keep you from cheatin' me outta what's rightly mine." As an aside to the audience he added, "Never can trust these shifty Redskins."

Rodger Hawkins never tried to steal another scene from Jack, but for the rest of the run he maintained his distance.

J. Murray & Company played in towns from Toledo to Cincinnati, from Lexington to Chattanooga, from Anniston to Vicksburg, from Natchez to New Orleans. The length of each stand was determined by the potential box office take. In the largest towns they'd play five days, giving both matinee and evening performances. In the jerk-water towns they'd do one-night stands. Business was good, and Murray raised Jack's salary to twenty dollars.

But once the newness of trouping had rubbed off, Jack grew tired of the routine. Being a performer was hard work and the frequent one-night stands were the worst. The company arrived at the town at dawn, or very late at night. While the rest went off to find breakfast, or rooms, or the local bar, Jack and McKinley unloaded the company's baggage at the opera house. This sounded grand, but it was usually only a large room above a store with a tiny stage and a piano at one end. Now Jack understood why Jimmy Ardell had appreciated his dank dressing room at the Toledo Regency. Most of these houses had no backstage area at all, or else tiny, filthy cubicles. In places that had no opera house, they'd play in a church basement. In Methodist or Baptist towns they'd play in the grange.

After Jack and McKinley set the stage, the company rehearsed the night's show, running through their paces as quickly as possible. After rehearsal there were free hours to sleep in their dressing rooms or see the town. But, except for Cincinnati, Vicksburg, Natchez and New Orleans, the towns were nothing special. Just appendages of the rail lines. They always had a barber shop, Chinese laundry, drugstore, dry goods emporium and, unless it was a dry county, a saloon. Jack found that although the audiences in these towns were starved for entertainment, the actors weren't otherwise welcome. The locals considered theatre people akin to side show freaks; they wanted to gawk at them, but only from the safety of the footlights. So, the actors kept to themselves. There was less trouble that way.

After each show Jack and McKinley struck the set and loaded the company's baggage onto the express wagon. They caught the next train out and slept on the B&O or Southern's gritty, unsprung wicker seats. On long hops they had berths, but usually their train trips weren't long enough to warrant them. The next day it started all over again in the next town. Jack grew tired of hearing himself say the same lines in the same play. He was tired of boardinghouse food and thin coffee, tired of washing his socks in men's rooms, tired of not belonging; but he never grew tired of the laughter and applause of his small-town audiences.

Once Mr. Murray learned how well Jack could dance, he featured him in two olios.

Jack constantly polished his routines, trying to build small laughs into the waves of sound that would wash over the stage. Depending on the bill, he either did a flash tap duo with Thora Roberts or a hot number with Jimmy Ardell. In the tap olio they wore green satin costumes with Thora showing plenty of leg, but the other olio was his favorite because it had lots of laughs. While the piano player vamped, Jack would crawl out from under the curtain, struggle to resettle the padding strapped to his chest, and begin an up-tempo song in which he described his lady love. "She's got hot lips. She's got black eyes. She's got long, brown curly hair. She's got me hyp-notized." Then he did a comic dance with his musket as a prop.

In the finish, he'd get very excited, look off to stage right and say to the audience, "And here she is now!" Then he'd wet his palms and slick down his coonskin cap and Jimmy Ardell would lumber on in the moth-eaten bear suit he'd discovered in an antique store in Cincinnati. Jimmy'd added a pair of red wax lips, a flowered hat and a pink tutu. They'd dance around, Jack making leering faces at the bear and at the audience. Jimmy danced as delicately as his bear suit allowed. The olio ended with Jack on one knee, proposing to his ursine sweetheart. *Well, this sure ain't high art*, Jack thought to himself, *but it always did get a laugh… and something more.* Jack played it straight and true, and in a strange way there was a kindness and empathy after the laugh. It touched the audience. Funny how funny isn't always funny but kind and endearing.

II
November 1926
New Orleans, Louisiana

Jack had known that it was risky to tell Hazel about J. Murray & Company, but he'd written to her anyway.

He'd been so proud to have a job as an entertainer and so homesick that he'd given her the troupe's itinerary. Father must have wormed the information from her because a few weeks later the letter from *him* arrived. Jack kept it several days before he opened it and after he read it, he put it at the bottom of his makeup kit. Whenever he prepared for a show he'd see the white envelope under his tubes of greasepaint. It was smeared with makeup and spotted with cold cream now, but it was a reminder that Jesse Whittridge had asked his son to come home. He'd even apologized for their fight and promised that if Jack came home he would send him back to college—all expenses paid. There was no mention of the stolen money. If the Old Boy suspected Jack as the culprit, he wasn't letting on.

Father wrote that, since Hazel was married and had gone East with her husband, the house was lonely. Jesse Whittridge suggested that he and his son could keep each other company. Jack didn't like the idea of sharing bachelor quarters with his father, and he didn't intend to ever go home to Columbus, but he'd saved the letter. He'd never written back and whenever he saw it at the bottom of his makeup case he thought, *If the Old Skinflint is ready to part with enough dough to send me back to school, he must be feeling real sorry for himself.* Jack remembered how cheap his father had always been and was pleased to know that his silence must hurt him now.

Since J. Murray & Company had reached New Orleans and thus, the end of the road, Jack didn't know what he would do next. He'd talked with Jimmy and Thora about forming an act. They'd even roughed out a routine based on the duo that Jack and Thora did as an olio. Jack taught Jimmy all the steps for "Two Boys and a Girl," in which Jimmy and Jack competed for Thora's attention, but no definite plans had been made. The uncertainty and apathy made Jack's stomach hurt.

After the evening performance Jack went directly to the room he shared with Jimmy. The other two had tried to convince him to go to the French Quarter for a celebration, but he'd felt like a third wheel. Their closeness made him jealous, on top of all the other negative emotions roiling around inside him. He didn't know which of the pair he resented more. It was all mixed up. Thora was a dish. Although she treated him like a younger brother, there was something in her manner that encouraged Jack. But he never would have a chance as long as Jimmy was hanging around. Jimmy made it plain that Thora was his property.

To make things worse, Jimmy was everything that Jack admired. Being with him made Jack feel invincibly larger than life, like a world-beater—a Genuine Up and Comer. But Thora took up most of Jimmy's time. They did everything together and often asked him to tag along, but Jack was tired of being a tagalong, only an audience, the perennial best friend.

More than anything, Jack just wanted to go to sleep that night. He decided that tomorrow was soon enough to make plans for the future. Maybe the three of them could find work at some club in New Orleans after the show folded for the season. He'd like to stick with Jimmy and Thora. They weren't perfect, but they were the best friends he had.

III

Jack was awakened by pounding on the door and Jimmy's voice saying, "Jack! Jack, wake up. Let us in."

He turned on the lamp and looked at the alarm clock. *Ten past four? What the hell was going on?* He heard Thora's giggle and more pounding. And then... they started to sing. "When the red—red—robin comes bob—bob—bobbin' along..."

Jack put on the shirt he'd worn the day before and fumbled with the chain lock, mumbling, "All right, all right. Hold your horses."

Jimmy and Thora sang louder, "WAKE UP, WAKE UP YOU SLEEPY HEAD." Jack opened the door on "GET UP, GET UP GET OUTTA BED."

"*Shh*. Shut up, you two. You'll get us thrown out of here." He pulled them into the room and took the bottle from Jimmy.

They continued, "Cheer up. Cheer up, the sun is red..." There was pounding on the wall from the adjoining room and they stopped, grinning guiltily at Jack.

Jimmy put his arm around Jack's shoulders and whispered, "Ol' frien', we've come to propose a toast." He filled the glass and lifted it towards Jack. "To the man who made it all possible. To Jack. Bes' frien' a guy ever had." Jimmy gave the half-finished glass to Thora, flopped back onto his bed, and closed his eyes. "C'mere honey." He stretched out an arm to where Thora sat on the bed next to him.

Jack became more and more irritated. "Would you two *please* stop talking in code and tell me what's going on? It's four in the morning, for Christ's sake."

Thora said, "Well, Jack, we wanted to come celebrate with you, because we owe it all to you."

"Owe what to me?"

"The fact that you are looking at the new dancing sensation of New Orleans. Roberts and Ardell."

"Ardell and Roberts," Jimmy's sleepy voice corrected.

"Sweetheart, we'll talk about that later." She smoothed the hair back from Jimmy's forehead. "Let's not worry about top billing right now," she said through a smile.

"Well, go on," said Jack hoarsely, fists clenched. But Jimmy was breathing deeply.

"He's out cold," Thora said softly, "Maybe we'd better let him sleep. He's had an awful lot to drink." She took off Jimmy's shoes and covered him with a blanket. "He's going to feel it in the morning. Thank God he can sleep late." She sat down on Jack's bed and continued, "Jack, it was the most wonderful night. And we really do owe it all to you. We've got work at a place in the French Quarter called *Le Chien Noir*. Has a band and a stage, and the manager was desperate for a dance team. We started shooting the breeze with him in the bar and when he found out that we were performers, he practically begged us to show him our stuff. So we did. And he liked us! And we've signed for seventy-five dollars a week *plus* meals. It's a terrific break."

Jack focused on the red, thin hand of the clock as it punctuated the passage of each second with a mechanical jerk.

"Well, aren't you happy for us?" she asked, nudging him playfully.

"Yeah, it's a terrific break, Thora. Just terrific," Jack said dully, wishing she would

The Dressing Drink

go away. "Now, if you don't mind, I'd like to get some sleep." He roughly got back into bed, pushing her off in the process.

Thora stood at the foot of his bed, looking at him. "Jack, why are you acting so funny? What's got into you? We thought you'd be happy for us."

"Thora, believe me, I'm delighted," he said evenly, all the while fussing to straighten the sheet. "Just delighted. Now will you let me sleep?" He reached over and turned off the lamp. He'd expected her to leave, but she didn't move.

After a while she said in a small voice, "You're mad, aren't you?"

"Of course not. I'm just tired." He faked a yawn, turned on his side and punched his pillow into a tight ball beneath his head. He wanted so much to let her have it at the knees and he knew he could do it. But he wanted to kiss her, and more, too. So many feelings took so much energy and Jack instead pent it up, told himself he was biding his time.

She left the room. Jack listened at the door, as thin as toilet paper, and heard her footsteps receding down the hall. He breathed a sigh of relief to have the darkness all to himself. *How could they have done this to me? That number belonged to Thora and me, and I thought it up. It's more than half mine. She could have at least asked if I'd mind if they took it. That would have been the decent thing to do. And what about all those plans for us all to work together? What about 'Two Boys and a Girl'? I guess I'm not good enough for them. Good for them,* they *got work, but what the hell am I supposed to do? Get some kind of shitty job around here? There's always work if you look for it, but it won't be in show business. And as long as I stay in New Orleans I'll be with them—just a third that nobody wants around. They don't really care about me anyway. And I think they're shitty. Just shitty.*

Jack lay in the darkness, imagining conversations in which he would tell them off. He'd make clear just how rotten they'd been—how careless of his feelings. He wished he'd blurted out all of his thoughts at Thora, sent her out sobbing, or kept her there, kissing. Then he stopped himself. *What's the use?* he thought. *They're so wrapped up in themselves that they forgot all about me tonight. That proves they don't care.* A thought that tormented him consistently, always dismissing his love of friends to protect himself, his emotions, and his mind. He needed to stay sharp, and part of that meant not wasting energy on people so self-involved. Jack was very good at turning it inward, holding resentment in his gut until it twisted back on him. He flipped onto his stomach and covered his head with his pillow. It was a long time before he fell asleep.

The next evening, as Jack removed his makeup after the final performance, his father's letter stared up at him from the bottom of his makeup kit.

I'd have done anything to get away from the Old Man, and now here I am ready to do anything to get away from here. I'll never get it right.

Thora's words burned in his brain: *"You just left your sister there? What if she's hurting?"*

Jack was always hurting. Who cared about that?

He collected his pay from Mr. Murray, shook hands, and decided to take the next train north to Columbus. Jack cleared out of New Orleans without saying goodbye to Thora or to Jimmy. He wondered if they'd notice that he was gone.

IV
The Ohio State University
Columbus, Ohio
October 1929

Jack lounged on a wooden seat in the topmost row of the lecture hall. From the podium below, Dr. Karp, Professor of Biology, was talking about oogenesis—the process by which a mature egg cell is produced. Karp was deep into his lecture and words such as *ootid, polar body, primary oocyte, secondary oocyte, mitosis,* and *meiosis* were splashed onto the chalkboard behind him. Tiers of students assiduously penned down Karp's every word. He did have a reputation for testing from his lecture notes, after all.

The class was composed of pre-med students and most of them took their studies quite seriously, but Jack doodled in his notebook, adding squiggles and flourishes to the face he'd drawn, changing it from a caricature of Karp to a bearded lady. His mind had wandered a few minutes after the professor launched into gamete formation and Jack became lost in the welter of unfamiliar words. It was as if Karp spoke another language. Jack usually took good notes, but today he didn't feel like it. He had other things on his mind and he really didn't care how mature eggs were formed. What was a mature egg anyway? An egg with a lot of poise? An egg that could hold its liquor? An egg with a wife, good steady job and three little omelets? Below Karp's picture he wrote, "What did the mature egg say to the sperm?" He jotted down:

"Fertilize me, baby," and "Know any good yolks?" Jack crossed them both out. He knew they could only be slightly amusing to a biologist.

Jack looked at the clock. The lecture would be over in ten minutes. Then he could meet the other members of the Red Mask Band at the campus coffee shop. He had great news for them—their agent had booked them into the Regent Theatre in Springfield that weekend.

This was the last semester of Jack's junior year as a premedical student at Ohio State and until now his grades had been excellent. It'd been a grind: attending classes, studying, even recopying lecture notes. Jesse Whittridge was proud of his son and had hopes that Jack would become the doctor he'd wanted to be. So far, Jack's father had kept his part of the bargain and had paid for everything: tuition, books, supplies, food, clothes, even pocket money. Things had been awkward when Jack first arrived home, but now that the Old Man spent most of his spare time with the mysterious lady friend, Jack seldom saw him. He liked it that way. Their lives were separate.

This semester was different from the previous ones because Jack had completed the liberal arts portion of the curriculum and was now carrying a heavy load of biology and chemistry courses. It seemed that he was always dissecting some misshapen, preserved creature, probing for faded remnants of arteries, veins and nerves. The perch, bullfrog, iguana and the pigeon hadn't been too bad. They were distasteful, but weren't much like people and you got used to the smell of formalin after a while. But now he was dissecting a tomcat in mammalian lab, and a pregnant rat in comparative anatomy. He kept imagining how it must feel to slice into a dead human and he didn't much like the idea. He doubted that he had what it took to be a doctor. For one thing, he hated the sight of blood. Once, he'd forced himself to watch as the nurse in the infirmary took a blood sample from his arm. He remembered seeing the sharp hypodermic pierce his skin and slide into his vein, and then purplish blood spurted into the syringe and then the room started swirling and Jack had fainted. He was sure that he'd never have the nerve to draw blood from a patient. He'd been accepted into Ohio State's Medical School but he wasn't at all sure that he really wanted to go through with it.

Lately Jack had let his studies slide because the Red Mask Band kept him busy. There were rehearsals and arrangements to make, to say nothing of performances. After successful appearances on campus and at clubs around Columbus, Jack persuaded an agent to book them. On spring vacation they'd piled all their scenery and baggage into a rickety Model T. They limped gaily from Cleveland to Cincinnati and then from Akron to Toronto. They hadn't made much money, but the Red Mask Band made a hit wherever it played. Jack was the master of ceremonies and custodian of the wisecracks. He knew their act wasn't too good and their jokes were old, but what they lacked in quality they made up in noise, spirit, freshness, and pep.

When Karp gathered his lecture notes into a neat pile and dismissed the class, Jack was the first out of the door. He couldn't wait to tell the guys the good news.

V

The Red Mask Band was a last-minute replacement for a troupe of Romanian acrobats that couldn't appear. They were third on the bill of this vaudeville house, sandwiched between Al Herman, the Assassin of Grief and Remorse; and Mildred and Dorothy Brown, Vaudeville's Dainty Young Misses. When Jack asked the stage manager what happened to the acrobats, the man had only thrown up his hands and spat out "Rumanians!" as if it were the worst curse he could think of. Jack didn't know and didn't care what happened to take the Romanians out of commission. It only mattered that he'd be backstage again, watching the sister act from the wings.

He'd seen the Brown Sisters before in some hick town in Tennessee. Murray's troupe had been playing down the street from them and since Jimmy Ardell knew them, he took Jack over one night to get acquainted. Jimmy and Thora had been fighting, and Jimmy really only did it to get Thora's goat, but Jack hadn't known that then. Jimmy brought a bottle of whiskey for the girls' mother and the four young people went walking.

Once they got to the edge of town, Jimmy gave Jack a wink and disappeared into the woods with Mildred, leaving Jack on a deserted country road with Dorothy. Back at their boardinghouse Jimmy had suggested that if Jack played his cards right, he'd have Dorothy right where he wanted her and gave Jack a sharp nudge in the ribs. Jack still winced when he thought of it, how tongue-tied and uncomfortable he'd been, making small talk and waiting at the edge of town for Jimmy and the other Dainty Miss of Vaudeville to come out of the bushes.

Back at the boarding house, Jack lied when Jimmy asked him if Dorothy had been wearing round heels. Jack didn't like to think of it now and pretended that he'd never met the Brown sisters or their mother.

Now, years later, he did see that they were still wearing the same old-fashioned, frilly, little girl outfits. The only difference was that their dresses were tighter beneath the arms and shorter than they'd been some years ago. Both girls still wore sausage curls, high button shoes and big pink hair ribbons. Their nasal voices and clog dance hadn't varied at all. Mrs. Brown had noticed him and was trying to catch his eye. He turned away from her daughters as they cavorted in a surprise pink spot.

Jack had forgotten how much he liked to be backstage, watching the nuts-and-bolts workings of a show: the stage manager hunched over the light board, the stagehands ready to pull the curtain, the dust that was everywhere, the clutter of props and scenery. Overhead hung hundreds of sandbags, counterweights for the many ropes and curtains. They reminded him of the first time he'd been on a real stage, at the Toledo Regency, and of how scared he'd been when he'd gotten lost trying to find Jimmy Ardell backstage. That was the first time he'd seen those sandbags and he'd been terrified that one would fall and brain him. He never thought about that anymore.

The band had done well that night. The audience liked them. Jack's adrenaline mixed with a shot of whiskey gave him chemistry with everyone. Between the band and the ladies lining up to fall all over him, he was in a kaleidoscopic whirlwind of laughter, success, and a well-inflated ego. It was a part, he was at the center of it, and he took to it like a duck to a June bug. They'd gotten some pretty good laughs! He'd been especially pleased at the laugh he'd gotten at the coronet player's expense.

The gag went: "You know fellas, Specs here has a new girlfriend."

Then the whole band said in unison, "Is she voluptuous?"

And Jack replied, "No, she's Polish."

The sister act had just taken its bows and the show was over. Jack was waiting in the wings, hoping that they and their mother would go to their dressing room without seeing him. He ducked behind some scenery to wait for the house manager and their paycheck, when he heard the stage doorman say, "Jack Ridge? Oh yeah, he's with the band. He's over there."

A pretty young woman came up to Jack and extended her hand. "I'm Winnie Lightner," she said, and paused to give him time to react. She obviously thought that he might know her.

Jack looked blank and she continued with a laugh, "Well, I don't suppose you've ever heard of me, but I also act. In fact, I'm playing just down the street at the Academy. I'd like to talk with you or with your manager. Do you have a manager?"

Jack shook his head.

"Well, that's not important. I just caught your show and I think you're pretty good. I need someone like you who can do funny stuff, and I want to make you an offer. My company's leaving for New York soon and I think you're good enough to join us. I'm willing to help you get started."

Jack hadn't expected to hear anything like this. He didn't know what to say. He'd never heard of Winnie Lightner and what she said sounded too good to be true. He thought he smelled a rat. The guys had played tricks on each other before. It was probably Specs trying to get even.

"Well, that's a nice offer, Miss… ah, Lightner. Tell the guys that I enjoyed their little joke, but they can't get rid of me that easily." He turned to walk away.

Winnie saw the house manager distributing paychecks and pulled him over to Jack. By this time Specs and Randy and the others had gathered around, a united front of Ohio State varsity sweaters and beanies.

Jack took one look at their puzzled faces and said, "Will you guys please cut it? You don't fool me one minute with those phony faces."

Miss Lightner interrupted him and turned to the house manager. She said, "Gus, will you tell Mr. Ridge just who I am and what I do for a living? He doesn't believe I'm on the level. He seems to think his friends here are playing some kind of prank. I haven't the time to convince him myself, I've got another show tonight."

Gus handed Jack the band's pay envelope, took the unlit cigar from his mouth and said, "Why sure, Miss Lightner. I'll be glad to set him straight. Boys, this here is Miss Winnie Lightner. I guess she and her family have been in this business for twenty years, maybe more. She was probably on stage before she was out of diapers, eh, Miss Lightner? And last year she made a real big hit in George White's *Scandals* on Broadway. She's legit and she's working The Palace circuit now. In case you didn't know... that means," here he jabbed Jack in the chest with a stubby index finger, "the Big Time. And she's a real lady besides, so don't get any funny ideas. Her family and me go back a long time. As a matter of fact, her dad, Newton Lightner and I, in nineteen-ought-seven, played in... lemme see..."

Miss Lightner interrupted him with, "That'll do, thank you, Gus. I think Mr. Ridge here will understand that I mean what I've said, and I don't have too much more time to convince him. Frankly, most performers just starting out would jump at the chance, but if you're not interested in my offer, Mr. Ridge..."

Specs and Randy had just figured out what was happening. Wide-eyed, while his bandmate tapped his foot and bit his lip, Randy said, "Now wait a minute, Miss Lightner, give the old boy here a chance to get accustomed to the idea. He's sometimes a little thick. Comes from an old childhood disease called stupidity. Takes him a while to catch on to things. Tell him more about it. I don't mean to horn in, Miss Lightner, but what would Fathead here be doing in your show?"

"Right now, I need a straight man. From what I've seen, Jack can dance, too. So I'd like to have him do that as well. This is our last night in Springfield. Tomorrow morning, we leave for St. Louis for a two-week run. Then we go on to New York."

"How much would you pay him?" asked Specs.

"I think fifty dollars a week to start would be fair."

Specs took a deep breath and said, "Jack, you'd be crazy not to do it."

But Jack still wasn't convinced. "Are you sure it's not some kind of trick? If I say yes and hear you holler '*sucker*,' Specs, I swear I'll wring your scrawny neck."

"No, honest, Jack. We didn't put her up to it. We've never seen her 'til just now. But it's a great chance! And you heard what Gus said. This kind of thing just doesn't happen every day." The boys were back slapping and grappling each other's neck, feeling good for all, just this once.

"Okay, Miss Lightner," said Jack. "I can't really believe this is happening, but I'll do it. It's a deal. When do we leave?"

"Meet me at six o'clock sharp for breakfast in the dining room of my hotel, across from the Academy. We'll get things ironed out on the train."

They shook hands and she added, "See you then. And don't be late."

She was almost out the door when Jack called out, "Wait a minute, Miss Lightner!" He ran after her, grabbed her hand and pumped it up and down. "Bye... and thanks." He watched her go through the stage door and then the boys crowded around, slapping him on the back and congratulating him, laughing that he'd thought they were trying to con him. Jack felt as if the breath had been knocked out of him.

A chance at the Big Time.

He had no idea what might happen tomorrow, but one thing was sure—he knew that his father would never understand.

12

Mother and I had a strange relationship. Though she was very distant, she was proud of me in her own way. She always took me everywhere—even when she was dying. Whenever Mother went out, to a cocktail party or to a house party, to a dinner or to any social event, I was dragged along. The host or hostess knew that I was Mother's inevitable companion. As a little boy I grew used to these grownup affairs. My first memories of these parties are of falling asleep amidst the fur coats that carelessly littered a big bed. It was comforting to snuggle beneath someone's sable, hearing the conversations drone in the living room. The monogrammed satin linings always smelled of faint perfume.

After a while I assumed a more definitive role. By age eight I could make a perfect martini. I knew how to coax even the most stubborn ice cubes from their trays, and always served from the left. I grew to enjoy going out with Mother and staying up late. If I were properly dressed in time, I could watch her transform in front of her dressing table. After deft touches of brushes dipped in mascara, eyeliner, eyeshadow, rouge, and lipstick, she could turn from an ordinary-looking woman into the most stunning creature. Her whole persona changed. A bit like the Wicked Witch in Snow White, *transforming into the beautiful-but-deadly Wicked Queen as she gazed into her magic mirror.*

I can still remember Mother's dressing table. A three-way mirror stood tall on the top, and an assortment of small drawers ran down the sides. They held the various accoutrements of her makeup. But the perfume compartment, a recessed box hidden in the top of the table, was the best part.

Mother usually wore Chanel No. 5, but sometimes she used more exotic scents. As a final touch to her transformation, she opened the perfume compartment and lifted and smelled the round glass stoppers of all the crystal and cut-glass bottles of amber fluids. It would take her a long time to select the proper fragrance, an exotic and purely feminine ritual that could not be interrupted. I can still see her red fingernails lifting the tops of those perfume bottles. Some stoppers were square, others round or octagonal. My favorite had a sphinx on it. Her fingers played across them as if they were the control knobs on an emotional console—a Pandora's box of potions that would assist her to cast any spell she chose. Sometimes I would be allowed to participate in this crucial decision… an acolyte in a mysterious, but significant, ceremony.

Thomas with his mother.

Mother was always perfectly groomed in a reserved sort of way. Minks and an armful of pavé sapphire and diamond bracelets, or her cuffs of gold charms were always featured. Her designer, Stephan, specially crafted all of her clothes. Yes, she could really be incredibly beautiful when she wanted to. Or at least it seemed this way to me.

Mother was never a demonstrably warm person. She would give me a peck on the cheek when I said goodnight and dismiss me quickly so she could return to reading the day's papers that were strewn over the satin duvet of her bed. I had lots of toys and unlimited access to Hostess cupcakes, my childhood idea of the perfect food. But there was no physical closeness. The only time she would hug me was when I was very small and would creep into her room at night, complaining of bad dreams. When I got older she never hugged me at all.

I remember one golden afternoon when we were living with the doctor, her third husband. After I begged and begged and begged her to play with me, she came downstairs and played a half-hearted game of catch. I can still see her in that late autumn sunlight: very tall, shading her eyes with one hand, waiting for me to throw the softball that she would fumble into the grass.

13

"Greenlea"
Bryn Mawr, Pennsylvania
December 30, 1941

    Dorothy Mary sat at her desk in the sitting room of the west wing of "Greenlea," the home of Chester's grandmother. She never thought of these ten rooms as her own home even though she and Chester had moved in shortly after their honeymoon. There was nothing of hers here, except this writing desk from her room at Denbigh—and it was the only piece of furniture in the whole place that she didn't loathe. The rest of the wing was crammed with Victorian/Gothic junk and gewgaws. If Chester let her, she'd have ordered the Salvation Army to haul it all away long ago.

    But Chester knew that would infuriate his grandmother. To Mrs. Kingwood Liddell this velvet-upholstered, horsehair-stuffed, mahogany-curlicued trash was a reliquary that held memories of the time when the Liddells had been a family of means, as well as social clout. Now that most of the money was gone, only this ugly furniture showed what the Liddell family had been a hundred years ago.

    Their first major battle had been over Grandmother. After their honeymoon, while Dorothy Mary was busy with her decorator, planning the renovation of the townhouse they had leased off Rittenhouse Square, the old woman invited Chester to a special tea. Dorothy had earlier made the mistake of telling Nana about the pink silk wall covering for the dining room and the scrumptious antique Anatolian rug she and the decorator had found. Nana told Chester that they were spending like young fools. They must be more sensible and more conservative, or she would revise her opinion of his ability to manage money. They should abandon this frivolous plan to redecorate an entire house, to say nothing of paying rent to a stranger. Why didn't they move into the empty west wing of Greenlea?

Chester saw that her offer had certain advantages. For one thing, they would save a lot of money. The west wing was already furnished, and Nana wouldn't expect them to pay rent. Also, Nana already had plenty of servants, so Dorothy Mary wouldn't have to hire or train any of her own. As a side benefit, it would only be a short walk to his greenhouses, instead of a daily forty-five-minute drive from town. But most importantly, Chester didn't want his grandmother to think him a spendthrift; then she'd never leave him a cent. He canceled the lease on the townhouse that day and accepted Nana's offer.

Dorothy couldn't believe what Chester had done without even consulting her. She fumed and sulked for weeks. All those plans for their own beautiful house, for nothing. She tried everything to change Chester's mind, but he was adamant. Eventually they moved into these quarters, and although Chester assured her that she was the most important thing in the world to him, Dorothy Mary realized she was a poor second to Nana.

In time, Dorothy Mary swallowed her anger. She assumed they could always move out if they didn't like living in this big old house. To compensate for the loss of her townhouse, she bought herself a sable wrap and a new pair of diamond earrings.

That had been a year and a half ago.

Dorothy Mary had only worn those earrings once before she discovered what a blunder it had been to let Chester and Nana have their way. She hated this place with its heavy curtains and unyielding sofas; on dreary days the furniture loomed in the shadowy rooms. It was neither a comfortable nor happy place. More than anything, Dorothy Mary disliked Nana's spying servants.

Although the old crone lived in the east wing, and they only saw her twice a week when she requested their presence at dinner, Nana seemed to know everything Dorothy Mary and Chester had done. She knew who they invited to dinner, how much they drank, what they ate, where they went, how late they stayed, what radio programs they enjoyed. *The servants must tell her everything.* Dorothy Mary knew all about servants. She could sacrifice her privacy, but Nana was horribly critical. And she had endless opinions about everything. Nana insisted that her extended household do everything the proper way. "Proper way" meant the Liddell way. Nana's way. She had endless inflexible rules. Dorothy Mary tried to be on her best behavior on Sunday and Wednesday nights when they were forced to eat with Nana, but somehow, she always fell short of the Old Lady's standards.

From time-to-time Dorothy still tried to convince Chester that they needed their own place, but he refused to confront his grandmother. Even though Dorothy Mary had given him control of her money, Nana was the key to his financial future. More than anything, he wanted to retain his position as favorite grandchild. Chester assumed that his young wife would adapt to their living conditions. The Old Lady couldn't last too much longer; then they'd be free as well as very rich.

Dorothy Mary couldn't see a way out of her situation, and she didn't want to think about it anymore. She had so much to do today: letters to write, a fitting this afternoon, then tea at the club with her mother and Aunt Jeanne. Thank God that Christmas was over.

Tomorrow night she and Chester would ring in 1942 at Denbigh with the Flaggs, then the holidays would be finished, and things would settle down. Next week she would meet with the steering committee of the Navy Women's Auxiliary League. Her mother was vice-chairman, and Dorothy Mary headed a committee to select a new uniform for the volunteer workers. She told Stephan, her designer, what she wanted, and his drawings and swatches of navy gabardine lay on her desk. She'd specified that he create something military chic that was also feminine. "These are wonderful. We can't have the Navy League heading into war for the first time since 1919 looking like a bunch of overgrown bluebirds, now can we?"

She was pleased with the sketches of a dress uniform with snug, hip-length jacket, slim skirt and peaked cap. Dorothy Mary knew it would look well on her. The right uniform was crucial. The workers would sell bonds, enlist blood donors, and chauffeur officers around town. They'd collect scrap, help with civil defense, and raise money for the Navy War effort. Shoes were a problem. She'd have to find some that were sensible but not too spinsterish. Perhaps navy oxfords with a nice heel would show off her legs to their best advantage.

Dorothy Mary liked her Navy League work. It took her out of Nana's domain, and it would help to win the war. It also gave her something to do that took her mind off Chester and their miserable, boring marriage. It was clear to her that unless some adjustments were made, their union would not last. She took one of their wedding albums from the bookstand at the side of her desk and leafed through the photographs, pleased to have at least this tangible proof that the ceremony and reception had been an enormous success.

When did it start to go wrong?

She turned to the photo taken just before she and Chester were driven from the Church of the Redeemer to the reception at Denbigh. She gazed lovingly at her image. In her ivory satin wedding gown, Dorothy Mary beamed at the camera, an enormous bouquet of lily of the valley trembled on her lap. Her voluminous train filled the foreground, billowing over Chester's knees and nearly engulfing him. Chester seemed a caricature of himself as he perched next to her on the edge of the rear seat. His top hat looked ridiculously oversized, and he clutched at his gray gloves. He was dumpy instead of elegant in his morning suit and, although he tried to smile, his eyes winced apologetically.

Dorothy Mary and Chester.

Even then he didn't know what to do with me, she thought. His faintly pitiful look reminded her of the expression that came over her Airedale puppy's face whenever she'd dressed him in doll clothes and tucked him into the baby carriage for a stroll through Denbigh's gardens.

The puppy could twist out of the bonnet in a second but was never able to escape the securely buttoned doll dress. He would eventually submit to this game, but his eyes would plead with Dorothy Mary to get it over quickly.

Taking a drag of her cigarette, she thought she could see the beginnings of their trouble in the uncertain eyes that peered from behind Chester's wire-framed glasses.

She had been an idiot to marry him.

Uncertain was a kind word to use to describe Chester's performance on their honeymoon. Although not exactly a virgin when they married, Dorothy Mary was no expert in sexual matters. But Chester was so inept that at first it had made her angry and then made her sad. She'd expected so much more. On their wedding night when she emerged from the bathroom, she expected Chester to be waiting to untie her chiffon peignoir and undress her like some long-anticipated, special gift. But Chester was beneath the covers and the room was dark. She slid into bed beside him and they began to kiss, the cardboard kisses she now knew so well. He briefly fingered one of her breasts, then wriggled out of his shorts, and as if it were an alchemist's formula, he whispered, "I love you," before he pushed her nightgown out of the way.

Remembering that nineteen-year-old Italian boy on the hillside overlooking Flume, Dorothy Mary took a deep breath and closed her eyes. She felt something inserted into her and Chester muttered, "It's finally in there," pleased with himself. He made two or three thrusts, shuddered, and stopped. He rolled off of her, kissed her in the manner in which he might salute a hostess after an evening of bridge, before yawning and picking his shorts up off the floor to wipe himself. Soon he was asleep in the darkness beside her.

Dorothy Mary went into the bathroom and took a long bath. The water in the tub was tepid before she grew sleepy. It had never gotten any better. She had explained the situation to her doctor, learned about premature ejaculation in sex manuals, even read the *Kama Sutra*. The doctor had suggested alternate positions. All the manuals said the small size of a man's genitalia was irrelevant in lovemaking, but Dorothy Mary couldn't help thinking that she'd married a cripple. One night, when she suggested there were things they could do to prolong their lovemaking, Chester grew silent and said he would try to do better. But, if he did try, Dorothy Mary never felt any evidence of it. It was always the same.

Now she was beyond caring.

II

That night Dorothy Mary dreamt of standing beside Chester in an elevator. A faceless operator jerked a lever to the left and the brass latticework doors slid shut with a metallic clasp. They descended to the masquerade, lozenges of red sequins arranged diagonally across the white and black halves of her harlequin costume. She slid the fingers of one hand up and down, caressing the sequins on hip and thigh. On the upward stroke they snagged her hand; on the downstroke they were smooth and slick, like the scales of a mermaid's tail. Chester was dressed as W.C. Fields' Micawber, replete with a huge, green top hat, flowing tie, and bulbous cherry nose. He held a Planters Punch in one hand and a short blue and red-striped cane in the other. He snickered, "My little chrysalis," and jabbed at her bottom with his cane. Irritated, Dorothy Mary snapped, "Goddammit, Chester. Stop. You'll wreck my costume."

The elevator doors slid back and the operator watched the couple enter the smoky ballroom. Chester raised his glass to her, tucked his cane beneath his belt and disappeared into the costumed crowd. Dorothy found herself waltzing with a tall stranger in top hat and tails. At first, she relished his close embrace, but then she felt strangled as his hips moved against her belly. She gasped for air and tried to say, "Cut it out, everyone will see," but no words came. He laughed down at her and pulled both of her arms to the middle of her back as she struggled to get free.

Chester's grandmother and her own mother were at a nearby table, costumed as Marie Antoinette and Napoleon. She overheard her mother exclaim, "She's just like her father," and their eyes glittered with judgment as they whispered behind their fans. Grizzy stood behind Mother's gilt chair wearing a hooked nose and horned cap with bells on ribbons. She called to him for help, but he only threw back his head and shrieked raucously. Grizzy's bells jangled as the patent-haired man pulled her down to the floor. Dorothy Mary wrenched one hand free and dug her nails into his eye. He screamed and the music stopped. Blood dripping from her hand, she scrambled away to the elevator; the crowd there would hide her.

Where was Chester? They had to get out of there. But she couldn't find him.

She pushed the elevator button again and again. Across the dance floor the man in the top hat stumbled toward her. Blood filled his eye socket and streamed down his face. Dorothy pushed open the heavy metal door next to the elevator with a grunt and raced up a flight of dark stairs. She heard footsteps behind her and glanced to see the top-hatted man leaping the stairs two at a time.

He's going to catch me, she thought.

She turned to face him. Supporting herself on the handrails, she kicked him as hard as she could with her spike heel. As it punctured his skull, it felt as if she were biting through the shell of a chocolate-covered cherry.

He grabbed for the banister but fell and rolled over and over, down the way he'd come. His scream echoed in the stairwell long after his body had stopped convulsing.

Dorothy looked down and saw Chester lying all crumpled in the light of the exit sign at the bottom of the stairs. His false nose was askew and a bloody hole gaped in his forehead. She ran toward him, but stopped short to pick up the top hat that had fallen on the stairs. Red and purple-flecked orchids sprouted from its upturned brim.

Dorothy Mary woke to darkness and the sound of Chester's regular breathing. Although she was relieved that it had only been a nightmare, her immediate reaction was disappointment that Chester wasn't dead. It would have been so much easier that way. Lying on her side, she drew her knees up, slept and dreamt no more.

III
"Denbigh"
December 31, 1941

Stanley Griswold Flagg plucked his monogrammed gold studs and cufflinks from his jewelry box and closed it with an efficient snap. Mr. Flagg liked to put his own studs into his shirts. It made him feel rather like an overgrown and ancient baby doll if Rodgers did it for him. He forced the studs into his starched shirt and thought about the evening ahead. He wasn't pleased with the prospect of spending the evening with his family. It would be a long night and he wondered what Marguerite was doing in her pink and beige apartment off Chestnut Street—the apartment that *he* financed. Did she think of him? He took a slug of the good Scotch, no ice, and imagined her dressing for a party, pulling sheer silk hose up those long, cool legs. But Marguerite was far away and the immediate problem was how to get through the night without murdering either of his sons.

If there were only something else they could talk about, but every conversational gambit from Pearl Harbor and Jap strategy to the shortage of good vintages due to the war was tinged with danger. Everything his family said, every joke, every pleasantry, made him angry these days—especially anything Grizzy and David said. That goddamn psychiatrist, Weintraub, had been right. May the bastard roast in whatever Hell Jews inhabited, but goddammit he had been *right*.

The psychiatrist's confidential report on his analysis of David and Grizzy was delivered in mid-September, and Mr. Flagg had been angry ever since. He didn't like dealing with Jews as a rule, but he made an exception in this case because Dr. Weintraub came highly recommended by old friends, members of his club. He'd requested that Weintraub interview and assess his sons, who had recently been hired as junior executive vice presidents at the family factory in Pottstown. Mr. Flagg wanted to make sure they were mentally sound before he gave them real responsibility. It would be their business someday; he wanted to know their strengths and weaknesses before he trained them to take over. It was his practice to subject new executives to emotional and mental examinations, so it was accepted as a matter of course. The usual tests were administered by the Personnel Department—but not with Grizzy and David. No, he wanted to supplement this information with the insights of a trained psychiatrist. If he'd only known what that little Jew was going to report, he'd never have started the whole business.

At first he hadn't believed what he read. He called the psychiatrist in for a conference. He became further outraged when he found the doctor was unreachable, attending a holiday called "circus" or something.

But Weintraub stood by his conclusions about the boys. If only he'd been able to make the psychiatrist retract those statements! But Weintraub was firm. He said, "You may not agree with my conclusions, Mr. Flagg. That is your prerogative. Nevertheless, it is my opinion that, at present, your sons are not fit for positions of authority. Griswold, Jr. shows a marked tendency for self-destruction. I see in him things that make me *extremely* concerned. Unless he begins analysis immediately and faces his problems, there's no telling what he will do. I cannot recommend such an unstable character for a position in which he will govern the lives and well-being of others! Put him into some kind of job where he works alone. Do *not* give him people to manage.

"As for the elder son, David, his problem is… more difficult. If you want to help him, you must somehow find a way to turn back the clock to his childhood. And you, yourself, *must* spend more time with him. He has been dominated by women all his life. He's a terribly nice boy but perhaps too considerate and self-effacing. He is weak. It would be a cruelty to place him in a position where he'll have to make decisions and hire and fire people. He has no business head. Let him be a scholar. He has an interest in history. You, with all your resources, can do this for him.

"As their father, it must be hard for you to accept the unfortunate truth. We expect so much of our children."

"Are you sure—dead sure—about these things?"

"I stake my professional reputation on it. However, they are far from hopeless. Both would greatly benefit from analysis, if they're ready."

"Well, Dr. Weintraub, thank you for your time. Your check will be in the mail." Mr. Flagg buzzed impatiently for his secretary and asked her to show the man out. They didn't shake hands.

Mr. Flagg thought, *I'll be damned if any son of mine is going to have analysis. 'Mark of weakness.' I've never had it and I'm fine, just fine. All those two need is a good shaking. Everything's come too easily to them. Do them good to struggle for a change.*

In the days and weeks since then Mr. Flagg had read and reread that confidential report until he knew it by heart. And he'd started to observe his sons' behavior.

He saw how Grizzy loved to make his underlings squirm. The way he liked to throw his weight around. Two secretaries quit.

He watched David and saw his nervous habits. How he bit his cuticles down until they bled. His fingertips were always bandaged. He noticed how David ducked his head when he entered the front office, as if expecting a blow.

Mr. Flagg was now sure that Dr. Weintraub had been right. His sons weren't fit to run the business. They were made for cocktails and tennis, not for boardroom politics and negotiating cutthroat deals. It was a simple fact: they'd never do.

The Dressing Drink

IV

As Chester parked their Chrysler sedan in Denbigh's curving driveway and switched off the ignition, Dorothy Mary turned and glared at him. The green dashboard lights reflected in the diamond pendants that sparkled at her ears, and the hood of her fox cape made an incongruous soft frame for her angry face. He had never seen her so upset. She hadn't spoken to him since their argument that morning when he'd broken the news. They had dressed for the night's party and driven to Denbigh in silence. Not even the usual dressing drink could anesthetize her irritation.

He gripped the steering wheel and tried one last time to make peace. "Sweetheart, be reasonable. Don't you see, I have to go. It's important that I do something in this war. Everyone else I know has enlisted or is planning to. Even Stewie Frazer. Liddells have always volunteered, and Nana expects it."

"Nana. It's always Nana. Nana this and Nana that. Why don't you marry Nana, for God's sake?"

"Come on, dear. Don't be this way. This'll be our last party for a long time. They'll be sending me to Egypt soon."

Dorothy Mary interrupted, as if speaking to a child. "Chester, you're a Quaker. Remember? Friends' Meeting and conscientious objection? Quakers can do other things in a war besides drive ambulances for the British Army."

"Yes, I'm a Quaker, but I'm only a Quaker because my family raised me that way. There are certain things I have to do, certain things the family expects; but I don't have to wait out the war hiding here in safe, old Philadelphia while all the other guys are putting their lives on the line. Can't you see how that makes me feel?"

Dorothy Mary snapped her thumbnails against her long fingernails. It was a nervous habit that made a sound like knuckles cracking. She knew Chester hated the sound and she did it on purpose. The wind against the snow-covered yews and the regular snapping of her fingernails were the only sounds in the car.

Chester grabbed her hand. "Please stop that. You know I dislike that unattractive sound."

She pulled her hand away. "Chester, this is imbecilic you going to Egypt to drive English ambulances. Face it. You're doing it for the same reason you married me. For the same reason you do everything. To please Nana. All the rest of what you say is bullshit."

"Sweetheart, I wish you wouldn't talk like that. It's not true. You haven't heard anything I've said."

"You said Nana expects you to volunteer."

"Sure, I did, but that's not my major reason for going. I don't want to sit around while everyone else is fighting, maybe dying. What do you expect me to do, roll bandages, or stuff ditty bags with your Navy Leaguers?"

"The fact remains that you don't have to go."

"I *do* have to go."

"Well, what am I supposed to do 'til you come back? *If* you come back."

Chester was touched. He now understood what she was so upset about. She was worried about him. He put his arms around her and tenderly put her head on his shoulder. "Darling don't worry about me. I'll come back to you. The war'll be over soon. I'll write to you and Nana every day."

At the word *Nana*, Dorothy jerked away from him and opened her car door. "Oh, that'll be just fine, Chester. You write to Nana and me every day. Cheery letters for home-front consumption. She and I can chuckle at your droll wit over our afternoon tea.

If you think I'm going to stay with her 'til you're ready to come home, you're nuts. And what exactly do you expect me to do with myself while I'm waiting for you? Knit argyles? Oh no, not this kid.

Fine, Chester, you go to Egypt and you do whatever you C.O.s do in a war, but don't expect me to be waiting when you decide that your war is over."

Dorothy Mary slammed the car door behind her and stomped across the snowdrifts to Denbigh.

After handing her cape and gloves to Rodgers, Dorothy Mary went into the library. Voices reached her from the parlor, and in the music room someone was playing the piano while others sang, but she wasn't ready to join the party yet. She needed a cigarette and a drink.

As she watched the rivulets of Scotch run over the ice cubes and added a sliver of lemon peel to her glass, things suddenly became clear to her.

There was a way out of this situation. There was a solution that would free her of Chester and of Nana and of goddamn Quaker Philadelphia forever. She sipped her drink, lit a cigarette and thought.

I don't have to live with Chester anymore. He'll go to Egypt soon and I can move back to Denbigh and let that old bitch rot in Bryn Mawr. Mother will let me move back here. Then I'll see the lawyers and file separation papers as soon as possible. If he isn't dead after six months, I'll get a divorce in Reno. It's supposed to be easy there.

She smiled to herself. Her life had suddenly become so simple. She rather liked the idea of being Dorothy Flagg Liddell, the divorcée. It sounded worldly, sophisticated, and slightly wicked. Then she could have a good time again, without Chester always at her elbow spoiling her fun. She would have her *own* money and be independent of everyone. Of course, it would scandalize the Liddells and half of Philadelphia. Nana might even disinherit Chester. But Dorothy Mary didn't care. She downed her drink and stubbed out her cigarette. In the hall she met Chester and smiled, then held out her hand.

"Come on Chester," she said. "Let's tell everyone your good news. They'll all be so proud of what you're going to do. Forget all that unpleasantness in the car and let's have fun. As you said—it's the last party we'll be going to for a long time."

Chester tucked her hand into his arm and smiled down at her. He'd never loved her more.

V

Throwing the lead was a New Year's Eve ritual at Denbigh.

Every year Stanley Griswold Flagg brought home a five-gallon smelter from the quality control laboratory of the pipefittings factory. It was set on a pedestal of bricks at one end of the music room next to a tub of cold water. Before the guests arrived, lead chips were poured into the smelter. By late evening they had melted into a pool of hot, silvery liquid. After midnight each guest was invited to throw a dipperful of molten lead into the tub of water. Tradition said that you could see your fortune for the new year in the shape of the cooled, solidified lead.

When she was the little girl who believed that if fern were sprinkled into her shoes it would make her invisible, the little girl who knew that fairies flew home to the western sky at each sunset, the little girl who tried to rescue the Lindbergh baby, her lead fortunes had had a mystic significance for Dorothy Mary. She treasured the silver talismans, kept them in a velvet-covered box in the top drawer of her writing desk and spent hours examining them, passionately trying to read her future. But now she no longer believed in throwing the lead. Like fern seed and fairies, its magic had evaporated. It was just another holiday custom, like candles in the windows, eggnog or Auld Lang Syne.

Mrs. Flagg had engaged a piano player and accordionist, and a crowd had gathered around them next to the tree in the music room, singing Christmas carols and popular tunes. Dorothy and Chester found Mrs. Flagg in the parlor where the older generation held sway. Here the talk was about the war, and the way the Japanese had conquered in the Far East. Dorothy Mary listened to Uncle Maurice recount Japanese victories. They'd taken Malaya, sunk the British battle cruiser *Repulse,* and the battleship *Prince of Wales,* off the Malayan coast. The second commander went down with his ship. Then the Japs took Wake Island, invaded the Philippines, and the day after Christmas, Hong Kong surrendered to the Japanese. MacArthur was fighting in the Philippines now. Dorothy Mary didn't have a clear idea of exactly where most of these places were, but she didn't want to dwell on the war or hear Uncle Maurice's gloomy predictions about how the Japanese were unstoppable. She'd seen pictures of Admiral Nimitz and General

MacArthur, and she trusted them. If anybody could squash the Japs, they could. She agreed with her father when he said, "Once we get this country mobilized, we'll wipe Tojo off the map."

The conversation turned to other topics: who was joining up, what Roosevelt would do, how stalwart the British had been. Then Dorothy Mary piped up, "Mother, Father, Chester has something to say to you." With a few curious glances, the guests on either side of Mrs. Flagg excused themselves.

Chester turned bright red. He hadn't told his grandmother yet, and she should be the first to know. But Dorothy Mary had forced his hand. "Mr. and Mrs. Flagg, I guess I'd better tell you, I'm going to Egypt or Libya next week as an ambulance driver with the American Friends Service Committee. I joined up just after Pearl Harbor. They notified me yesterday."

"But, Chester, isn't that terribly dangerous?" gasped Mrs. Flagg.

"You might get shot at, or even killed."

"I suppose you're right, Mother Flagg, but I think it's important." He looked at Dorothy Mary. "I… that is, we, thought you ought to know."

Mr. Flagg clapped Chester on the back. "Congratulations, Chester. We need more young men like you. Not afraid to sacrifice for their country. Good luck."

Dorothy Mary smiled at Chester. "Good. Now that we've gotten that over with, would you dance with me, Daddy? It may be our last chance in 1941 and they're playing a waltz. Would you excuse us, Mother, Chester." Dorothy Mary took her father's arm and they drifted into the music room.

"Daddy, I have a favor to ask."

Mr. Flagg put down his drink and they began to waltz past the piano, past the singers, past the Christmas tree adorned with tinsel.

"Well, ask. I've never known you to be reticent, Dorothy Mary."

"Well, Daddy," she said, looking up into his eyes with her most appealing face, "when Chester goes to Egypt, I'll be all alone in that big house with his grandmother. Do you think it would be okay if I moved back here to Denbigh with you and Mother?"

"Is that all you wanted?"

"Yes, it would make me feel a lot better."

"Why certainly, Dorothy. Don't you worry about Chester, he'll be just fine. Do him a world of good to see some real fighting and find out what the world is about. He'll come home a new man. I'm sure your mother will be pleased to have you back. Between the two of you, the Navy League can really get rolling."

"Thank you, Daddy." Dorothy Mary smiled up into his eyes. "Happy almost New Year."

The waltz ended and Dorothy Mary and her father joined the singers at the piano. David and Grizzy were there, Grizzy with his arm around a tiny brunette, his hand resting on her hip. When he saw his father coming across the floor, he moved it to her waist.

David sat beside the piano player, turning pages for him. He smiled up at Dorothy Mary and his father. Mr. Flagg stared at Grizzy's date, at her low-cut black satin dress. Then he glared at his son. "I don't believe I've had the pleasure of meeting your friend, Grizzy."

"Oh, yes. Father, this is Miss Trixie Hayward. Miss Hayward, my father, Griswold Flagg."

"Pleased to meet you, I'm sure," said the girl and extended her hand as if she expected Mr. Flagg to kiss it. "Oh, you're the senior and Grizzy is the junior, right?"

"Good evening, Miss Hayward. Grizzy, David, come into the library. I have something for you."

The three excused themselves to the library, where Mr. Flagg closed the doors behind them and poured himself a drink. "Sit down, boys." He took two envelopes from the inside pocket of his dinner jacket and tapped them against the fingers of his hand. Grizzy eyed his father's clenched jaw, the rise of his shoulders, and knew he was angry. He tried not to delight in it.

"Before we begin this conversation, how many times have I told you not to bring your tramps here, Grizzy? When we've finished I want you to take Miss Trixie Hayward back to South Philadelphia and leave her there. Your cheap, theatrical friends aren't welcome in my house, especially at a family gathering. I don't care what you do on your own, but I will not have you parading it in front of your mother."

He thrust one envelope at Grizzy and the other at David. David protested, "Father, please. Not another present. You've already given us too much for Christmas."

"David, this isn't a present. At least the two of you won't think of it as one right now. Someday you'll see that I was right to do this, but now you'll probably be quite upset by what I'm about to give you. I can't help that." Each son tentatively took one of the proffered envelopes. "A month's severance pay."

"Severance pay? You get that when you're fired," David said, a little wide-eyed.

"Well, that's exactly what the two of you are. As of right now, you no longer work for me. I've given both of you a fair trial and I've watched you these last months. I've decided that you don't have what it takes to run the company. I wash my hands of you. They told me that both of you are unfit for business. At first I couldn't believe it. After all, you're my own sons. But I've seen enough and have decided that you're both wrong for the company.

"Come in on Monday and get your things from the office. I'm sorry that it has to be this way, but business is business. You're on your own now."

"But Father..." said David.

"I don't want to discuss it further, David. I've made my decision. I think it's for the best and I intend to stick with it. Someday you'll thank me for it." Mr. Flagg picked up his drink and left the library.

Grizzy opened his envelope and laughed. "Well, Father doesn't miss a trick. He's even deducted Social Security." Turning to his brother, he said, "David, dear boy, we have just been what is technically called 'royally buggered in the ass.' I don't know about you, but I'm out of this place. Happy New Year." He downed his drink and left David sitting alone in the library, turning the white envelope over and over in his hands. What could he have done to deserve this?

Dorothy Mary appeared at the library door. "Here you are—come on, David, it's almost the new year."

He got up and followed her out into the music room where all the guests were assembled in front of the grandfather clock with their horns and tweeters and party hats. The clock chimed out, one after another. On the last bong everyone shouted, "Happy New Year," and the piano player started "Auld Lang Syne." Someone handed David a container of confetti and he threw it up into the air. He looked at the white envelope his father had given him and slowly tore it into long strips, then tore those strips in half and in half again. He threw the little pieces of his check high into the air, put his arm around Dorothy Mary's waist and joined in the last phrases of the song, "…take a cup of kindness yet, for Old Lang Syne." His eye caught his father's across the circle of singing friends, and David yelled, "Happy New Year, Father."

Mr. Flagg turned away to kiss Aunt Jeanne's wrinkled cheek. He didn't seem to notice that David had spoken to him.

Mrs. Flagg made her way over to Dorothy Mary and Chester. "You two must be the first to throw the lead. And you *must* do it together." She led them to the smelter and waited expectantly as they filled the dipper with the molten metal and Dorothy Mary hurled it into the tub of water. The metal hissed as it entered the water and sank to the bottom of the tub. Chester unbuttoned his cuff and pulled the dripping, glittering mass from the water and handed it to his wife.

"Here, let me see, Dorothy Mary," said Mrs. Flagg. She took the shape from Dorothy Mary's fingers and adjusted her glasses. "Well, it's certainly interesting. It looks like something that might fly. It must mean an auspicious year for the two of you. Happy New Year, darlings." Mrs. Flagg kissed her daughter and son-in-law, and called to the next guest to throw the lead and read his fortune.

"I don't know about you, dear, but I'm starving. Shall I get you something?" asked Chester.

"Yes, that would be lovely," said Dorothy Mary. After he'd left, she stood facing the fireplace and examined her lead fortune. After one look she knew exactly what it was. A twisted bird, with one wing long and pointy, built for soaring, and the other malformed, gnarled. Mother was wrong. This bird could never fly. Dorothy Mary threw it into the fire and helped herself to a glass of champagne from the tray that Rodgers was passing. She caught sight of her reflection in the floor-to-ceiling mirror at the end of the room. Keeping an eye on that other Dorothy Mary, she raised her glass and silently toasted herself and the New Year.

Dorothy Mary Liddell in evening gown.

14

Welcome to the Big Show. It's strange to have a visitor in this tent. There's only myself to blame—I invited you in to see the show, and I suppose I have an urge to confide in you; although I don't know why I should trust you. After all, I barely know you. And I don't really like you sitting there watching my performers with that impassive look. It's only because I'm out of practice. I'm not used to an audience—solitude is my more usual companion. Solitude and time. There's plenty of each in this tent. Day after day I sit and listen to the wind tug at the canvas and I think about my life. There's plenty of time to regret things that I've done. Plenty of time to edit conversations with the dead—conversations in which I always have the winning hand, in which I soar into eloquent rhetoric, brilliantly justifying the things I've done and not done. Oh yes, there's plenty of time here, time to wish I could change so many things.

You see, it was my fault that I never got to know my father. I didn't realize who he was until years after he was dead, a victim of the incompetence of some white-coated cipher in a New York City hospital who mismatched his blood. The idiot gave him a transfusion of the wrong blood type. He died of it.

Now that he's gone, I think of him often, but when he was alive I was more interested in Cassie, his nineteen-year-old wife. Father was nice enough, but Cassie was pure, distilled, 150-proof sex. When she was around—and she was always around—I thought only about her. My mind revolved around my crotch, or hers. Perhaps I'll tell you about it sometime, if you're interested. The important thing is that I wasted the only year I was given to learn who my father was.

As I said before, Father died from a transfusion of the wrong kind of blood, but the thing that actually killed him was his cheapness. He'd insisted on going to one of the city hospitals because they were less expensive than New York's private hospitals. Father could stretch a dollar further than anyone I've ever known. He seldom picked up a check; never bought anything he could get for free; never left a store without shoplifting a present for himself. It embarrassed me that he insisted on bargaining with shopkeepers, but he was usually so funny that they'd reduce the price of whatever he wanted.

He was also known as a cheapskate in show business circles, but the first time I met him he broke his old habit and invited eight people to Sardi's for dinner. After we ate, he astounded his old friend John Raitt by asking the waiter for the check. Raitt stood up, banged on his water glass for silence and gleefully announced, "Friends, this is an historic occasion. JACK GOODE IS PICKING UP A CHECK!" The entire restaurant broke into cheers and applause. Every person in that restaurant knew Jack was meeting his son for the first time that night. Father (and, in retrospect, I) recognized that those cheers weren't only because he agreed to foot his table's bill for the first time ever. Father took a bow.

His cheapness was the despair of his more open-handed friends. But the same cheapness that killed him has enabled me to get to know him, because it also made him the packrat that he was.

When I moved in I found that the basement and attic of the house, as well as the loft of the barn, were crammed with forty years' worth of things that he couldn't bring himself to throw away. He saved everything. There were trunks filled with funny hats and trick shoes and plaid jackets with outrageous green and orange lapels, and bowties that lit up and spangled serapes and uniforms and motheaten evening clothes and tap shoes of all colors and styles, and an ancient black leather makeup bag with used tubes of grease paint. And toupees—there was every kind of toupee. Father hated his bald head because he thought it made him look old. He always hid it with a hat or a toupee. In the bottom of one trunk I even found a crewcut toupee. Think about that for a minute—a crewcut toupee.

For me, the final proof of his cheapness was that he even kept the boxes that his toupee plasters came in. In the attic I found a huge carton filled with hundreds of tiny boxes from Lambert's Toupee Plasters. All were empty. But his show business paraphernalia was only the beginning. He also collected furniture that he'd intended to refinish, as well as antique firearms and crockery. As you can imagine, it took me months to sort through all this junk, deciding what to sell, what to give away, what to discard, and what to keep.

One afternoon in the attic, amidst carpet of dead blue bottle houseflies, wasps and hornets, and busy orb-weavers, I found a worn cardboard box crammed against the eaves. It was the kind of long, flat box that people use to store things beneath their beds. I found that Father's whole life was summarized in that box of ancient newspaper clippings, reviews, scripts, playbills *and letters. He never kept scrapbooks the way that Mother had. Instead, he piled everything into this box, and the box was eventually stored in the attic.*

The clippings were in a rough chronological sequence, layer upon layer of yellow, brittle newsprint that crumbled beneath my fingers. They went back to the late '20s when Father got his first real break from Winnie Lightner.

It took me weeks to sort the clippings. After reading them all, I got my first impression of the man I had ignored. Father had been more than just a funnyman. He'd actually been a great comedian and Broadway star, and I'd been too busy sniffing around his wife like a dog around a bitch in heat. I'd bungled my only opportunity to know who he really was.

Most of what I know about Father is a mere recital of names of shows and a chronology of his career. I could name-drop forever, ticking off the greats and near-greats of show business that he worked with. Perhaps it might impress you. But the names aren't really important. You should know that the critics called Jack Goode one of the greatest comics and best dancers on Broadway, that audiences loved him, and given half a chance, he could stop a show with his clowning. If you've watched reruns of The Honeymooners *on television, you know how funny he was.*

Father worked all of his life in show business; on Broadway, in vaudeville, in summer theatres all across the country; on radio, in films, on television. But today no one remembers his name. I don't know what kept him from achieving the kind of superstardom that makes an actor's name a household word. He certainly had enough talent. He certainly had the drive. Everyone expected it.

If I could have the chance, I'd find out what kept him from the kind of success that should have been his. But now I'll never know the answer. I never bothered to get to know him. I lost my only chance.

Little Tommy being held by his father.

15

September 1943

As soon as the curtain closed, three stagehands hustled to front, center stage and deposited a small table and sturdy, wooden chair. One put a seltzer siphon, a tumbler, and a whiskey bottle filled with strong tea onto the table, and just as the curtains began to reopen, they sprinted off into the opposite wings. Jack heard the pianist begin his music.

This was his cue.

He ambled onstage wearing a baggy checkered suit, porkpie hat and floppy, orange bowtie. The follow spot was full on him and when he looked out into the house, he could just barely see the halos outlining the heads of the director, the producer, and their assorted hangers-on. Except for this small audience, the theatre was empty at this dress rehearsal of *Full Speed Ahead*.

Suddenly, Jack saw the bottle. It seemed to magnetically drag him over to the table. He stealthily glanced over each shoulder to see if anyone were watching, poured himself a drink and downed it in one swallow. Then he looked out front and did a doubletake as he noticed the audience for the first time. A cheerful, but guilty grin spread slowly across his face as he transformed from the clandestine drinker to the epitome of the jovial barfly.

Motioning towards the bottle, he said to the audience, "Do you care for a drink?"

Receiving no answer, he tried again, this time louder and with elaborate diction, as if he were speaking to a deaf foreigner. "I beg your pardon, but would you care for a jai alai ball?" As he rolled out these last three words his mouth gaped slackly, like a goldfish gulping air at the surface of a pond. Then in a mutter that reached to the back of the house he said, "I think I'll have just a teensy little one myself."

He poured a glassful and added a splash of seltzer.

As an afterthought he spritzed some seltzer into his hair and rubbed it in well. Then he splashed a little at each armpit and energetically pumped his arms back and forth. He finished his toilette with a dainty dab behind each ear. Refreshed, he lifted his glass and toasted the audience with, "Cheerio… over the gums," then swallowed and added, "Look out stomach, here it comes," a drumroll punctuating his final word.

Jack poured himself another, but before he downed this drink, he paused to sniff its bouquet. He said, "Quite good, but not very strong." He drained the glass, there was another drum roll, and Jack fell flat on the stage. He heard the performers in the wings snicker. Hat and tie askew, he fought his way to his feet by clambering up the chair rungs. When he was finally upright, he weaved a little and said to the audience with that instant intimacy of drunks, "I know what you're talking about. I've had my share of marital struggles, too."

The full orchestra came in as he sang in a slurred, but understandable alcoholic baritone:

"The other night, I came home tight
and what a fight we had.
She packed her clothes, her shoes and hose.
She left and I feel bad!"

Dancing, he launched into the chorus. His first steps were merely tentative shuffles to the left, but as the chorus continued, his dancing grew more confident, flashy and expert. He sang:

"My wife has gone and left me. Gee, but I feel blue.
Ha ha ha ha ha ha ha. Oh Gee, but I feel blue.
My wife has gone and left me. She took her mother too!
Ha ha ha ha ha ha ha. Oh Gee, but I feel blue!
I always took her with me, and here's the reason why:
I couldn't stand to kiss that ugly face of hers goodbye!
My wife has gone and left me. I'm sad and that's a fact.
Ha ha ha ha ha ha ha.
My God! She might come back!"

Jack stopped dancing and the orchestra accompanied him pianissimo while he said, "I don't see anything wrong with a couple of fellows having a drink. The other night a fellow said to me, 'You look miserable.' I said, 'I am. My wife and I had a fight and she said she wouldn't speak to me for thirty days.' He paused before delivering the punchline, 'But today's the last day!'

"A policeman says to me, 'You're not going to drive, are you?' I said, 'I'm in no condition to walk!'"

Next, Jack pantomimed a drunk walking home. He was the driver of a truck who madly tried to avoid a drunk pedestrian as well as the drunk who was nearly run down. He finally reached the opposite curb by doing a high-speed crawl.

"Finally, I went home and there was my wife, *burning* at the window. Getting her daily exercise by jumping to conclusions! She said to me, 'You're drunk.' I said, 'I am not. No man is drunk if he can lie flat on the ground without holding on.'"

The orchestra came full up again as Jack turned front and finished his number with some spectacular kicks. He sang:

"Oh, my wife has gone and left me. Gee, but I feel blue! Ha ha ha ha ha ha ha. *Gee, but I feel blue!*"

He concluded with a big, boozy grin and took off his mangled hat to the audience in a sweeping bow. Then he picked up his bottle, patted it tenderly and veered unsteadily into the wings.

Darrel, a chorus boy, ceremoniously wrapped a white towel around his neck as if he were bestowing a medal of honor. He squeezed Jack's shoulders for emphasis as he lisped, "Jesus, Jack, that was a scream." Then he raced to his place onstage, ready for the number that closed the first act. Once on his mark, he smiled at Jack. In response Jack rolled his eyes, gestured broadly with one limp wrist and mimicked Darrel's lisp, saying, "You're such a sweet person." Darrel and the two dancers next to him were watching and they all began to giggle uncontrollably. The other dancers, waiting onstage for the curtains to open, looked over to see what was so funny but by that time Jack was standing in the wings, innocently wiping his neck with the towel. He grinned mischievously at the three little fags onstage and pretended his towel was a feather boa, producing another wave of giggles. The three regained their composure as the curtain opened and their number started. Jack watched them selling their song and thought, *They're okay. At least three feet short of a yard, but okay.*

From the wings Jack had an unobstructed view of the chorus. Both the boys and girls wore pert sailor hats and clinging satin sailor suits as they sang and danced to the show's title song. He was thinking what a good-looking girl that was, third from the left, when he suddenly realized that the person he was admiring was a boy, not a short-haired girl. It reminded him of the dreams he'd had just before his second marriage. They were strange, recurring dreams all about men: about following them down dark alleys, kissing them, being kissed by them. Jack would tell himself that it was only a dream and he'd struggle to wake up, but the mere fact that he'd dreamed them made Jack wonder about himself. Did they mean that he was some kind of secret faggot? Some Jekyll and Hyde kind of monster? He didn't understand because he'd always been a ladies' man—in fact, he'd prided himself on being something of a lady killer.

When the dreams continued, Jack decided that he'd been without a woman for too long. He hunted for someone suitable for about a month and then met and married Ruth Wiedle, a secretary from Indianapolis. Thank God those dreams had stopped, and he felt his virility had been affirmed. His ability to satisfy Ruth, who knew more about sex than any other woman he'd ever encountered, gave him the He-Man Seal of Approval. But, as he watched the chorus onstage, he was disturbed that he'd mistaken a boy for a girl. He tried to joke about it to himself. *Well, Old Fella*, he thought as he watched Darrel go through the routine, *whatever you once had is on its way out*. He wiped his hair with the towel, saw the brown strands that clung to it and thought, *Yup, you're losing it, but not as fast as you're losing your hair*. But the joke fell flat.

It wasn't funny anymore.

Jack stopped himself, and thought, *Jesus Christ. What am I doing?* He glanced around to see whether anyone had noticed him staring at the chorus boys and then vigorously scrubbed at his face and hair with the towel. *Is there something wrong with me? Does that little fag, Darrel, suspect something? Did he spend all afternoon helping me move into my dressing room because he thinks I'm like him?*

Jack took Darrel's towel from his neck and draped it over a piece of scenery. He didn't want anything to do with it. From now on he would discourage Darrel's friendship, as well as avoid all the other queers in the cast. Darrel smiled at Jack from the stage, but Jack ignored him and turned to go upstairs to his dressing room.

The stage doorman met Jack near the lightboard and handed him a telegram, saying, "This came for you a while ago."

"Thanks, Sammy," Jack said, hoping it was from Irv. *He said he'd let me know as soon as he heard anything about Harris' new show.*

Jack ripped open the yellow Western Union envelope. The telegram began "Greetings," and in a few short sentences his draft board told him that he would be inducted into the Army at Fort Benjamin Harrison in Indiana. He should report for duty in a week.

Damn, Jack thought. *Just when things were looking up. Just when I've got work again for the first time in years.*

He reread the name and address again. And again. The telegram belonged to someone else. It had to. But there was no mistake. "Damn!" Jack burst out.

In a haze, each of his own footsteps echoing through his brain, he went to the front of the theatre, to the director in his orchestra seat. The first act was over and the house lights were up. He watched his own hand rise up to give the telegram to the director. He said, "It's a good thing I've only got a few sides in this show. My Uncle has plans for me."

II
Fort Benjamin Harrison
January 1944

With an olive drab towel around his neck and a wooden rifle on his shoulder, Jack nodded and the piano player at the other end of the mess hall began the medley of military marches that was the overture for *Khaki Kapers*.

Jack surveyed the line of recruits that the Army had given him as a chorus, and they watched him right back. He'd taught the men the steps to their first number in small groups. This was the first time that all thirty were assembled for a rehearsal, and Jack had to make them all work together. If he couldn't mold them into a team, then the show had little chance of success.

Jack knew it was important to show them who was boss. The whole show depended upon his ability to make these guys respect him.

He watched the men listen to the overture and decided that since he wasn't General Patton, since he'd never had any experience as a leader of men, he'd just have to treat these guys like any other audience. If they threw cabbages he'd know how to run for the wings. All he could do was his best.

The pianist finished the overture and Jack said, "Okay, now you make your first entrance." He nodded to the piano player once more and this time a syncopated march echoed against the bare walls of the mess hall that had been converted into a rehearsal space. Jack ran to a spot he'd previously indicated was backstage, smiled and yelled to the guys, "Now imagine that I'm not just one dancer, but a whole line of hoofers." He waited 'til the third bar of the march, standing at strict attention, emptying his mind of everything but the dance he was about to do. When the third bar started, he made a smart right face toward the men, and went into the tap routine that would open *Khaki Kapers*.

From what would have been upstage left—if there had been a real stage—Jack danced toward the men with his quick-kneed, ankle-flapping, limber-jointed grace. The slightest movement of his feet produced staccato bursts of metallic clicks that counterpunched or double-timed the rhythm. From time to time, he switched the rifle to his opposite shoulder or twirled it before him. He smiled at his audience of recruits in the most infectious way—selling the routine, selling himself. He was showing off and he loved it. From the grins on their faces, he could tell that the men liked it, too. This routine was his baby—he'd *created* it. It felt good to show the boys how an expert handled it.

When he repeated the routine a second time, he was more sure of his audience and couldn't help trying for easy laughs. After one complicated set of steps, he said, "Make it look easy, huh?" And just before he twirled the rifle while doing a double-time step he said, "Here's the tough part." His throwaway lines made the would-be chorus boys smile, laugh and nudge each other. Until now they'd never seen him dance. Oh, he'd demonstrated steps, but there had been nothing like this performance. The admiration and surprise on their faces made up for the hours he'd spent perfecting the routine and trying to pound it into them. At once he forgave them for the way they ground his sophisticated steps into the boards. He demonstrated the whole thing once more and then stopped, slightly out of breath.

The men started to applaud, but he raised his hand for quiet. Taking a deep breath he said in a rush, "See? Not so difficult—the main thing is to believe that your feet know what to do, muscle memory. You've been practicing the steps for a week now. Whether you realize it or not, your feet, your muscles, they remember what to do. But you have to let them dance. You do that by concentrating on the rhythm and being loose at the same time. Sounds complicated and I can see that some of you don't believe me, but it's true. You'll see.

"Now, from the top. Line up, please, for your first entrance. Okay, men, on the count of four, follow me." He turned his back, signaled the pianist to start, shouldered his rifle and as the accompanist pounded through the second bar, Jack yelled, "One, two, three, and…"

With his back to them he repeated the whole routine once more. Then he stopped to look behind him and his shoulders sagged.

Jesus. They danced like paraplegics.

Some men were off count. Jack ran over and had them clap out the rhythm, yelling out the count. They improved. Other guys had their heads down. Jack ran up to them and yelled, "Look up—up! Look up at the clock on the wall. Look at me. Don't look at your feet. That's better. Chin up." Some men were shuffling when they should have been stamping or vice versa. Jack danced next to each, yelling encouragement over the thunder of inexperienced tap dancing. Six or seven men knew what they were doing, and they handled the routine well. Jack brought them to the front where the rest could see them to imitate. *Monkey see, monkey do.*

The pianist looked at Jack quizzically as if to ask if he wanted him to repeat the number and Jack nodded. The second time through Jack noticed a tall blond fellow in the back row. There was something rustic about him. He looked as if he ought to have a wisp of straw between his teeth and didn't give the impression of great intelligence. Jack watched him pawing the floorboards with his left foot in what looked like an imitation of Clara the Counting Mare. *Jesus. Where the Hell did the Army get this guy?* Jack looked at his men hopping noisily around the floor, wiped the sweat from his brow and wondered how in God's name he would ever mold this mess into a chorus line in only three weeks. Except for the six good dancers in the front row, the rest of these clodhoppers had two left feet. Well, he'd been ordered to make them into dancers, and he'd do it if it killed him. But it wasn't going to be easy.

Jack walked over and told the piano player to stop. In a loud, smart-ass voice, he said, "You in the back row," and pointed to the big hayseed, "What's your name?"

"Private Yankelevitch," was the answer.

"Well, men, I want you to know that you're all rotten dancers, but Yankelevitch here has the dubious distinction of being the worst amongst you. But at least he's got an excuse—his brains and feet are separated by six and a half feet of Yankelevitch. But the rest of you don't have that excuse.

"Now, Yankelevitch, come up here. We're going to have some private lessons. The rest of you. Try it again on the count of four, and..."

By this time Yankelevitch was at the front of the group of men. Jack grabbed him by the hand and said, "I'm not trying to get fresh... Now, follow Father. One, two, three, *and*..." Jack tapped out the routine as simply as he could so that Yankelevitch could follow. He dragged the big soldier through the steps, trying to make him feel the rhythm. Yankelevitch was embarrassed at being singled out and his neck and ears grew hot. All the guys were watching him and laughing at how clumsy he was. Although he tried to follow Jack's steps, he moved like an arthritic moose on a frozen mill pond.

Exasperated, Jack yelled, "Cut! Stop! Cease! Desist!" The pianist finally silenced in the hall, and Jack, hands on hips, barked like Top Sergeant, "What the hell are you guys trying to do? Maim each other? Send me to an early grave? I've been in show business all my life and I thought I'd seen the worst. Once I saw an audience in Paducah nearly lynch the Flying Farfans and their Dancing Pigs. But this 'performance' of yours takes the cake. Without a doubt, you are the *worst* imitations of dancers that I've ever seen.

"Just a minute ago I said that Yankelevitch was bad, but I want to retract that statement. At least he's trying to learn the routine. I'm not sure what the rest of you are doing, but one thing's for sure: you're not dancing.

"Fletcher, Toomey, Hessler, Baumgarten. Front and center. Each of you take a squad of six men and drill this routine into them. I'll be back in two hours. If they even faintly look like a chorus line, we'll break for chow and stop for the day. If not, we'll have another call after dinner and we'll keep at it all night, and *every* night till they can do this routine in their sleep. Remember, we've only got three weeks, and this is only one of three routines. You've got your work cut out for you, so get on with it. Yankelevitch—try it with Toomey's group. We'll see how you're doing in a while."

As Jack walked to the front of the hall, he heard groaning and muttering behind him. Someone said, "What the hell does he think this is, the Marines, or something?" Then the piano started again, and instead of sixty feet tapping in synchrony, he heard the same stampede. Jack smiled to himself. If they had to rehearse after dinner, they'd miss the camp's Saturday night movie. Perhaps the threat of being kept after school and deprived of *Casablanca* would get these deadbeats on their toes.

The four other principals of the show, Vince, Carl, Al, and Smilin' Jack Porter, were arguing in a small room off the front of the hall. He could hear them criticizing and revising the first draft. As usual, Vince and Carl were at each other's throats. They never agreed as to what was funny. Jack decided to wait outside until they calmed down.

All of them had been in the Army for only four weeks. They hadn't even learned how to reassemble their rifles before a smart second looie in the Classification Department discovered that, by chance, a lot of theatrical talent was concentrated at Camp Benjamin Harrison. There was the Broadway dancer and comedian, Jack Goode, as well as Vince Daniels who'd been a comedian in George White's *Scandals*. There was Carl Baker, a radio funnyman, Al Hodges and Smilin' Jack Porter, musicians at the local NBC station in Indianapolis. This information passed up the chain of command at the Fort, and before long the top brass ordered them to create an original revue that would tour the country to sell war bonds and raise military morale. They were assigned a group of bandsmen, thirty recruits, and the Army would foot the bill.

So they had set to work on *Khaki Kapers*. Al got him to let them use some of his created dance routines for three productions with two specialty numbers: the drunk scene that he'd prepared for *Full Speed Ahead*, and "Hiya Jackson," a rapid-patter skit with Carl Baker that revolved around booze and broads. Jack also would do specialty dancing with the chorus in their three big numbers. In effect, he was to be the choreographer, director, and star of the show. The book was still not finished, but as Jack listened to the four authors haggle over a skit, he was sure they'd have the rough sections smoothed soon. But that *chorus* was another matter.

Jack watched them rehearse in small groups. If he'd had a professional chorus this routine would have been perfected and polished within a week, but with these guys, the task looked difficult, at best. But Jack wasn't willing to give up on them yet. Even if they never learned the steps properly, these stumblebums might still be worth a laugh. Or, if worse came to worst and the routine was too hard for them, he'd work up a marching sequence and use the few who could really dance in front. There were lots of possibilities. He wasn't licked. Not by a long shot.

Yankelevitch was watching Toomey and trying to mimic his movements. But the big guy's eyes were on his own feet when they weren't glued to Toomey.

Jack yelled, "Yankelevitch! Look up, not at your feet."

The boy looked up, grinned self-consciously at Jack, and determinedly fixed his eyes on a spot somewhere above Jack's head. But in a few minutes, his eyes were back on his bootlaces. When he realized his mistake, he quickly glanced to see if Jack was still watching. Although they were both only privates, Yankelevitch looked embarrassed, shot Jack a salute and redoubled his efforts to learn the routine. He'd decided to show that smooth talking, smart-assed Jack Goode that he could learn this dumb dance just as well as anyone else. He might be big and clumsy now, but he was determined to learn this routine. He'd show 'em.

III
Fort Wayne, Indiana
March 1944

With opening night behind them, the cast of *Khaki Kapers* was eating breakfast in the dining room at the Fort Wayne Grande Hotel. Their first performance had raised $10,000 in bonds. The buzz of conversation and clink of tableware were interrupted by a whoop, as Yankelevitch found their review in the *Fort Wayne Sentinel*. In an excited voice he said, "Hey, guys, look what the papers say about us. Here's the headline: '*Khaki Kapers Pleases Large Audience at First Performance.*'

"It says here," he looked up and caught Jack's eye across the table, "'Private Jack Goode, whom the old timers tell me is a very reasonable facsimile of the great Willie Howard, led a cast of soldiers from Fort Benjamin Harrison and a chorus of Indianapolis debutantes through an entertaining variety show as *Khaki Kapers* opened a two-day run at the Shrine Auditorium before a capacity audience that purchased war bonds to obtain seats for the production.'

"Hey, Jack. Listen to this," Yankelevitch continued. "'Private Goode was all that his name implies and more, as he clowned his way through two acts and 14 scenes of the show, which is labeled a satire on Army life, but which still had its serious sides. The versatile comedian and dancer has been in the Army only a short time, and was practically the show itself. Probably his best number was a clever pantomime about a drunk. He had the audience roaring with a bit where he tried to get across a street.'"

Yankelevitch continued reading the review which mentioned the other principals and Hoagy Carmichael's music. The review was quite long and Yankelevitch read every word. Jack stopped listening after a while. He'd read reviews all his life and, although it was nice to have a good one, reviews were really only important on Broadway. The opinion of the theatre critic of the *Fort Wayne Sentinel*, who was probably also in charge of judging the quality of livestock at the County Fair, hardly mattered. Jack did note that, in addition to the bonds that had been purchased as tickets, the insurance company that conducted the bond rally during intermission had raised an additional $200,000. Jack was pleased that their opening night had gone so well and that they were doing their bit for the war effort. Raising money was almost as important as killing Germans.

The chorus wasn't perfect, but in the final week of rehearsal they had pulled into shape. Now they did his routines almost as well as any Shubert line. Tonight there was another performance in Indianapolis, and then they'd return to camp. The top brass would handle the engagements for the show and they'd leave on their cross-country tour in about a week. Jack finished his breakfast and watched Phil Yankelevitch crow over their notice. He felt bad that he'd made him the butt of so many tall jokes and dumb farmer jokes in the last weeks, and decided to try to be nicer to him in the future. He was a likable kid and deserved to be treated better.

IV
Indianapolis, Indiana

"Boys, I want you to meet someone who's near and dear to my heart," Jack said. He stood in the midst of a group of cast members from *Khaki Kapers*. They'd just given a second successful performance and were celebrating in the Monkey Bar of the Imperial Hotel in Indianapolis.

Jack put down his drink, and with the flourish of a magician plucking a bouquet of rainbow silks from out of nowhere, pulled a ragged, yellowed rubber chicken from his breast pocket and flopped it, breast up, onto the bar. There was a roar of surprised laughter as Jack pretended to be astonished at the nakedness of Agnes, his rubber chicken. He tried to cover her with his tie. The guys all liked Jack. He was a Live Wire—a Real Card. He always had something up his sleeve.

Everything was going well until Jack made a slight error in judgment. It would have been better if he'd used Agnes as the focus of jokes. He could have gotten away with either a flurry of one-liners or a string of low-down and dirty stories. Or he could have just used Agnes as a dancing partner. The guys all envied Jack's skill as a dancer and his professional reputation was now a community myth. They all knew about his Broadway successes, that he'd choreographed Shirley Temple's dances in *Little Miss Marker*. They were impressed that he'd rubbed shoulders with Fred Astaire and Ginger Rogers, and they were certain that he'd slept with whole constellations of Hollywood starlets. Jack's mere presence lent legitimacy to *Khaki Kapers*. It proved that their show was a cut above the pathetic hopefuls on the Amateur Hour.

The boys would have stayed to watch him dance or to hear his jokes, but Jack misjudged their mood. Tonight, they didn't have the patience to watch a pantomime.

When that tiny brunette teetered into the bar, Jack realized his impromptu performance was going sour. He felt the men's attention shift as they watched her struggle to get aboard a tall stool and order a sloe gin fizz. She wasn't special looking, not a stunner or anything, but her skirt-hoisting effort to seat herself, combined with her shrill giggle, threw off Jack's timing. It wasn't long before several guys sauntered over to her. When other girls joined her, they were introduced and more of Jack's audience abandoned him. Finally, the band started to play in the next room and Jack was left alone at the bar with Agnes, the wreckage of his pantomime, and Phil Yankelevitch.

Jack felt like an idiot. He hated being ignored, especially by these second-raters. He crushed the rubber chicken into a ball and shoved it into his pants pocket. He'd been trying too hard and he knew it. The only thing to do to preserve his self-respect was to pretend that the whole thing had never happened. Never look back—that was his motto.

Grabbing his drink, he sat down at the bar next to Phil, counting the bottles of whiskey, gin, rye, vodka, and liqueurs behind the bar. He didn't feel like celebrating anymore and he was determined to keep a low profile for the rest of the evening. In the next room the band played "Green Eyes," and Jack was grateful that the melody filled what would have been an uncomfortable silence. Yankelevitch wasn't a great talker. In fact, he hardly ever said anything.

The band segued into "Tangerine" and the two men sat, sipping their drinks and listening to the sounds around them. Jack wished he were part of the animated conversation at the end of the bar, but he felt compelled to keep Yankelevitch company.

Finally, Jack said, "So, how are you, Phil?"

Phil looked at his drink and said, "Okay."

"I guess I made pretty much a fool of myself just now."

There was a silence while Phil seemed to consider this remark. Then he replied, "Yeah, I guess you did."

Jack didn't know what to say to that. Following another silence, Phil took a deep breath and spat out, "What the hell do you care what I think? I'm just the dumb farmer who couldn't dance, remember?"

Phil threw back his drink and got up to leave the bar.

Jack grabbed his arm and said, "Let's get something straight. I'm sorry for riding you so much at rehearsals. You've got a right to be mad—you probably should have just punched me a long time ago. That would have fixed everything."

Then Jack had a brilliant idea. He stood up and said, "Listen, why don't you take a poke at me right now? Then you'll feel better and I'll feel better. Go ahead." He put his hands on his hips, straightened his uniform, stuck out his chin and closed his eyes. He was a caricature of a man braced to absorb a blow to the jaw. Eyes closed, Jack pointed to his jaw and said, "Okay, Yankelevitch—here's the target. Don't keep me waiting. I can't stand the suspense. Go ahead. Hit me."

But nothing happened. He indicated his chin again and again, saying, "Come on, Yankelevitch. Let's get it over with. Come on. Hit me. Hit me."

Still nothing happened and Jack opened one eye to see Phil shaking with that strange soundless laughter that he'd seen before. It was an opportunity too good to waste.

"Afraid of me, are ya?" said Jack, springing around the floor in a fighter's crouch. He thumbed his nose, whirled around and shadow boxed with his fists held at arm's length like Gentleman Jim Corbett. "Come on, Yankelevitch. Give me your best shot. Don't hold back. I can take it."

Yankelevitch extended one long arm to put his palm against Jack's forehead, holding him off as Jack swung recklessly. His uppercuts, jabs and hooks landed in the air six inches from Phil's chest.

Jack sprang away from time to time to deliver funny lines that made Phil double up and laugh in his silent way, but whenever Jack got close enough to try to land a punch, Phil would hold him off. Soon a crowd had gathered, watching, laughing, and applauding.

Now that he had an audience, Jack needed an exit. He couldn't keep this up all night and he didn't want them to get bored again. Then he remembered Agnes. In their next clinch, he whispered his plan to Phil. When Jack sprung away for the last time, he pulled the rubber chicken from his pocket and swung it around his head. He conked Yankelevitch over the head with her and Phil obligingly crashed to the floor. Jack raised Agnes overhead, yelling, "The winnah and still champeen." He accepted the crowd's applause and made Phil get up to take a bow. After that they bought drinks for each other 'til the bar closed. They got stinking drunk, traded biographies, told each other lies and became friends.

V
Fort Benjamin Harrison
Indianapolis, Indiana
March 1945

Jack was furious. Why did the War Department have to be so damned secretive? *For God's sake, we're only a traveling show, not some crack troupe of commandos. Why can't they just tell us where we're going? Are the Nazis or the Japs really interested in* our *movements?*

He opened his locker and jerked his uniforms from their jangling metal hangers. When he'd removed everything, he kicked the door closed, went to his bunk and dropped everything on to it. He'd have to be packed and out of this dump quickly. The bus left in a half hour.

Jack folded his uniforms, packed them into his duffle bag and thought how this overseas duty would have been an adventure if Phil were coming along. But that Yankelevitch was a stubborn bastard. He said he'd had enough of show business and wanted to get into combat. Although Jack tried to convince Phil to stay with the show, Phil was determined to have his chance to be a hero. Only a few minutes ago he'd left by bus for some unidentified post. But because the Army was so secretive, *Phil* didn't even know where Phil was going, and, to make matters worse, they hadn't given anyone APO numbers yet. He wouldn't even be able to write to Phil for at least two months. *Goddamn this Army.*

Although Jack would never have admitted it to Phil, he was worried about him. Jack had never been under fire, but *Khaki Kapers* had entertained in plenty of Army hospitals and he'd seen what bullets and bombs could do. The thought of Phil shot or maimed made Jack's stomach twist. He absolutely refused to think that Phil might get killed. They'd made plans for after the war. He forced his extra shirts into his bag and told himself over and over, *Phil will make it through this. I know he'll be okay.*

Jack and Phil were now best friends. On the year-long tour they'd shared a room, and soon had become an inseparable pair. This was unusual for Jack because he hadn't had a close friend since Jimmy Ardell.

Over his years in show biz, he'd grown accustomed to being a loner. Loneliness was as much a part of his business as applause, curtain calls, and memorizing lines. To fill his empty hours he'd learned to refinish antique furniture and repair antique guns. When these hobbies paled he chased women, and most of the time, he caught them. Women seemed to find Jack irresistible while he considered them just another hobby, a way to kill time.

His first marriage had been ruined by a travel schedule that kept him and his wife apart so much. Florence Lake had been his college sweetheart. They'd married in 1933, just after Jack's first Broadway success in *Hello, Paris*. The show lasted only thirty-three performances, but the contract he'd signed with the Shuberts guaranteed him $10,000 a year for the next three years. At that time, it seemed like all the money he and Florence would ever need. Florence wanted to be a movie actress and Jack wanted Florence. So, against everyone's advice, they eloped and went to Hollywood where she'd been successful. Her work at the studio kept her busy and she hadn't minded when Jack went back to Broadway, and then to a tour of the Midwestern summer theatres that were a part of the Shubert empire. She knew he was happy, and they both had work. Florence began to resent his absences, however, when she'd been forced to stop acting to have their child. She begged Jack to return to Hollywood, to give it another try—but Jack refused. He'd had his fill of the movie racket.

He'd been in a few films. He'd had a part in the chorus of Fred Astaire's *Swing Time*, and in *Flying Down to Rio*. He'd also had bigger parts in a few forgettable RKO shorts. His career in the movies had looked promising until that day the casting director at RKO slid his hand into Jack's crotch and made it clear that unless he received certain explicit sexual favors, Jack was finished at RKO.

Enraged, Jack punched the faggot. He remembered the wave of satisfaction when he saw the creep spit out blood and one bloody tooth. Jack left the studio in a huff and soon the word spread that he was poison. Those faggots stuck together, that's for sure. Jack decided that he'd had enough of movies and that Hollywood was a perverted place to make a living. When the Shuberts offered him summer work at the MUNI in St. Louis, he'd been happy to take it just to get away from California.

Florence had their baby all alone in a Hollywood hospital. She was disappointed that Jack couldn't be with her but she was a trooper, and knew that the show always comes first. When she found out about his dalliances with chorus girls at the MUNI, however, and that he didn't intend to ever come back to Hollywood, it was too much for her. And in true Hollywood fashion, she divorced him, moving on to be the starlet she dreamed of being on her own.

Jack was sad about the whole affair. He was sad for Florence, and for Joyce, his baby daughter. He sent them money whenever he could, but at the tail end of the Depression he was too broke to send them anything. Now that he was no longer expected to be husband and full-time father, Jack vowed to steer clear of the marriage trap forever. He only wanted to work, to make audiences laugh, to play golf, to fish and hunt on his farm in Ohio, to collect guns and refinish antiques—with no interference from anyone, especially a demanding wife and squalling brats. In short, he wanted to fish and fuck at random.

He did marry again—and again, and again. Seven times, actually. He was to become a sort of professional husband. But Ruth, his second wife, was very different from Florence. In fact, Ruth was different from any woman Jack had ever met. She wasn't a nest builder at all. Perhaps the best thing about her was that she didn't expect Jack to act like a husband. They'd gone to bed that first night and had stayed there all weekend. As Jack finished packing his duffle bag, he wondered why they had bothered to involve the State of Ohio in their affair at all.

Ruth turned out to be just as independent as Jack.

She knew what she wanted and she was no dummy, either. She'd always been stage-struck, and had used Jack's contacts to launch her own career. After he'd been drafted, they'd lost touch. The last time he'd heard from her she was appearing on the Starlight Circuit in *Hit the Deck*. In many ways she was just like him; she demanded nothing and didn't interfere in his life at all. Their marriage was only for mutual convenience. Although Jack had enjoyed their lovemaking and was grateful to have been reminded what it was like to be with a woman, Jack didn't miss Ruth or write to her or even think of her. Mostly he thought about his friend Phil Yankelevitch, and wished he'd been able to convince the stubborn Russian bastard to stay with the company.

After checking beneath his bunk to make sure he'd packed everything, Jack zipped up his bag, put on his coat and cap, and joined the other members of the troupe on the bus that would take them to the train station.

As the bus pulled away from the curb and Jack sighed, wishing Phil were there, it didn't occur to him that for the first time in his life, he was in love. He and Phil complemented each other so well and they'd made so many plans. Phil had been raised on a dairy farm in Wisconsin and knew all about farming. After the war he was going to manage Jack's farm in Ohio, and they'd split the profits.

The bus passed the mess hall where *Khaki Kapers* had been born. Jack remembered the way Phil had stood in the back of the chorus: awkward, clumsy, shy. But after the first wave of tenderness, his main emotion was anger. He was angry that the damned Army didn't know who to trust. He was angry that there was so much red tape. It would keep Phil from writing to him and it would prevent him from knowing if the man he loved was safe.

As the bus swept through the main gate of the fort and the cast headed for some secret destination in the Pacific, Jack listened to the musicians in the back of the bus begin their interminable poker game, and all he could think was, *Damn. Damn this war. Damn the Japs and the goddamn Nazis. And damn this stinking, disorganized, shit-for-brains Army.*

Thomas in his early acting days, a young Jack Goode Jr.
Photo by Chris Alexander

16

From San Francisco the army flew *Khaki Kapers* to Hawaii, where they boarded a carrier bound for the Solomon Islands and for Guadalcanal. The Marines had captured that island and its airstrip in the fall of 1941. The fighting had been over for years on Guadalcanal and now it served as a strategic air base, a stopover on the way to the Philippines or Japan. Japanese navy planes still sporadically attacked Henderson Field, but in 1944 Guadalcanal was well behind the front lines and a relatively safe place in the Pacific. The main problem was getting there.

The carrier took a zigzag course designed to confuse the enemy and foil submarines that might be trailing her. These jogs out of the way prolonged the voyage, which would have taken three weeks in peacetime, to an agonizing ten weeks. The troops gambled, wrote letters, polished their bayonets, and drilled while the cast worked frantically at a different sort of duty. They had been ordered to present their shipmates with a different show each week. They performed matinee and evening performances for the men on Friday, Saturday, and Sunday. The other days of the week they invented and rehearsed routines for the new show. By the time they finally disembarked at Guadalcanal the cast had given sixty performances and Jack figured they were the theatrical equivalent of Marine Raiders.

In the States, the chorus had numbered thirty men but there were only fifteen of them now. The band had been similarly whittled down to only five musicians: drums, trumpet, sax, cornet, and bass. Because a piano was a rare commodity in the Solomon Islands, Joe Vera, the piano virtuoso, had dropped out. This left only four principals with the show: Al Hodges, Carl Baker, Vince Daniels and, of course, Jack Goode.

Jack was the company's ace-in-the-hole. Without him they would never have been able to produce a new show each week for ten weeks. He had a phenomenal memory for songs and he could recall nearly every gag or bit of business that he'd ever seen as well as most of his dance routines. Moreover, he had no trouble creating new skits from his repertoire of vintage material. Jack had a sixth sense for what was funny. He used bits from his first jobs with J. Murray & Company and with the Red Mask Band, as well as routines from his more recent Broadway and summer circuit appearances. The guys grew so accustomed to learning new material under pressure that by the time they reached Guadalcanal, Jack thought that if they were given at least two hours' notice they could perform anything, anywhere. He figured that, after their frantic pace aboard ship, it would be simple for them to do the same show night after night on Guadalcanal. And, if it hadn't been for the mud and the rain and the mosquitoes, Jack would have been right.

Years later, Jack would forget most of what happened on Guadalcanal. He would forget the bugs, the daily doses of Atabrine to ward off malaria, the lizards that clung by their toes from the rafters of every mess hall, threatening to drop into some poor sucker's soup. He would forget the hard work to erect and strike the set at each camp. He would forget how often they got lost or delayed because of breakdowns of their ancient, dilapidated truck. But Jack would never forget the rain, the mud, and the mold.

It was raining when they arrived on Guadalcanal. It was raining when they outfitted the truck that was to serve as both transportation and backstage area. It was raining when they first rigged the camouflage-spotted canvas that formed the backdrop for their set. It continued to rain when they first erected Al Hodges' specially designed, portable stage. It was raining when they first spread the huge tarp that sheltered the GI audiences who sat beneath it in their dripping ponchos. It was always threatening to rain or else raining on Guadalcanal. The roads linking the Army encampments were churned into a reddish-brown goo that sucked at their boots with each step. Merely traveling from one camp to another became an accomplishment. Their truck had four-wheel drive, but Jack lost count of the times that he and the others had to attach ropes to her axles and haul her out of the mud.

The ceaseless rain made everything mildew. Their canvas had been treated with a fungicide and was guaranteed by the Army not to mold, but after about a week it smelled as if rancid mushrooms were flourishing in its folds. The drummer complained that his drums wouldn't hold a pitch. Soon the drumheads collapsed, eaten through by a blue, fuzzy growth. The sax player's spare reeds turned green. The veneer warped off the back of the bass fiddle. But these were only minor problems caused by the rain and continual damp. Somehow, between hands of their endless poker game, the musicians were able to cope.

From the constant effort to entertain officers and men under these conditions, the health of several members of the troupe began to suffer. Carl Baker developed the ear fungus that troubled so many soldiers on the island. The growth seemed to be impervious to the sulfa drugs the medics administered. When Carl complained of being dizzy and nauseous all the time, the doctors said that the fungus had spread to his inner ear. He wasn't funny anymore in the "Jackson" skit. In fact, Jack hated to look at Carl. The pieces of cotton that were stuffed into his ears were always soaked with yellow pus. After two months of Guadalcanal, Carl left for an Army hospital in the States. Jack kept their routine in the show, but he did it alone, wearing two hats and doing both parts. The GIs loved it.

A short while later Vince Daniels got a fungus infection beneath his nails. His fingers and toes were swollen to double their size and were an angry red. He limped around camp and was only comfortable with his feet up. The medics at Henderson Field drilled holes into his nail beds to administer sulfa powder but it didn't do Vince much good. He was always in some kind of discomfort and was terrified that he was going to lose his fingers and toes—which would have been the end of his livelihood as a horn player. He left the troupe, and Jack assumed control of the show.

He changed the schedule, allowing more time for travel between camps and putting in rest days. But, as the rain continued, three members of the cast came down with malaria. Atabrine hadn't done them any good. Because they were so short-handed, everyone had to do more of the manual work required to move the show from camp to camp, and they too, became exhausted.

Jack was helping rig the canvas drop, hurling the sodden, moldy canvas over a rope strung between two coconut palms when he felt the first twinge in his back. The pain was sharp enough to take his breath away, but it faded and he helped finish the job. The next day his back was stiff, but Jack thought nothing of it. He'd been a dancer all his life and was used to painful muscles. They came with the job.

He was crouching over to adjust the bolts on the stage when a second bad spasm gripped his back. He found it difficult to straighten up and this time the pain didn't go away. He lay down on the stage and let the others finish the job. He decided to lay off the heavy work and let his back rest for the night's performance.

That night the pain was worse and he limped through his part. Walking was agonizing, and nothing seemed to help. For the next several weeks he stoically ignored the pain, expecting it to get better. When the troupe played at Henderson Field and the pain had only grown more vicious, Jack decided to see a doctor.

II
Henderson Field
Guadalcanal
1944

The doctor held the X-ray up to the light and pointed to white blocks that Jack recognized as vertebrae.

"Here's the problem, Jack. These growths of bone between and alongside your lumbar vertebrae... they're compressing the nerves that emerge from your spinal cord. Here, here, and here. The pads of cartilage between the vertebrae in this area are swollen, too, and to make things worse, the bone growths are also pressing on the cartilage. It's gotten inflamed. It may possibly be infected, although I doubt that. I don't know right now. You've only got a low-grade fever, so there's probably no infection. To make a long story short, all the pain you've been having comes from the calcium deposits pressing on the nerves and on the pads of cartilage between your vertebrae."

"What can you do for it, Doc?"

"Well, to tell you the truth, not much right now. We'll see what aspirin will do for you, but Jack... This is the most severe case of spinal arthritis I've ever seen. You've probably had this condition all your life. Deposits like that don't grow overnight. It's gotten gradually worse over the years and now the rain and humidity here on Guadalcanal have aggravated it. Have you always had back pain?"

"No, not always, but everyone who does my kind of work has pain from time to time. You get used to stiff joints. It's a part of the job."

"Well, I'm sure it's not going to be part of your job for long. You're being admitted to the hospital here on the base. Right now, you're kidding yourself if you think you can get around for much longer without constant pain."

"But, Doc, can't you give me something? I've got to go on with the guys."

"No, Jack. You're going to stay in bed right where you are. Dancing is out of the question."

"But how long will I be laid up? I'm afraid you don't quite have the picture, Doc. I *have* to keep in shape. I have to exercise *every day*. It's my job. My livelihood." Jack tried to sit up so he could look the doctor straight in the eye, but a spasm in his back made him exhale suddenly from pain.

He found that he couldn't sit up at all.

The doctor said, "See what I mean? You've got to take this seriously. It's not just a pulled muscle or a stiff joint. The X-ray shows that your back is in serious trouble. If you don't watch it, you may create a problem that will keep you bedridden for the rest of your life.

"The orderly will give you something to help you relax, and forgive me if I seem abrupt, but I've got a lot of other patients and you've got to cooperate. Lie still. The less you fight it, the quicker those swollen joints will heal. Then we can decide if we're going to operate. But we have to wait till the swelling goes down."

"Are you going to operate here?" Jack asked, incredulous.

"No, back in the States. We'll put you in traction for a while and see how you respond. Then you'll fly home to an Army hospital where the orthopods will know what to do with you."

As the doctor turned to pick up the chart at the next guy's bed, Jack thought, *This guy probably doesn't know shit from Shinola about backs. I'll see a real doctor, a specialist, when I get home.*

He tried to remain motionless, closing his eyes to relax, but one index finger found a loose thread on the hem of his sheet and twisted it round and round. Jack thought about those white blocks that were his vertebrae and the gray, hazy areas that were cartilage. He willed his back to heal. He didn't want to be an invalid. He didn't want this pain. He wanted to get back to the States to see Phil. He wanted to play Broadway again.

Jack never returned to the show. He was almost always in pain now and sometimes thought he'd go crazy from having to lie in bed. But after a while the pain began to subside. He graduated from traction to a back brace and was shipped home to a veteran's hospital near Phoenix, Arizona. Then came mornings when he woke up and found that his back didn't hurt. The surgeons said that if he kept improving, it might not be necessary to fuse his vertebrae. He knew enough about backs to know that might end his dancing career. The end of his life.

III

Dear Phil,

There was something about those two words that didn't sound right to Jack. They sounded too intimate, too girly. They made him nervous, and he crumpled the sheet of airmail paper and tossed it into his bedside wastebasket. It landed with a hollow *thwunk*, and he began a new letter on a fresh sheet of paper.

Dear Pvt. Yankelevitch,

(Or is it Cpl. Yankelevitch? Or possibly Cpt. Yankelevitch?)

Certainly, it is Yankelevitch S.O.B. By now the Masterminds that run this Flying Circus called the U.S. Army have surely discovered at least one or two of your flawless leadership qualities and have raised you to a rank more celestial than mere Private. It's been so long since I've heard from you that you might be running the whole damn European Theatre for all I know. But the papers say that some guy called Eisenhower is in command. (Maybe he reports to you.)

All kidding aside, while you are gaily killing Krauts, I am still stuck in the VA hospital in Phoenix. I've been here for three months now and, believe me, except for the tan I've gotten from sitting in my wheelchair in the sun, I'd rather be in Philadelphia. No contest.

My back is healing—finally. The specialists here tell me it's a miracle, but let me tell you, I've been praying to anybody who'll listen. I don't relish spending the rest of my days in a chair. They say that I have to forget about dancing. And after what I've been through, I'm not taking any chances. I intend to follow the doctor's orders to the last semicolon. For a while there I thought I'd go crazy—when you're flat on your back and it hurts to even turn your head, you really appreciate what it is to be able to do things for yourself. I've been walking with a cane for three weeks now, and if I'm a good boy and follow orders, they say they're going to let me out of this joint—under my own steam. I can't wait to get home to the farm. It'll take a while to get things arranged with Ruth, but she's always been reasonable, and it isn't as if she's attached to me or anything. If worse comes to worst, I know a judge very high up in Ohio politics. He'll be able to help, I'm sure of that.

I haven't heard a word from you since I've been in the States, but they tell me that the snafu is standard—mail from the Solomons is always months late. So, I hope this finds you well. It looks like it'll all be over soon. Boy, am I ever glad you're not with the Marines in the Philippines.

Have you counted up your points? Personally, I think their whole system is screwy, but maybe it'll work to your advantage. Seems to have fouled up everyone else I've heard of. Anyway, it's only fair that a hero like you should be getting out soon. Sure would be nice if you got out the day after you get this letter and flew to Phoenix to help your old dancing teacher hobble home.

As far as I'm concerned, the deal is still on about the farm, only now, I'll be living there as well. My career as the toast of Broadway and three continents has been terminated. I suppose I should be sad. But I'm not. I've spent a life in this business. I'm just glad that there's you and the farm to fall back on.

Why don't you break down and send the Old Cripple a letter? That's if you aren't too busy with your many admirers. Look forward to hearing from you.

Adieu, a bientot and Creamed Rats on Toast,

Jack

Jack reread the letter and made corrections here and there. Overall he was pleased with his effort. It seemed to strike the proper tone: friendly, but not mushy. He didn't think the letter revealed how worried he was about Phil. It had been months, but because there was no official word that Phil had been wounded or killed, Jack reasoned that no news was good news. It was just like Yankelevitch not to write. He probably had other things on his mind—like staying alive. But, goddammit, he could send something—even a crummy postcard would be better than silence.

In the month after Jack wrote that letter to Phil he kept exercising and strengthening his body. Soon he could walk more freely, using his cane at only irregular, unsteady periods. He was discharged from the Army and arrived in Ohio a day after the war with Japan was declared over.

Jack Goode is holding young Thomas at Christmas.

17

Father began to dance again, but this time his dancing was more athletic. He developed a stunt in one of his routines in which he ran across the stage at full tilt, and the momentum carried him six or seven feet up a concrete wall that was part of the stage—walking the arch, as it was called. My Aunt Hazel told me all about this. She said that after the war he built himself up furiously, and then, even though the doctors told him not to, he went back into show business.

One thing that Aunt Hazel didn't tell me was about Father's affairs with men. I'm sure she had no idea, but I learned that men either loved or hated Father. When I questioned old friends of his—some of them show business legends—I either got a royal welcome or the bum's rush at the mention of his name. I got the feeling that they knew something I didn't and that they weren't willing to tell me.

When I did find out that my Father developed a taste for men as well as women, I was astounded. The only context I'd had for this man was the one of a picture of suave manliness that didn't fit at all with this new knowledge. And the fact that he hid it until the day he died only confused and angered me more.

It happened long after he was dead. Somebody told his "unsavory" little secret to me in the guise of kindness. But it wasn't a kindness. It destroyed the image of the man I'd only barely gotten to know in the last year of his life. There has been nothing to replace it.

When Father went back into show business after his disappointment over Phil Yankelevitch, he fell into the arms of his co-star in a show that toured the country. That gentleman co-star is still an active singer and comedian to this day, as is the role that he is unwaveringly heterosexual. But Father created a whole new set of habits. Acting upon his

The Dressing Drink

bisexuality was only one of them. I'm sure that when he died, he hoped what he considered to be his sordid little secret would be buried with him.

Father settled into his life as a civilian and began to reorder things to make room for Phil Yankelevitch. The immediate thing he had to do was begin divorce proceedings against Ruth Wiedle. It wasn't difficult for him to win that divorce case. He was a crippled veteran. I'm sure he went into the courtroom and played his part to the hilt. By the time he returned from the war, Ruth had shared a bed with many of his show business friends. Some of them testified against her and Ruth didn't have a chance of either contesting the divorce or getting alimony. Exit: Wife #2.

Father waited patiently for Phil to arrive. He kept looking for letters and finally wrote to the Army. One day he got a tersely-worded message from the Department of War: Records. Private Philip Yankelevitch had received an honorable discharge in October of 1945. But Phil never appeared at Father's farm in Ohio and he never contacted Father. He was untraceable. Perhaps he was as scared of their potential relationship as Father was.

One thing I am certain of is that the solitude began to grate on Father's nerves. He wrote to Aunt Hazel telling her that he was lonely. He hated the sounds of the insects droning outside in the trees. There were cicadas in the daytime and katydids at night. Their continuous racket might have gone unnoticed by someone else, but it drove Father crazy. He wasn't built for solitude.

His doctors told him that dancing would aggravate his spinal arthritis. But as the months passed and as he finished all the projects he had started, Father couldn't resist getting back into shape. Soon he had built his back and leg muscles to the extent that he could walk and even run without pain.

An 18-year-old Thomas K. Flagg
Photo by Donna Reed

18

As soon as Chester shipped out to join the American Friends' Service Committee as an ambulance driver attached to the British Army in Egypt, Dorothy Mary vacated the west wing of Greenlea and moved back to Denbigh. She was happy to be out of that Victorian mansion and, to celebrate, she had completely decorated Denbigh's third floor. She chose feminine but sophisticated furnishings and transformed her old rooms and the adjoining nursery into an office, sitting room, and bedroom. Her new abode was the antithesis of Nana's gloomy monstrosity.

Things were quieter at Denbigh now. One evening in front of the fire in the library, David told Dorothy Mary how Father sacked Grizzy and himself. He was very matter-of-fact about it and emphasized that Father had been correct to do so. David had known all along that he wasn't suited to be an executive at the family factory. He'd enlisted as a second lieutenant in the Army and Mother had wrangled a nice desk job for him in the States. But in a few months David had joined a fighting unit in Europe. Mrs. Flagg and Dorothy Mary were worried about him. His last letter was from Normandy and there hadn't been any word from him in months.

Grizzy joined the Navy but they didn't expect any letters from him. He was angry at the family, even at Mrs. Flagg. No one knew where Grizzy was stationed, or even if he was alive. Although Dorothy and her mother were concerned about the boys, Mr. Flagg never mentioned them. It was as if he had no sons.

Dorothy Mary embraced the war effort like a long-awaited lover. It gave purpose and color to her days and she began to fill a new set of leather-bound scrapbooks. But the newspaper photos and clippings that she saved were different from those of her debutante years. Now she was always dressed in the smart Navy League uniform that she had designed.

She never smiled languidly into the camera as she had as a debutante, but instead, was always pictured as concentrating on the task at hand. The war effort and her volunteer work were serious business. Now the society columns made no mention of parties, gowns, sparkling repartee, or tea dances. Instead they lauded Dorothy Mary as a tireless worker for the Navy League. She sorted and tagged binoculars loaned by her peers for wartime use. She rode with the Navy League Bicycle Corps as they trained for messenger service in the event of air attack. She chauffeured Navy brass around town in her convertible. She packed parachutes and collected cigarettes, razor blades, Kleenex, chocolate bars and spare shoelaces for ditty bags for the Seventh Fleet. She sold war bonds in the Navy League booth at 30th and Broad Streets in downtown Philadelphia. Within a year of Chester's departure Dorothy Mary was a leader of the younger women in the Navy League, and a solid member of the best set of patriotic young Philadelphians. Her mother couldn't have been more proud. Dorothy Mary found that she didn't miss Chester and seldom thought of him.

After a while she found herself getting just a bit bored with her patriotic role. She wanted to do something more dramatic but didn't quite know what that was.

Then the League gave her a special assignment. In addition to everything else, she was asked to organize, write, and host a Navy League radio program. It would originate on radio station WFIL and would be called "The Navy League Hour with Mrs. Chester Liddell." The program was to emphasize what Philadelphians were doing, or should do, to help defeat the enemy.

Dorothy Mary (left) with colleagues at the Navy League Radio Show.

Like most people, Dorothy Mary knew how to turn a radio on and off, but that was all. The rest of radio production was Terra Incognita to her. She'd never been inside a radio station and had no idea how important time was. On one of her first programs, while she reviewed the script with the WAVES and WACS she was to interview, a harried man, previously introduced as the production director, kept interrupting their conversation. He reminded her again and again to watch the clock because the station had to take an identification break every fifteen minutes. Dorothy thought he was unspeakably rude. By airtime the man had repeated this warning so often that she was thoroughly annoyed. Just to show him that she knew the value of time, she hurried through the interviews and signed off the air eight minutes early.

After she learned what she'd done to that harried little man, Dorothy began to take her show more seriously. She spent hours at the station watching the production crew. Soon she knew exactly how to manage the time allotted to her and she grew fearless in front of the mic. She learned to elicit answers to controversial questions. Her show gained popularity. She interviewed Navy personnel from recruiting officers to ships' cooks, to vice admirals. She wanted to give her listeners a true picture of how Navy men and women were faring in the war.

Dorothy Mary receiving honor (left) and with fellow colleagues (right).

There were also shows devoted to practical ways the citizens of Philadelphia could cope with sugar and gasoline rationing, shows about conservation of paper and fat, shows about scrap metal drives and bond sales. She interviewed people who cultivated victory gardens off the Atlantic coast. She sponsored a program to aid orphans in Italy, Belgium, France, and Holland. "The Navy League Hour" was a sustaining program. In the radio business this meant that it was unsponsored and aired as a public service first on only one station, WFIL. As it gained popularity WBIG, KYW, and WHAT carried it. Like other wartime-sustaining shows, "The Navy League Hour" was heard in midafternoon or early morning. It was no competition for shows like "The Thin Man," "Terry and the Pirates," "Gangbusters," or "Break the Bank," but it did attract a wide audience, and Dorothy Mary felt rewarded for her time and effort.

In 1943 her volunteer work was interrupted for a month when she and her mother traveled by train to Reno for the divorce. Dorothy had to record shows ahead and had the satisfaction of hearing herself on the radio at Denbigh before she and her mother left for 30th Street Station. Mrs. Flagg was horrified that Dorothy Mary was bringing this scandal into the family after all she had done to improve their social standing.

Dorothy Mary paid no attention to her mother and stuck to her plan. She had filed separation papers as soon as Chester left town. It was nearly a year before the lawyers advised her to go to Reno. The divorce and the grounds of mental cruelty made a big splash in the Philadelphia, Baltimore, and New York papers. It was exactly the sort of publicity that Mrs. Flagg had feared. Dorothy Mary was furious when she read the gossip columns that made her sound like a backstabbing shrew who had divorced her patriotic husband while he risked his life in the war. None mentioned her own war work.

For a year after the divorce Dorothy Mary found that she was ostracized by many of those "close friends" who had hitherto found her presence essential for their dinner parties. Those fastidious hostesses thought she had an unfortunate disease: chronic notoriety. Dorothy continued with the volunteer work and with her radio show. Since she was in the public eye and did such conspicuously good work for the League, it wasn't long before she was once again welcomed in the best circles. But Dorothy Mary never forgot those fair-weather friends. She began to ridicule Philadelphia and Philadelphians. William Penn's statue, atop City Hall, always looked as if he were pissing on all of Philadelphia. She thought it was a fitting gesture and looked forward to the time when she could move on to bigger pools and better fish.

After the divorce she was billed as Dorothy Flagg Liddell, instead of Mrs. Chester Liddell. That name meant something in Philadelphia and New York: shop girls gave a Liddell better service; headwaiters swept a Liddell to the best table; hotel clerks fell all over themselves to oblige a Liddell. It was the only worthwhile thing she'd gotten from Chester.

The end of the war came and WFIL announced that "The Navy League Hour with Dorothy Flagg Liddell" would be cancelled—but they offered Dorothy Mary a chance at a different kind of show. The management liked her voice and poise. To them she was a rare bird... an expert interviewer who had the power and glamour of high society. And she was a snob's snob. She looked like a pretty Philadelphia matron but they knew she was also tough, quick-thinking, and stubborn. She could hold her own in any circle, especially in show business. She wasn't awed by celebrities.

One day they called her into the executive meeting room of WFIL and propositioned her.

"We'd like to see you host a weekly fifteen-minute celebrity interview show, from the Ocean Room of the Drake Hotel. Your job would be to track down show business folk who are visiting Philadelphia and convince them to appear on the air. Do you want the job?"

Dorothy Mary thought about it for almost a minute before she pushed back the ash blonde pageboy that framed her face, smiled her best debutante smile, and said, "Yes."

II
Denbigh, Pennsylvania
Radnor, Pennsylvania
February 1946

Mrs. Flagg had her gardener's plan book on her lap and was leafing through seed catalogues, searching for perennials for the flowerbeds that flanked the pool. She usually used sweet alyssum, ageratum, phlox, and lilies, but this year she wanted something more special. The doctors said that David might be out of the hospital in the summer—he *would* be—and she wanted the gardens to be especially nice for his homecoming. He appreciated the flowers and the poor child had suffered so much. Perhaps she could put in beds of pink and yellow lady's slippers—that would be unusual and would set the Garden Club of Ardmore on its ear.

Her husband sat in the wing chair facing her, listening to the seven o'clock news on the radio and leafing through the evening paper. It rustled and snapped as he thumbed through it, but Mrs. Flagg hardly heard the radio or her husband's restless noises. She was thinking about David.

As the Allies moved in to liberate Paris, David had gotten captured behind the German lines.

The Nazis sent him to a camp.

When Germany fell David had been liberated, reconditioned, and sent to the Far East to join MacArthur's assault on New Guinea. He'd been with MacArthur's staff until the Jap surrender in Tokyo Bay. The letter from the psychiatrist in the Army hospital in Santa Barbara said David was suffering from battle fatigue. She had written back to the man, saying that David would be so much better at Denbigh. He would be infinitely more comfortable, and she would personally look after him. But the doctor refused. He said that such a seriously disturbed man needed trained psychiatric support. Mrs. Flagg didn't quite understand. Was "battle fatigue" a euphemism for insanity? Had David gone crazy? Mrs. Flagg had no answers to her questions and could only hope that her eldest son was healing and would be home soon. She wished David would write or call, but there had been no word from him. And the doctor had specifically asked the family not to try to contact David.

Grizzy was a different matter. He'd never seen active duty. An accident in the Navy shipyards in Philadelphia had sidelined him and he'd eventually been given a medical discharge. He married and lived with Libby, his wife, at Tiptonbrook, her farm in Chester County. Mrs. Flagg had hoped that Grizzy would settle down after his marriage but that didn't seem likely now. The elder Flaggs had only been invited to Tiptonbrook once, and the evening had been a disaster. Both Grizzy and Libby were drunk when the Flaggs arrived. The meal had been badly prepared and was hours late. Grizzy passed out in the bathroom before dessert was served. Mr. Flagg had driven home in a reckless fury. All the way to Denbigh he cut corners too sharply, drove too fast and ranted about Grizzy, calling him a wastrel, a drunk and worse. He'd threatened to cut him out of the will.

Mrs. Flagg looked up as the clock struck seven-thirty. Mr. Flagg liked everything to be punctual: cocktails from seven to eight, and dinner promptly at eight. Her husband took out his pocket watch and frowned. If Dorothy Mary didn't arrive soon there would be another scene.

"Did Dorothy say she would be late tonight?" asked her husband.

"No, she said she would be home in time for cocktails. She should be here any minute. Don't be hard on her, dear, she's been doing such good work. Her drive for the orphans resulted in 350 boxes sent to Belgium alone. And there's her program on top of that. And, you know, she's never kept a penny of that money. It's all been given to the League."

"Hmph. Still doesn't give her an excuse to hold up dinner." Mr. Flagg returned to the paper. He was hungry but, more than that, he was irritated. It had been a bad day. The plant was months behind in production and he'd had to threaten the plant manager that day. He'd just read more about the rumors of a coal miner's strike. The miners' demands were unreasonable, and John L. Lewis should be shot. If there were a coal miners' strike, that would make steel prices skyrocket. If it was a long strike, steel shortages were inevitable. You can't make steel without coal. This would make the pipe-fittings business even worse.

On top of everything else, Marguerite was being difficult... sulking, pouting, complaining that he neglected her. The woman was impossible. You'd think that after all these years she'd understood their relationship. And after all he'd done for her. After all he'd given her. Had the whole world gone nuts? He'd come home hoping for a little peace and quiet, and now his daughter was late and dinner would be delayed. Where *was* that damned girl? Ever since she'd taken on that celebrity radio show, she'd become such a flibberty-gibbet. Not dependable. But, everything considered, she was the best of the lot. Grizzy was an unspeakable drunk. Every word out of his mouth was foul, crude. David had something wrong upstairs. Dorothy wasn't perfect—she'd divorced Chester Liddell, but what self-respecting girl wouldn't have done that?

The news went off and *The Shadow* came on. Mr. Flagg listened as Lamont Cranston opened the creaking door to spin another murder mystery. When intermission came he looked at his watch again. A quarter to eight—you'd think that blasted girl would have sense enough to call if she were going to be late.

Dorothy Mary slammed her car door and hurried into the house. She knew she was late and that Father would be annoyed, if he were home. But she hoped both her parents were there. When they heard the news they would forget that they were mad. It was *such* good news! She was going to be famous as well as very, very rich. They'd be so proud of her.

She found them in the library. Father snapped off the radio and Mother glanced up from her perennial border plan as Dorothy entered. "Evening, Mother. Hello, Daddy. I'm sorry I'm late, but traffic from town was impossible. I'm dying for a drink. Do I have time?" Without pausing for a reply, she went to the bar and poured herself a martini from the silver shaker. She turned back to her parents. "I thought of waiting until after dinner, but if I don't tell someone soon, I'll just *burst* with the news.

"Daddy, I especially wanted you to be here. You're going to be so surprised. I've finally *made* it. WFIL wants me to do the show five nights a week instead of just one. They've got a sponsor and today I signed the contracts. I'm to be the spokeswoman for Pirandello Champagne." She went over to her father's chair and sat on the embroidered footstool next to him. "And, Daddy, guess how much my contract is for?"

"Tell me, Dorothy," her mother interrupted.

"A hundred thousand dollars for the next three years!"

"Before or after taxes?" her father asked.

"Well, before, I guess," she said hesitantly.

"Too bad it isn't after. But congratulations, Dorothy. This calls for another drink. It's the first good news I've heard all day."

"Dorothy, that's simply marvelous!" said Mrs. Flagg. Her perennial border was forgotten. "I can't wait to tell the League. We can certainly use the money for the relief effort in Europe."

Dorothy Mary put her glass on the table next to her father's chair and turned to her mother. "Wait a minute, Mother. Let's get this clear right now. I'm *not* donating this money to the League or to any other charity. They've gotten every penny I've earned since the war—I thought that was the least I could do since the League really gave me my start in radio. But that's all over now. I've paid my debt. Any money I earn from here on in is mine. And I intend to keep it." She got up from the footstool and went back to the bar at the side of the room.

Mrs. Flagg closed her gardening book with a slap and objected, "Dorothy, you have no business keeping that money. We simply don't do such things."

"No, Mother, *you* don't do such things, but I do. I'm sick to death of Philadelphia and what *it* thinks is proper. From now on I'm through with devoting myself to volunteer work. From now on my number one charity is me. Me."

"But, Dorothy, how can you? Using our name to endorse products is so common. How you can even consider it after the way you've been brought up is beyond me."

"Mother, we're not talking about a thousand dollars or just five thousand dollars. Billy Feldman says that I may earn a million from endorsements in the next seven years. The champagne account is just the beginning."

"So, we're going to see you hawking car polishes and chewing gum and face creams?"

"Mother, I'll sell anything they'll pay me to. Besides, it's too late to argue about it. I've already signed the contracts. It's all set. I have two weeks off and then the show goes into production. WFIL has even given me an office and a secretary." She turned on her heels to her father. "Daddy, you haven't said a word. What do you think?"

There was a pause and he looked from his wife and said, "Dorothy, on principle your mother is right. But…" Here he paused significantly. "I've observed that the smartest people are never any better than they have to be. So, I'll tell you what I think." He got up, walked over to his tall daughter, placed one hand on each of her shoulders and turned her to face him. "I think you should give it a try. I don't think you have a prayer of making that million. But if you do, I'll pay the taxes on it for you."

Dorothy felt his hand grip her shoulder. As she grinned at him she knew she had won a major victory and that, perhaps for the first time in her life, her father was proud of her.

19

"Denbigh"
Radnor, Pennsylvania
May 1946

    The David that came home that spring was frail, thinner than anyone remembered, and extremely quiet. But, at least at first, he seemed to be glad to be home. David and Dorothy Mary had always been especially close and perhaps, if she hadn't been so preoccupied with her radio program, she might have seen that something was wrong with her brother. If she'd been able to devote any time to him, she would have noticed that his eyes were different—they didn't smile anymore. His open, slightly mocking expression had been replaced by a frightened look. His hands had a slight tremor, which he tried to hide by clasping them behind his back or thrusting them into his pockets. But Dorothy Mary had no time for David. She was in Philadelphia or New York most of the time and she didn't realize how greatly the war had damaged him until it was too late.

    David had always been the quietest of the Flagg children and now he behaved like a deaf mute. He sat alone for hours staring into space, lost in contemplation of some inner landscape. If someone disturbed him it was a while before he could respond. He surfaced slowly from these private depths, like a crippled fish swimming painfully up toward sunlit waters.

    Although Dorothy Mary was too busy to notice these changes in her brother, Mrs. Flagg knew there was something very wrong with her son. She was surprised he hadn't been more appreciative of the things she had done to welcome him home to Denbigh. For example, he hadn't noticed that his rooms were newly decorated, and he begged her to cancel the dinner dance she had planned in his honor. David said that he couldn't face any of his old friends just yet. Worst of all, he only mumbled a vague "thanks" when his father gave him the keys to the yellow Jaguar convertible that was his welcome home present from the family. The old David would have acted so differently. He would have said something about the new colors of his rooms; he would have danced all night at his party; he would have insisted on taking everyone on the estate, even Rodgers, for a spin in his new sportscar.

Although Mrs. Flagg was surprised that David hadn't been more demonstrative about her efforts to welcome him home, the only thing that really hurt her was that he ignored the flowers she had planted for him. She had thought he would instantly understand that the masses of pale, pink lady's slippers were her special gift to him. They'd come from the New Jersey Pine Barrens. It had taken her two days of grubbing in the dirt on hands and knees to plant them, and the flowers themselves had cost a fortune. David sat by the pool every day sipping a drink, staring at those flowers. He must have known they were for him. It bothered Mrs. Flagg that he never said a word.

David always wanted to be alone these days. He wasn't interested in tennis or polo or even in women. This was odd, because before the war he'd been one of the most active, sought-after bachelors on the Main Line. For several weeks after his return the phone had rung constantly. All of David's old friends wanted to entertain him. But he refused everything and now even his best friends had stopped calling. Lately he'd formed the habit of driving off with no explanation. When he returned, he'd only say that he'd been to New York and then he'd shut himself in his rooms. The son that Mrs. Flagg had raised would never have been so thoughtless, so selfish.

Mrs. Flagg called Dr. Klauber at the sanitorium in San Diego and described David's behavior. What was still wrong with him? Could the family do something for him? Should he be seeing another psychiatrist? Dr. Klauber was reassuring. David was fine. He was only having a problem readjusting to civilian life. After all, he'd had a pretty tough time in the prison camps and now he needed time to feel his way back into the real world. Above all, David shouldn't be pressured by the family. They should just leave him alone. Mrs. Flagg tried to find comfort in Dr. Klauber's advice but she couldn't help worrying about her eldest boy. To make matters worse, he was drinking too much.

If Grizzy weren't an alcoholic, Mrs. Flagg probably wouldn't have given David's drinking a second thought. But since he'd returned, David drank all the time. In the morning he had Bloody Marys or Bull shots; in the afternoons, whiskey and sodas; before dinner it was Scotch. Then there was wine with dinner and neat whiskey or brandy on into the night.

After that disastrous evening at Tiptonbrook, Mr. Flagg had indeed written Grizzy out of his will and forbidden his wife to invite him to Denbigh. Mrs. Flagg kept in touch with her favorite by phone, but she never visited him, and she missed him and his confidences. It would be unbearable if David also disinherited himself. So, Mrs. Flagg kept watch on the supply of liquor in the bar. She noticed that it disappeared much more rapidly since David had come home. She hoped her husband didn't notice.

Of course, drinking itself was no crime. One had to possess this social skill just as one had to know how to sit a horse or manage a receiving line or make small talk. But alcoholics were tedious and sloppy. Thank God that David was never noticeably drunk. Mrs. Flagg could only watch and pray that soon the old David would return from the war.

II

For the thousandth time the familiar nightmare started again.

David felt the beam of a flashlight stab into his brain as the guards shook him awake and ordered him out of bed.

Once more they cuffed his hands behind his back and marched past the other prisoners.

Again, David heard the sounds made by dozens of men asleep. If his fellow prisoners were aware that the guards had come for him, they made no sign. They knew when to keep their mouths shut.

The guards marched David down the main street of the quiet, deserted camp toward the light that spilled from the window of the commandant's quarters. That unforgettable pool of light that David had seen so many times night after night. Occasionally they nudged him in the small of the back with the snouts of their rifles. David knew that the commandant often took prisoners away in the middle of the night, but he had thought he was immune to such things. After all, even in war there were rules: David was an officer, a gentleman, and an American.

But now he was worried and scared. What were they going to do with him? What did they want? The idea of escape was hopeless. His hands were tightly bound. Once again, he tried to work his hands free and felt the panic rise in his chest when he realized his arms were useless to him now. Even if there were someplace to run, the guards would cut him down before he had gone two feet. It had been more than a year since he had a cigarette, but now David was desperate for one.

They climbed the few stairs of the commandant's bungalow. The guards knocked, opened the door, and shoved David inside. The commandant was expecting them. He looked David up and down and smiled a cold smile. He nodded to the guards and in slow motion David saw him begin to unbutton his tunic. Once more the commandant said, "Perhaps this will teach the American dog his place. He should be more respectful of his betters."

Once again David was paralyzed by terror. He knew what would happen next and he wanted this nightmare to stop.

At the hospital, Dr. Klauber told him that he was okay now. He had shaken hands with David and pronounced him completely cured. David remembered all those afternoons, listening to Dr. Klauber's antiseptic voice in that beige office of his. He remembered the doctors reassuring him that just because he had been raped in prison camp didn't mean that he was perverted. David could make the dreams stop if he wanted to. He could be a whole man again. But David knew the psychiatrist was wrong—he didn't have all the facts.

David had been ashamed to tell him what always happened at the end of the nightmare. So, he knew that the doctor's well-remembered words didn't have enough magic to dispel this awful dream. They faded as if they had never been spoken into that beige room, and the scene in the commandant's quarters continued to unroll as it had so many times before.

The guards ripped off David's clothes and flung him face down on a cot in the corner of the room. As he fell, his mouth smashed against the iron bedstead, filling with metallic-tasting blood. He tried to roll over and get up, but a guard sat on his lower legs and pinned him to the cot. David twisted and thrashed his upper body, trying to throw the guard off his legs, but months in the camp had made him weak. His mouth throbbed and someone straddled him from behind. He felt like a dazed mouse suffocating in the coils of a viper. He couldn't breathe. Black flecks swam before his eyes. But the throbbing of his bloody mouth and the panic of his claustrophobia were abruptly forgotten in a pain greater than any he had ever imagined. He thought he would be ripped apart, as something too big forced its way into his anus. He tried again to twist away, but that only made it hurt worse. Shame welled in him. He could hear the commandant's hoarse breathing above him and the pain came in waves as he plunged up and down.

And once more David screamed and screamed because, as the nightmare continued, he looked up over his shoulder and saw that the commandant had his own face and smiled his own mocking smile.

III
Radio Station WFIL
Philadelphia, Pennsylvania
November 1946

Dorothy Mary yelled to the outer office, "Virginia, come on in. Let's get this finished quickly."

It had taken some time, but after firing three other candidates from WFIL's secretarial pool, Dorothy Mary had found Virginia Peraino. The others had possessed the necessary secretarial skills, but they lacked the savvy for dealing with irregular hours, a hectic schedule, quirky show folk who had to be alternately charmed and threatened, as well as a temperamental boss who demanded perfection from her second-in-command. Virginia did more than type letters. Each week she helped produce the Mary Liddell Hour. Together they combed *Variety*, contacted agents, and kept the program supplied with show business personalities who were visiting the City of Brotherly Love. Virginia was a tough, thirty-five-year old divorcée who had been raised in South Philly. She had none of Dorothy Mary's upper-crust polish, but she was tenacious, fearless, and loyal. And she needed her paycheck. She entered the office with her clipboard and pencil.

"Okay, Virginia. Let's hear the schedule for next week."

"Monday is Sophie Tucker."

"Good grief, Virginia, not that old battle axe again. She was just on a month and a half ago." Dorothy threw her pencil down onto her desk. "I swear, if I have to interview her once more… well, I don't know exactly what I'll do, but I know it'll be violent. That woman is arrogant and pompous *and* she's boring. And that *voice*. It belongs to a female impersonator. Really, Virginia. How can you do this to me? You know how I feel about her. You've got to cancel her and get someone else. I simply can't face her again."

"Mary, I can't. We owe Bob Kappel a favor. Remember last Spring, he got you Bing Crosby?"

"Yes, but can't you talk him out of it, Virginia? Maybe he'd settle for a column in the *Inquirer* instead?"

"Not a chance. You'll just have to do Sophie Tucker on Monday. There's no way out."

"Well, I hope there's something better for the rest of the week to make up for that overblown windbag. Please, Virginia, remember—*never* again. Got it?"

"Okay."

"Who's on for the rest of the week?"

"Tuesday is Xavier Cugat."

"Good. Cugie is always a peach."

"Wednesday, Dorothy Lamour."

"Fine. Did you get Spike Jones for Thursday?"

"Yes, and Friday you'll have Betty Grable and Harry James. Their agent confirmed it today."

"Well, it looks like the week is all set and we can relax a little. Except for Two-Ton

Tessie on Monday, it should be swell. What about the following week? Are there any problems I should know about?"

Virginia consulted her clipboard. "Well, don't forget that next Tuesday you're going to be at the Navy Yard to christen the *USS William R. Rush*. As far as the show goes, I'm trying to get the principals of *The Desert Song*. It opened last night and the reviews weren't bad. So far neither Iris Whitney nor Edward Roecker have called back. I'd like to have one or both of them. If they can't make it, then Jack Goode, the show's comic, will be with you. He's making a comeback after being injured in the war. There's a good story there in case we have to use him."

"That sounds fine, Virginia, but don't give up on the others. I'd really rather have Iris. She's temperamental, but she's a doll. Besides, we can't have two comics in a row. Don't we have Red Skelton on Thursday?"

"Oh, I'd forgotten about that. I'll try to get Iris, but I can't promise."

Dorothy was clearing the top of her desk. "Is there anything else before I leave? Oh, and see what you can dig up on Spike Jones. Betty and Harry are easy. We can always talk about horses, if nothing else. Did you know that they raise thoroughbreds on their farm in California?"

Virginia wasn't ready for small talk. She continued, "Let's see, on Monday you have a sitting at 12:30 for the new Medaglia d'Oro campaign. Then the agency wants you for lunch. Here are your tickets for *The Desert Song* for tonight. And don't forget your fitting with Stephan tomorrow in New York. That's about all I can think of, Mary. Oh, and yes, there's this." She handed Dorothy Mary a slip of paper. "Some man called Padrosche called long distance from New York. He's probably some new boy with William Morris. He left his number and said he'd call back. We're all set and unless you have more for me, I've got to get going. I'm being taken to lunch by a tall, dark, and terrific agent who handles the Amana account. How do you think I look?" Virginia patted her hair and posed as if she were modeling a bathing suit.

Dorothy Mary sat looking at the piece of paper. Absentmindedly, she said, "Okay, bye, Virginia. And thanks." But by that time Virginia was out of the office door and down the hall, thinking that sometimes society people are so rude.

Dorothy Mary picked up her phone. When the operator asked, "Number, please," she placed a long-distance call to New York. She wanted to talk person-to-person to Mr. Joseph Padrosche. After static and a series of clicks, the phone was ringing in New York. A female voice answered, "Good morning, Spanish Embassy."

The operator asked for Mr. Padrosche and the secretary replied, "I'm sorry, the Ambassador is not available right now. Who may I say is calling?"

Dorothy Mary said, "Thank you, operator," and hung up. She drove home to Denbigh, packed an overnight bag, gave her tickets for *The Desert Song* to Rodgers, and took the next train to New York.

The Dressing Drink

Somewhere between Trenton and Newark, Dorothy Mary finalized her plan. She would ask Pat Roebling to help her find Joe this weekend. Pat was not only her best friend, but also president of the First National City Bank. In the past, she had arranged for Dorothy to meet people who had been helpful in her career. She knew everyone. Pat had contacts all over the Eastern seaboard. Best of all, this would appeal to Pat's matchmaking streak. If anyone could wrangle her an invitation to whatever social function Joe might be attending this weekend, it was Pat. She would get her on the phone as soon as she reached the Carlton House.

Then, Stephan must be persuaded to fit her new clothes tonight instead of tomorrow. If Pat came through with an invitation, Dorothy Mary would need them the next day. She hadn't brought more than the bare essentials and her best jewelry, and when she met Joe again she wanted to look perfect. Not just pretty or well dressed, but *perfect*. If Stephan failed her, there was always Bergdorf's, but it was only a last resort. After all, anyone could shop at Bergdorf's, but only a very small and select circle of clients could wear Stephan's designs.

Dorothy Mary looked at her watch. It would be an hour before the train pulled into Penn Station.

She stubbed out her cigarette, gathered her purse and went to the ladies' lounge to repair her makeup. She scrutinized her image in the clear daylight that filled the room. Joe hadn't seen her since she was eighteen. Would he notice that she was beginning to get lines beneath her eyes that didn't immediately disappear after her smile faded? Would he still think she was pretty?

She decided that her hair was a mess, that she needed a facial and that her nails were grubby. Her hairdresser, Robbie at Elizabeth Arden's, would be booked solid for today and tomorrow. But maybe she could coax him to come to the hotel tonight, after the salon closed. Perhaps Rosa would come along with him to give her a facial and manicure. It would cost a fortune, but it would be worth it. She dabbed powder on her nose and rummaged in her bag for her sunglasses. She vowed to remember to wear them whenever she went outdoors. Goddammit, why did it have to be such an effort to keep looking well?

Feeling angry with herself she returned to her seat in the club car, lit another cigarette, and watched the ugly backside of northern Jersey slide past the window. Absentmindedly, she fingered the charms of the gold bracelet that was her trademark. One of her beaus had given her a tiny man dressed in a tailcoat and top hat. He was a hunchback and she remembered that the nuns in Florence had told her that touching the hump of a hunchbacked orderly at the hospital would bring her good luck. Now she sat playing with the little charm, hoping it might bring her luck with Joe. Had he changed much over the years? Was he married? Why had he just disappeared that summer ten years ago? She wished the train would get to New York so that she could begin to put her plan into action.

It was three-thirty by the time the train arrived at Penn Station. Dorothy Mary took a cab directly to the Elizabeth Arden Salon on Fifth Avenue. She told the cabbie to wait and hurried past the doorman, past the astonished receptionist who wailed that she couldn't possibly see Mr. Robbie right now: he had another client. She strode determinedly to Robbie's cubicle and interrupted an anecdote he was hearing from a dowager draped in pink towels.

Dorothy Mary recognized Mrs. Hadley Hadrington beneath all that wet laundry, paid her respects, and apologized for stealing Robbie. Dorothy Mary took his arm in both her hands and looked pleadingly into his eyes. "Robbie, I know there's no time, but something very, very important has come up and you *simply must* help me. After work today. Please come to my hotel room and do my hair, and bring Rosa to do my nails and give me a facial. Honestly, Robbie, this is the *most important thing* in the world to me, and if you won't help me, I just don't know what I'll do."

Robbie was taken by surprise. "Why Mary Liddell, I've never seen you in such a swivel. *Who's* the big attraction? *What* is going on?" Robbie whispered into her ear, "Is it the Aga?"

Dorothy Mary shook her head, and smiled her most conspiratorial smile. "Uh-uh. Come after work to the Carlton House and I'll tell you all about it." She knew that if anything would influence Robbie to cooperate, it would be the tantalizing promise of gossip.

But he was playing hard-to-get. "Well, I don't know, Mary, dear. This week has been too screamingly hectic. I'm nearly dead on my feet, and sweetheart, you don't know how these dogs are barking. But tell me," again he whispered in her ear, "... is it Errol?"

"Please, Robbie. I understand and I wouldn't ask you if it weren't so important."

"Well, I won't be able to leave this dump before six. Anything before that is out of the question."

"Six then." She had him. "Robbie, you're a perfect lamb. You've saved my life." She gave his arm a triumphant squeeze, smiled brightly at Mrs. Hadrington in her turban of laundry and said, "Darling, Mrs. Hadrington, so good to see you again. He's done *wonders* with you," and raced out of the salon, sweeping past the icy glare of the receptionist, and ordered her taxi to the Carlton House.

Once in her suite she called Pat and asked her to find out anything and everything about Joe Padrosche. Then she called Stephan and told him to send his boy over today with her new things. Stephan was a prima donna and was upset with this sudden change of plans. She explained that if he wanted to be in on the Medaglia d'Oro account, he'd simply have to make any alterations tonight and tomorrow morning so that she could wear his designs tomorrow. Stephan was a gifted designer, and he was greedy. He agreed to send over her outfits.

The Dressing Drink

Pat was her usual efficient self. She wasn't the first and only female bank president in the United States for no reason. She called back in twenty minutes and got right to the point. "Well," she said, "don't you think it's about time you let me in on your little secret? How is it that you know this Romeo? Have you ever actually met him or what?"

"Wouldn't you like to know?" Dorothy Mary countered.

"I can't believe it, you've actually got a crush on this guy. Do you know who he is?"

There was an expectant silence.

"Well, I don't have time to be coy. He works at the Spanish Embassy to the UN. And he's not just any ordinary, run-of-the-mill civil servant. He's the Spanish Ambassador. He also belongs to one of the oldest, richest families in Europe. He's got a list of titles a yard long. And he's a war hero, too."

"Is he married?"

"Nope. In fact, he's one of the most eligible bachelors in New York. My spies tell me that every hostess in the city wants him as an extra man."

"Where does he live?"

"That's the one thing I couldn't find out—or his home phone. No one will give out that info. Security, I suppose."

"Anything else?"

"Well, be ready and waiting in the lobby of your hotel tomorrow night because you, me, and Dudley, the old dear, are going to the party Bruton Wetherill is giving. It's for the Opera Guild, and I'm sure you won't mind making a slight contribution. Padrosche will be there. It's one of his charities. We couldn't get tickets for the benefit that follows, but surely no one will mind if three such distinguished friends of the opera just crash." Hand on the hip, she continued, "Now level with me, Mary, when did you meet him and why have I gone to all this trouble for you? Apart from the fact that you're my dearest friend in all the world. Just who *is* this guy?"

"Well, I met him the year I came out and then one day he just disappeared. He broke my heart."

"Well, he must be really something if you're still interested after all these years. If you're willing to go to all this trouble just to say hello to Padrosche, I'll tell you what… you can have Dudley for the night, and I'll take the Ambassador."

"Over my dead body, Pat Roebling."

They both laughed and said goodbye.

Dorothy Mary finished trying on the black tulle gown with the rhinestone bodice that Stephan had made just for her. She might have a few more lines in her face, but she was still as slim as when she was a debutante. She turned to and fro in front of the mirror, luxuriating in the swishing yards of tulle. It fit perfectly, a model of elegance, and black was one of her best colors. Pulled sharply together, astoundingly feminine, the minx was irresistible and unattainable. Thank God she'd remembered to bring her diamonds. She called room service and ordered refreshments for Robbie and Rosa. They'd arrive in an hour and everything was going to be just perfect. They were going to make her beautiful. And she would see Joe again.

Robbie and Rosa were gone and Dorothy Mary felt like a new woman. Her hair was glossy and elegantly coifed. She hoped it wouldn't fall by tomorrow. When she had told Robbie that she was seeing her first sweetheart he said that he could come over tomorrow afternoon and give her a touch up if she wanted it. He was a doll. Her nails gleamed Cherries in the Snow and her skin felt tingly after her facial and bath. The evening stretched languidly before her. She knew that if she were smart, she'd just go to bed—but she was too keyed up. She decided to go to Scribner's on Fifth and get John Hersey's new book. She was scheduled to interview him in two weeks.

She put on the outfit she'd worn from home: a Gunn tartan kilt, navy turtlenecked sweater, long socks, and loafers. Thank God she had her mink to hide it all. She probably wouldn't see anyone she knew and would only be gone for about forty-five minutes. Besides, she couldn't dress up if she wanted to—not unless she wanted to wear a gown to the bookstore.

She stood before the elevator bank and admired her new hairdo in the mirror. For all his bitching, Robbie was a genius. She pushed the button for the lobby, and as she did so, caught the reflection of a familiar stranger who opened the double glass doors that led to the elevators.

Joe.

She immediately fumbled in her clutch bag for her dark glasses. She wasn't prepared to see him and hoped that he wouldn't recognize her. But before she could locate her glasses and turn up her coat collar, Joe walked past her, pushed the elevator button, turned, and smiled.

For a moment she thought she was safe. He stood facing the elevator, mirrored as she was in the wall. He wore a dark blue cashmere coat. His hands held a gray Hamburg and gloves. Then she felt him staring at her and she grew uncomfortable. Where was that blasted elevator? She turned to go back to her room when he said, "Good evening, Dorothy Mary. Don't you remember me?"

She whirled toward him, smiled and too coyly said, "Have we met?" Instantly she wished she hadn't said that.

He came forward, took her hand, lifted and kissed it. "My God, you're a beautiful woman. And, if you'll forgive me," he added, still holding her hand and looking directly into her eyes, "you're a rotten liar. Furthermore you, my dear, should be severely punished for breaking my heart."

"How are you, Joe? It's good to see you," said Dorothy Mary, back-pedaling as fast as she could.

"Why didn't you answer my letter?"

Regaining her composure, she ignored his question and observed, "You're looking very well."

"Perhaps you didn't hear me. I asked why you didn't answer my letter."

"What letter? I don't know what you're talking about."

"The letter I gave Grizzy to give to you when I went over to Spain for your mother."

"Huh?" Dorothy was mystified. "Grizzy never gave me any letter. I don't understand."

"Well, all I know is that Grizzy came to me with a large sum of money from your mother's charity group and sent me over to Spain with it. I gave him a letter to explain why I would be away that summer. Surely you're teasing me?"

"Honestly, Joe, this is the first I've ever heard of it."

"Well, let's forget it for now. That was a long time ago. The important thing is that we're together again. And it is wonderful to see you, Dorothy." He looked into her eyes and held onto her hand until the elevator opened.

Dorothy Mary felt the passengers staring at her and was embarrassed. She asked, "Are you going down?" and got inside. As they descended, she thought, *What a dumb thing to say. He'll think I'm really a cretin if I keep this up.*

They walked out of the hotel onto Madison Avenue and Joe asked, "Will you have dinner with me?"

"Joe, I don't think so. I'm hardly dressed for it. I can't change—these are all the clothes I have with me." Joe took her arm and steered her toward the curb to hail a taxi. He said, "Dorothy, any restaurant that wouldn't take you exactly as you are, is crazy. Don't you know that you're beautiful, no matter what you're wearing?"

He helped her into the cab. She couldn't take her eyes off him as he got in beside her, and she felt beautiful because she saw herself mirrored in his eyes.

They ate at a Spanish restaurant where Joe knew the proprietor. Dorothy Mary sipped her Scotch and tried to memorize the sound of Joe's voice as he ordered their meal in rapid-fire Spanish. She pretended to be interested in what he was ordering, but she didn't pay too much attention. In reply to his question, she said that she ate anything except octopus and left everything else up to him. She was busy watching Joe, thinking how marvelous he looked, and imagining how it would feel to be in his arms again.

He looked much the same as he had that summer when they had first met. He was a bit heavier now; there was a spider's web of fine lines about his eyes and a touch of gray at each temple, but he was even more attractive than she remembered. She could understand why hostesses such as Marie Clayborg, who could have her pick of the most eligible bachelors on the East Coast, besieged Joe with invitations. He was the ideal Extra Man. The sort who was accustomed to the best of everything, yet he wasn't an egocentric brat like most of the playboys Dorothy Mary knew.

As she watched him, Dorothy Mary wondered if she could make him fall in love with her. Thank God that at least she'd been done up before they'd met at the elevator.

Joe acted like a smitten man. He wanted to know all about her. His eyes were fastened upon her face as if he, too, were observing, evaluating, wondering. Something told her that his old feelings for her were intact, masked by this urbane surface. She began to relax and enjoy the evening.

She had lots of questions about him and wanted to know the answers all at once. Where had he *been* all these years? How had he become the ambassador to a government that he'd opposed during the War? Was he married? But she decided to see if he would answer these questions without her asking them. After all, he'd made her wait for years. She could afford to be a little mysterious now.

Once finished with dinner, they planned to go to a jazz club. They were walking near Washington Square Park looking for a cab when Joe said, "By the way, I'm really disappointed in you. Just where were you raised? Didn't they tell you at one of those fancy finishing schools that you're supposed to say thank you when someone takes you to dinner?"

Dorothy Mary squeezed his arm and said, "Sorry, darling. Thank you. It was a wonderful meal."

Joe was quiet for a minute and then he said, "That's okay, but it's not exactly what I had in mind. I suppose I'll have to teach you everything. Now, here's how you say thank you in the proper manner."

He pulled her into a shadowy doorway, lifted her chin and just before he kissed her, he said, "Lesson One."

For Dorothy Mary it was like coming home when there was a fire burning in the library fireplace, like eating peach ice cream on a hot summer evening, like finding a gold ring she thought was lost forever.

IV
"Denbigh"
January 1947

Dorothy Mary stomped the snow from her suede boots, handed her coat to Rodgers and asked, "Where's my brother right now?"

The Dressing Drink

"You'll find him in the library, Miss Dorothy."

"Is my mother home?"

"No, Miss. She'll be out for the afternoon. Will there be anything else?"

"No. Thank you, Rodgers."

Dorothy Mary found David in the library, watching the flames of a smoky fire. He didn't look up when she entered the room.

"My God, David. What have you done to your face? "

A purplish bruise stained David's left eye and cheek.

He said thickly, "Pretty ugly, aren't I?"

"How did you ever do that? It looks like someone slugged you."

"Not a chance. I fell on the ice in the driveway last night. Knocked myself silly. Forgive me if I don't say too much. It hurts. This helps kill the pain though." David held up a half-finished glass of Scotch.

"I'm sure it does. Have you seen a doctor?"

"No, it's nothing, really. Looks worse than it is." He smiled weakly at his sister, as if he were trying to convince himself of the truth of his words.

Dorothy Mary pulled up the footstool next to her brother's chair and sat looking at his misshapen, swollen face. "Are you sure you don't want an icepack or something?"

"No, thanks. But maybe you could just hand me the Pinch. That way I don't have to get up. It hurts to move around."

Dorothy Mary handed him the decanter and put two fresh cubes of ice into his glass. "I think we'd better go to the doctor, David."

"Honestly, Dorothy, it's not so bad. It'll be gone in a few days. You'll see."

"All right. Anyway, we've got to talk. There's something I need you to do for me."

"What's that?"

"I want you to get an apartment in New York with me. We both won't live there, but otherwise Mother and Father will have fits. Remember Joe Padrosche, from years ago?" David nodded and winced. "Well, he's back in town and I just spent the weekend with him, and he wants me to move in with him which, of course, I can't do. Unless you help me, that is."

"Why don't you two do something simple—like get engaged or married?"

"Oh, there's some complication with his job at the Embassy and with his family. He's explained it all to me over and over, and it's too tedious to go into now. Besides, what have I got to lose? And anyway, I rather like the idea of being a Fallen Woman. David, he's wonderful and we're redoing his apartment. He's taking me to Antibes this summer. I want you to meet him and get to know him. He will adore you."

"I'd like that very much. Let's have dinner sometime when I'm feeling better. Now, how do I fit into this whole thing?"

"Well, because of his post at the UN there can't be any hint of scandal. It would ruin him. So, I want you to move into the city with me and share an apartment."

"But, Dorothy, it takes months to find a good place."

"I've got one all picked out. We can go see it as soon as you like. It has nine rooms and two entrances. It's in a good building on Park and 70th. I'll pay half the rent and all I want is one little room to store things in. All the rest is yours. I'll decorate it for you, if you want. Oh, David, please say you'll do it. It's high time that both of us got out of Denbigh. They must be wondering when we're going to leave the nest. You're feeling all right, aren't you, David? I mean after the War and all?"

"Don't worry about me. I'm fine. A little clumsy, but fine. I suppose it would be good to have a place of my own and some privacy."

"Oh, you'd have plenty of that. And just think of the traveling time you'll save. You do spend a lot of time in New York, don't you?"

David looked quickly at his sister. Did she know?

Dorothy Mary paid no attention to his scrutiny and continued, "I promise you, I won't ever barge in on you unannounced. It'll really be your apartment, David. Only my name will be on the mailbox, too. And I'll sign the lease. Will you go and look at it with me?"

"Sure, Dorothy. I'd be glad to."

"Oh, David. You're a love. Thank you so much. I'd kiss you, but I'm afraid it might hurt your face."

And so, against the protests of Mrs. Flagg who wanted David to stay at home where she could keep an eye on him, David and Dorothy Mary moved into their apartment on Park and 70th. Dorothy continued her radio show from the Ocean Room of the Drake Hotel, only now she taped all five broadcasts on one night so she would only have to be in Philadelphia for a day or two at a time.

She endorsed Pirandello Champagne, Medaglia d'Oro Espresso, Amana Refrigerators and Dishwashers, Woolite, and a host of other products. Remembering what her mother said about chewing gum, all but condemning a gum-chewing woman to Hell, she turned down an offer from Wrigley's, but eventually Billy Feldman's prediction came true.

In 1950 she made her first million dollars.

Although he complained that she'd made that million by pandering to show business people who were common as dirt, her father kept his part of their bargain and paid the taxes on that million for her. To celebrate, Dorothy Mary and Joe flew to Rio.

While they were away, her father suffered a stroke and died in his walnut-paneled office at the factory in Pottstown.

The Dressing Drink

Dorothy Mary Liddell, endorsing *Roylprints* Paper Place Mats.

Dorothy flew home for the funeral. She had never been allowed to be close to her father. Although she felt sad at his death, she was pleased that he had lived long enough to see her win their agreement.

Mr. Flagg had made no secret of his plan to leave Denbigh to the Episcopal diocese, with the single proviso that it never be sold to the Catholics. Too much of the Main Line belonged to them already. Mrs. Flagg made plans to move from Denbigh to a smaller, more convenient house in Ardmore. When she received the news that her husband had died, relief overcame Mrs. Flagg more so than sadness. Now she would never have to tiptoe around his temper at dinner again. She would be *free*.

After the funeral, her solicitors sold the family business and she also asked them to inquire if Marguerite had been provided for. She had known about her husband's mistress for years and had even been grateful for her existence. Like all of the other servants, Marguerite was given what amounted to a pension.

Now that his father was dead, Grizzy was constantly at his mother's elbow, consoling and offering advice while drinking her whiskey. He helped reorchestrate her life. They had a special understanding. They were confidantes, and he was such a comfort to her.

Six months after Mr. Flagg's death, the will was read.

Livid did not even begin to describe Grizzy when he learned that his father had disinherited him. He would get only $10,000 while Dorothy and David each got trust funds worth millions. The lawyers told Mrs. Flagg that her husband had changed his will in favor of Dorothy Mary and David shortly after that disastrous night at Tiptonbrook. Mrs. Flagg felt sorry for Grizzy. He'd been so faithful to her of late, so she promised to make it up to him.

Dorothy Mary and Joe were skiing in Switzerland when Mrs. Flagg moved from Denbigh to Ardmore. But Grizzy was there to see that Mamma didn't get her blood pressure up. Since her husband's death, she was often emotional and would cry at the least upset. The doctor told her to try to keep calm and to watch her diet.

Once the move was over, Grizzy became a fixture at the house in Ardmore. He wasn't too popular at Tiptonbrook these days; Mamma's bar was well-stocked, and he wanted to ingratiate himself as favorite child. He gave his mother a pair of black standard poodle puppies to keep her company and to further cement their new relationship. Their special joke was that the poodles were better company than Father had ever been. At least they slept in her room.

V
New York City
September 1948

David was in better spirits than at any time since the War. Shortly after he moved to New York, he began psychotherapy again. Only this time he told his therapist everything.

David now viewed his preference for men as just another facet of his personality, like his sense of humor or his fair complexion. He'd had one long-lasting relationship with Richard, a waiter in a West Side bar, but that had broken up and now David was frequenting bars in the Village, prowling for another lover. He found a partner for the night at the White Horse. They had drinks and David invited him back to the apartment on 70th Street.

David had only been looking for casual sex. Cautious by nature, he had chosen a boy that he thought looked both sexy and harmless. Thus, he was surprised to be awakened in the night by the sound of someone rummaging through the bureau drawers. He lay in bed without moving, wondering whether it was better to be robbed or to fight. He'd been beaten up before by other boys he'd brought home. He was about to let the fellow have what he wanted until he saw him take the Lalique crystal frog from the top of the bureau and stuff it into his jacket pocket. Dorothy Mary had given David that trinket, a souvenir of her last trip to Paris, and David didn't want it stolen by a bar boy, no matter how pretty he was or how tight his little ass had been.

The boy's back turned, he was searching through David's pants pockets now. David took the opportunity to get out of bed and grab him from behind. They struggled and for a moment David thought he would be able to pin the boy's arms to his sides—but David had forgotten that the boy was fifteen years younger and stronger, and he also hadn't considered that, unlike society fags, pretty pickup boys often carried knives.

David never knew what severed his aorta. He never even felt the blade pierce the skin between his ribs. In the light that spilled from the bathroom, he grappled with the boy he had made love with only a few hours earlier. He saw the light reflected off the boy's wet eye, saw the perspiration bead on the gentle curve of his upper lip. Then he felt something warm and wet on his leg and looked down to see blood spurting from his side and dripping onto the carpet. He didn't see anything more.

The boy went into the bathroom and washed his hands. He wiped his handprints from the crystal frog and dropped it on the floor next to David's body. He closed the bedroom door behind him and wondered what to do. He hadn't meant to kill the man. He'd stabbed him without thinking, almost like a reflex. It had all been a mistake. He let himself out of the apartment and the door locked behind him. He went down the service entrance—the same way he and David had entered the building. No one had seen them enter the building. No one saw him leave.

20

I was a petulant, bossy child, given to quarreling with the few friends I had. As a consequence, I spent much time alone and felt extremely sorry for myself. On those interminable Sunday afternoons when there was no one to play with and nothing to do, I would often amuse myself by building towers with the special slotted cards that Mother had brought me from Switzerland. I also had an Erector Set that I could build with, but I liked the cards better. For one thing, I was never able to make the intricate mechanical toys shown in the instruction booklet. The cards were much easier to use and I didn't have to worry about being scolded by the maids. Those little nuts and bolts from the Erector Set had a habit of escaping and lurking in the carpet 'til Mrs. Pitz approached with the Electrolux.

The cards fit together in various ways, and I could build tall structures with them. I'd carefully arrange each layer, some horizontal, others vertical. I built higher and higher, waiting for that inevitable moment when the tower would grow top-heavy, buckle, and then collapse. Sometimes the cards just slithered down into a messy pile. Other times there was the swift, satisfying splat of destruction as all the cards fell at once onto the glass table.

David's death was that inevitable moment for the Flagg family.

Mother was the one who found him as he lay on the floor of his bedroom, the beige carpet around him stiff with his dried blood. Of course she never told me about it, but I overheard a conversation she once had with Aunt Kay. I was in a corner of the living room, lying on the floor behind a wing chair, seemingly engrossed in an Iron Man comic, but actually eavesdropping.

I can't remember the exact words, but I do remember that there was something strange in the way Mother described finding her brother's body. She was so calm about it. So very, very calm. She said that she knew the moment she saw him that he was dead and that she didn't want to touch him. Somehow David was telling her to go away and to leave him alone. She said that she'd wanted to do something for him, but the only thing she could think of was to pick the crystal Lalique frog from the carpet beside him and carry it out of the room. Then she called Joe and he'd taken charge. She said she didn't know how he had arranged it, but David's death was never investigated by the police.

I have David's crystal frog now. It sits across from Mother's photograph on the top of my bureau. When she was alive it used to crouch on her bedside table and the blue-gray room would swim upside down in its protruding eyes.

I suppose that those clear eyes saw David bleed to death. I know they watched Mother die slowly and painfully from cancer. The frog even saw my "Aunt" Pat Roebling introduce Mother to Father.

Aunty Pat is still alive today and sometimes I'm pleased that she tried to cheer Mother by bringing Father into her life. But other times, when there's no one to talk to and nothing to do in the interminable Sunday afternoon that always simmers in this tent, I hear the silent croaking of that crystal frog, peer into his blind eyes and want to smash him down into Aunty Pat's skull.

Petulant little Thomas with his pals.

21

New York City, N.Y.
September 1948

David hadn't answered his phone for three days, and Dorothy Mary knew something was wrong. At first it had been merely irritating to call him again and again and listen to the phone ring on, unanswered. She was sure that something strange had happened but she told herself it was silly to panic before she'd checked his apartment. He might be there sulking, hiding from one of his numerous male admirers. She searched through her desk for the keys to his apartment and took a cab uptown.

As soon as she unlocked the apartment door she spotted his trench coat draped over the arm of a sofa. He must be home. Why hadn't he answered the goddamn phone? Could he be sick or hurt?

She called out, "David? It's only me. David. David? Where are you?" But there was no reply. It was quiet in the third-floor apartment. Closing the door behind her, she began to look for her brother.

She walked through the living room, dining room, kitchen, and hall, calling to him. She looked into the bathroom and into her storage room, but all were empty.

Then she noticed the sickly-sweet odor when she reached the hall that led to his room. The smell got stronger when she opened David's bedroom door.

From where she stood in the hallway the room looked messy, but rather like David's room always did. The cleaning lady only came once a week and David had never learned to put away his clothes or make his bed. At Denbigh there had always been servants to do things like that, so once on his own, his bed was always jumbled and his clothes were usually on the floor where he dropped them.

God, the smell was awful! Dorothy Mary's stomach jumped and she gagged. She had to get some fresh air. As she crossed the room to open the window, she noticed that the rope soles of her espadrilles dragged against the carpet, as if gum was stuck to them, or as if they were wet.

She looked down and gasped when she saw that she was standing in the midst of a maroon stain that covered the beige carpet between David's bed and the window. The toes of her yellow shoes were stained the same dark red. *Oh my God*, she thought. *Blood. David.* Then she saw his outstretched hand and realized that he was lying on the floor, partially hidden by the skirt of the double bed. She took a step towards him and called his name, but he didn't move. That awful smell grew stronger near him. His face was turned to the wall, showing the cowlick on the back of his head that he'd fought ever since he was a boy. Now it stood stubbornly erect as he lay there motionless. His skin was a peculiar yellow-gray. It stretched tautly over his ribs. One of his legs was drawn up to his chest and one arm was flung out, reaching for the crystal frog that lay on its side beyond the perimeter of the bloodstain.

Dorothy didn't stop to wonder why the frog was on the floor because, more than anything, the color of David's skin reminded her of the tableau of Jack the Ripper and his victims that she'd seen in a wax museum in London. She'd never been able to forget those ashy, yellowed faces that grimaced in fright and pain. She was grateful she couldn't see David's face now. It was awful enough to know that he was dead.

Tears streamed down her face, and she wanted to do something for him. She pulled the sheet from the twisted pile of blankets but couldn't quite make herself go near enough to cover him. She was afraid he would suddenly rise, or move, or turn over and show her his grinning, bloody death mask.

Suddenly she had to get out of the room, to get away from this awful-smelling thing. She dropped the sheet and picked up the crystal frog that her brother seemed to have been reaching for before he died. She would take care of it for him. Dorothy Mary took one last look at the back of David's head, his stubborn tuft of hair, the vulnerable curve of his neck, and hurried out of the room. Slamming the door behind her, she ran to the living room to call Joe. Her hands were wet, and the frog slipped from her grasp and rolled heavily on the living room floor.

She took several deep breaths and dialed Joe's number at the Embassy. She tried to sound calm but could hear the hysteria in her voice. "Please. Please come over here right away. I'm at David's. Something terrible has happened." After a pause, she then said, "I think he's dead." Another pause and then she broke in, "I don't know. Please. Just get here." She hung up without saying goodbye.

Who could have done this?

She remembered how David would surface after nights of crawling from one homosexual watering hole to the next. She remembered the times he had been beaten by men he brought home. She remembered his sweet face with bruised eyes and swollen mouth. David would lie and say that he'd only fallen or cut himself, but Dorothy Mary wasn't fooled. She knew he liked his lovers to play rough. *Oh, David*, she thought, *you stupid fool. You finally found someone who played too rough. Just a little too rough.*

She picked up his trench coat from the sofa and thought about hanging it up. When would Joe get here? Then she noticed the smell of David's aftershave in the folds of the coat. She folded it over and over until it was the size of a pillow and hugged it to her and sobbed, rocking back and forth.

Oh God. Not David. It isn't fair. It just isn't fair. How could someone have hurt him? He was always the good one. So sweet. So considerate. He used to make her laugh. She remembered how he would defend her when Grizzy would pick on her. She remembered when Grizzy splashed her dress on purpose at her coming-out party.

Joe found her there in David's living room, her face red and swollen, her mascara smeared into black clots and circles beneath each eye. He had seen shock victims in the War and recognized the symptoms. He put his arms around her and held her for many minutes before he asked, very gently, "Where is he?"

She didn't seem to hear him, but rocked and sobbed against his shoulder. It was a while before she gasped an answer between sobs. "Oh Joe, he's my brother. My best brother."

Joe phoned Pat Roebling and asked her to come over as soon as she could and to bring a sedative if she had one. If she would watch over Dorothy Mary, he could deal with this mess. First of all, he would have to do something about the body and the smell of decay that filled the apartment. Soon the neighbors would notice and then the police and the papers might find out. After he opened all the windows, Joe and his chauffeur rolled David's body into a sheet. They tied blankets around the sheet and rolled the whole thing up in the bloodstained carpet. They arranged for a panel truck and, later that day, carried the carpet out of the building. The chauffeur drove David's body to a funeral home in Bala Cynwyd that some of Joe's underworld friends had recommended as sympathetic.

Joe got his own physician to verify that David had died of natural causes, explaining that, although the family was aware of David's peccadilloes, they didn't want all of the Main Line to know that he had probably been stabbed by some faggot he had picked up in a bar. The doctor charged a substantial fee for this service, but the money wasn't important.

David's body was cremated and a few days later his ashes were buried in the Flagg family plot at St. David's church, next to his father's grave. Only the immediate family attended the funeral. The murder was never reported to the police. That seemed pointless. It would only cause a scandal and it would never bring David back.

The Dressing Drink

Mrs. Flagg was remarkably composed during the funeral, but afterward she was filled with grief and remorse. She was convinced that if David had never taken that New York apartment, he would still be alive. She should have forced him to stay with her in Ardmore. David hadn't been well. He'd been too trusting. Such a good boy—the best of her children. She had pangs of guilt but mostly felt sorry for herself, and she mourned for David with an intensity that had been absent when her husband died. She was soon exhausted from grieving, but she wouldn't be comforted, couldn't stop crying, and refused to accept David was dead.

Dorothy Mary was concerned when she saw how hard her mother was taking David's death. Dorothy Mary missed David too, but she had commitments. There was business to do. She asked Grizzy to watch over their mother until she could arrange to spend more time with her in Ardmore. Grizzy had all the time in the world. He never had held a job, and now fancied himself a gentleman farmer, but that was only a pretty façade. Grizzy really spent his days drinking whiskey, puttering about his property, and quarreling with his wife, Libby. Grizzy agreed to look after Mamma. When he couldn't visit her in Ardmore, he would phone her at least twice a day.

But things didn't quite work according to Grizzy's plan.

That first night when he visited his mother in Ardmore, he drank himself senseless. Mrs. Flagg watched him get more and more inebriated until he passed out in a corner wing chair in the living room. She found his performance disgusting. and decided to leave him there to sleep it off. He would have a terrible hangover in the morning and she would have no sympathy for him. Grizzy was not her favorite anymore. She decided to call her solicitor the next day to revise her will. Giff had been right. Grizzy was a bad seed. He should have died instead of poor, sweet David.

Mrs. Flagg turned off the light, leaving Grizzy snoring in the darkness. His head was tipped as far back as it would go. As she made her way upstairs, she listened to the bubbly sound and wondered if he would strangle in the night. She gripped the banister hard and continued slowly up, panting from the exertion, hearing her own heart pound with each step. She was showing her age. She'd have to start taking it easy. Near the top of the staircase her knees got weak, and a sudden hot pain stabbed her temples. Her hands flew up to her head and she lost her balance and fell backwards. She bumped down the staircase, hitting her head against each step. She was unconscious before she reached the bottom of the stairwell.

The sound of her fall nearly woke Grizzy. His bubbling snores stopped with a snarl, but then the silence lulled him back to sleep.

The next morning Rodgers found Mrs. Flagg, lying beneath the open window on the first-floor landing. Her skin was cold, but she was still breathing. He called an ambulance and she was rushed to the hospital.

The doctors told Dorothy Mary if it hadn't been for the freezing air blowing onto her all night, Mrs. Flagg would have died. The doctors said she was lucky, but everyone who knew how much the stroke had damaged Mrs. Flagg thought otherwise. For the rest of her life, she was confined to a wheelchair, semi-paralyzed and speechless.

With her mother so sick, Dorothy Mary had to assume the responsibility for running the house and servants in Ardmore, as well as continue her mother's charity commitments, until other arrangements could be made. She visited her mother in the hospital every day. Mrs. Flagg seemed so disoriented and frail that Dorothy Mary was convinced she was going to die. She took an indefinite leave of absence from the radio station and divided her time between visits to her mother and renovations to the house in Ardmore. She got the idea that, if she readied the house for her mother, it would work like a magic charm to keep her alive. So, doorways were widened to accommodate a wheelchair; a ramp was built alongside the front and back stairs; the bathrooms on the lower floor were renovated.

It was a difficult, anxious time for Dorothy Mary, and she had never been more grateful for Joe. He was especially thoughtful and tender. He knew how worried she was and traveled to Ardmore to see her as often as his work at the UN would allow. They talked on the phone every day and spent weekends together whenever possible. He was an angel.

The doctors suggested that Dorothy try to help her mother learn to speak again. There was one excruciating session with a speech therapist in which Dorothy observed her mother's pathetic attempts to say "duck" when the therapist pointed to a fluffy yellow duckling, or "cow" when he pointed to a picture of a Guernsey. Dorothy couldn't stand to hear her mother say, "Ow, ow, owww." over and over. It was too humiliating. Flaggs always took care of themselves. It would be better for Mother not to talk than to have to go through those lessons, and so Dorothy canceled the speech therapist.

Instead, she concentrated on developing a kind of sixth sense for what Mother wanted to say. It was sad to see what had been a regal, active woman, imprisoned in the body of this feeble invalid. But as long as Joe was around, as long as she could snuggle next to him or talk to him on the phone, she knew she could face anything. She had never loved him more.

II

Mrs. Flagg was to be released from the hospital the following week and the house was ready for her return. Dorothy had hired two nurses to care for her and had given herself the weekend off. She took the afternoon train to New York, and was looking forward to spending the entire weekend with Joe. Her leather shopping bag was filled with his favorite foods: a jar of Beluga caviar, two beautifully aged steaks, a big tin of macadamia nuts, and a wedge of Stilton.

The apartment they shared was empty when she arrived. She put the groceries on the kitchen counter and went into the bedroom. There was time for a leisurely shower before she would imbibe her liquid courage and dress for dinner.

After she came out of the shower, she noticed an envelope on her pillow. She immediately recognized Joe's handwriting and his heavy cream-colored writing paper with the family crest embossed on the envelope flap. What a wonderful man. He'd written her a love letter. She sat down on her blue, watered-silk bedspread to dry her hair and read what Joe had written.

My Dearest Dorothy,

For weeks now I have worried about how to tell you. I had planned to get it over with in June, but then there was the shock of David's death and after that your mother's stroke, I didn't have the heart to tell you then. Lately you've been in Ardmore so much, and I've been busy tying up all the loose ends here at the Embassy. And now, it seems I've waited too long, and I've run out of time. My plane leaves in only four hours and so I must take the coward's way out and tell you in a letter.

Forgive me, Dorothy. Forgive me, if you can.

There is no way or time now to really explain—what could I say anyway that would or could ever really explain. Sometimes I don't understand it myself. So, how can I expect you to understand? Perhaps the kindest thing is simply to tell you. To get it over with quick and clean, like a rapier slash. Perhaps that way in time it will heal, leaving only a small scar. As you can tell, I am really trying more to convince myself of this, my darling. I fear I will never begin to convince you.

The short of it is that by the time you read this I will be en route to Madrid. In a few days I will be formally engaged to the absurd child my parents insisted I marry. Their will has finally prevailed, and I have agreed to marry Maria Therese. She is of a very old Castilian family. I have only seen her once. My father is anxious for grandchildren and is now willing to give me my inheritance, after all these years of poverty and difficulty. But, in order to get it, I must knuckle under and marry the girl of his choice. He gives me no alternative. It must be Maria Therese. In some ridiculous way his honor as a nobleman is involved.

I suggested that he and Mama meet you, but he refused and we have had serious quarrels over this in the last four years. Now he has given me an ultimatum: either I marry immediately, or else everything will go to my sister, Elena.

You and I have shared so much these last five years, and I have never been happier. I know that this will sound ludicrous to you, given that I am now about to marry Maria Therese, but please know that I do love you—no matter what happens you will always be very dear to me. I wish that my family would consent to our marriage, but as you are not Catholic and are a divorced woman, it is out of the question. My lawyers will make the details of my affection more explicit after the marriage takes place next month.

If it is of any consolation, know that I did try to convince them that you would make a better wife for me than Maria, but they would not consent. I am sure you will understand this family of mine. After all, you know how Philadelphians are. Spaniards aren't much different.

Please do not try to contact me. Prolonging the pain will make it only that much harder to bear. You will find another man, perhaps one who is more worthy of you, and perhaps a better man, but you will never find anyone who loves you more than I.

I wish there were another choice. I will always love you.

Joe

Dorothy Mary couldn't believe it. She put down the letter and laughed. It must be some kind of bizarre joke. "You've *got* to be kidding, Padrosche," she said aloud, and resumed drying her hair. But in a minute she snatched it up again and reread it, looking for some indication that it was a spoof. There was none.

She called his number at the Embassy, the private line at his desk that only she and a few close friends knew. The receptionist answered. She recognized Dorothy Mary's voice and said wasn't it awful how he'd left so suddenly. He had resigned and now was just a private citizen. She had personally placed the call to Pan Am and booked his flight to Madrid.

Dorothy Mary hung up, dumbfounded. Why hadn't he told her? It was too awful to find the letter without any kind of warning.

Then she remembered his love of practical jokes, sat up and wiped the tears from her eyes, and said out loud, "Okay, Padrosche, you bastard. You've had your little laugh." She knew he was hiding. "I'm going to get even with you for this, you creep." She ran over to his walk-in closet and whipped open the louvered doors. She had heard a noise and knew that he was hiding there, laughing at her. But the closet was empty. The hangers moved, banging softly against each other.

All his clothes were gone.

She was suddenly very tired of it all. She closed the bedroom curtains against the late afternoon sun. She drew back the covers on Joe's side of the bed and lay down, smelling his scent on the pillowcase. As she fell asleep, she hoped that he would wake her.

The Dressing Drink

III

But it was a call from Pat Roebling that woke Dorothy. Before she was fully awake Dorothy Mary didn't remember that Joe had left her, but as she was listening to Pat's plans for the weekend, she saw his letter on her bedside table and she began to cry.

Pat heard Dorothy's breathing begin to come in gasps, like she was struggling for air. "Dorothy, are you all right? You sound funny. Are you crying?"

There was silence. Dorothy didn't want Pat to know that she was upset.

But Pat knew that something was wrong. "Look, kiddo, don't do anything—just sit tight. I'll be right over. Let me in, okay? I know that Dora's off today."

Between sobs Dorothy managed an "Okay," and hung up. She cried into Joe's pillow until she was sick to her stomach, went into the bathroom, vomited, then lay down on the bed again. *How could Joe have done this?*

When Pat arrived she found Dorothy in the bedroom, sobbing uncontrollably. Pat read Joe's letter and couldn't help hating him for being such a goddamn coward. It was amazing to her what men would sometimes do in the name of kindness. She made Dorothy a drink and tried to calm her, tried to sympathize, but her words didn't help. Dorothy would just have to live through this. There wasn't anything that anyone could say or do. "Dorothy, you let it all out, and you'll be back on top in a day or two. You always are."

Then Pat listened to Dorothy Mary sniffle and sob and carry on, before making her take two sleeping pills. Dorothy's sobs dried up to hiccups, and soon she was asleep. Pat covered her with a blanket and decided to stay in the guest room, concerned that Dorothy was so upset, she might do something awful.

Pat broiled a steak for herself and thought that there was no real need to worry about Dorothy. Look at how she'd bounded back from her father's death, David's death, and she'd been wonderful when her mother was sick. She'd be herself in a day or two. This hysterical crying would stop. No one could keep it up for too long. For one thing, it was too tiring.

As it turned out, Pat was wrong. Dorothy Mary got sadder as the days passed. She lost all interest in her job, her friends and herself. She dictated a letter of resignation to Virginia over the phone. She told Billy Feldman not to accept any more jobs for her and to find someone else for anything that still had to be done. She was quitting the business. She called Grizzy and told him to take care of Mother. She wouldn't be going to Ardmore for a long time. Grizzy should tell Mamma that she was sick.

Dorothy Mary didn't leave her bedroom for days. Most of the time she sat in bed, reading Joe's letter, looking at the scrapbooks she had compiled of their trips together, and weeping. She ate little. When Pat came to visit there were no wisecracks, no funny remarks. Sometimes she would just start to cry, because something would have reminded her of Joe. One evening Pat found her sitting on the floor next to the phonograph, playing the song "Joey" from *Pal Joey* over and over. It had been a favorite of Joe's. They'd seen the revival twice.

Two weeks passed and Dorothy Mary had still not left her apartment. She didn't glance at the papers or magazines that Pat brought. She didn't want to watch TV or listen to the radio. She said that she just wanted to be left alone.

Pat tried to be patient with her friend, enduring the hysterical crying and sobbing. She'd even taken time off from the bank to be with Dorothy Mary. She'd done almost everything she could think of to cheer her friend, but Dorothy Mary refused to get over Joe. She wouldn't get dressed, wouldn't come out of the apartment. She looked awful, as if she'd aged fifteen years in as many days. Pat began to think that something was wrong, *really* wrong, with Dorothy Mary. This mourning for Joe had gone on too long. Maybe she should see a doctor. Maybe she'd gone crazy. There *was* that in her family.

Pat began to investigate psychiatric nursing homes and learned that only a relative could commit someone. She decided that unless Dorothy Mary had improved by the end of this week, she should tell Grizzy about his sister's breakdown—but that was a last resort. Before that, there had to be other attempts to bring her around. Dorothy Mary was too good a person to ruin her life over a love affair that ended badly. Something had to be done.

Pat was in her office at the bank, on the phone with Lee Shubert, President of the Shubert Theatrical Management Corporation. Lee wanted a loan and she'd been his banker for years. While they were discussing the terms the bank was willing to make, Pat got an idea: Dorothy Mary had made a career on the fringes of show business, maybe a clown or a comedian could cheer her up. Since she wouldn't budge from the apartment, maybe Shubert had someone who would make a house call. She abruptly changed the subject of their conversation.

"Listen, Lee, I just thought of something that you may be able to help me with."
"What's that?"
"Well, I have a very close friend who needs to be cheered up."
"Male or female?"
"Female."
"Pretty?"
"Yes, pretty, in an upper-crust sort of way."
"I get the picture."
"No, Lee, don't misunderstand me so fast. She's not looking for a date. Listen, the poor kid's been crying for weeks and nothing helps. I've tried everything. I thought maybe you might have a really good comedian in your stable who would go over there and make her laugh. Maybe some stranger could get her mind off her troubles."
"So, you want a clown?"

"No, not a circus clown, squirting carnations or whoopee cushions. What I need is just a very funny man. He's got to make her laugh. Then maybe she'll get better."

"How about Jack Goode?"

"Never heard of him. Is he funny?"

"Ever watch *The Honeymooners*, with Jackie Gleason?"

"Yeah, sometimes."

"Well, when Art Carney and Jackie Gleason go to the Raccoon Lodge, Jack is the Grand Poobah—the guy in front who runs the lodge meetings—he wears a cap with five raccoon tails."

"Never seen him. Lee, all I want is for you to send over the funniest guy you've got and tell him to make her laugh. If you think that Goode can do it, then fine."

"Tomorrow might be soon enough?"

"How about tonight instead?"

"It's pretty short notice, but for you and only for you, Banker Lady, I'll call him. What's your friend's address?"

Pat gave him that information and hung up. When he hadn't called back in fifteen minutes, she was sure that the comedian was all arranged. She phoned Dorothy Mary, and in her most officious Bank President voice, she said:

"Now listen to me, Dorothy Mary Flagg Liddell. For the last two weeks I've been patient and good. I've held your hand and been as sympathetic as I could. I've tried my best to help, but you won't meet me halfway. You're so busy feeling sorry for yourself that you've no idea of how tired *I* am of all of this. You've been weeping for two solid weeks and it's getting more than a little ridiculous. Sure, Joe acted like a shithead, but now that he's left you flat, *your* life has to go on. I can tell you one thing—if you're not willing to make some effort, to take some interest in things, I hope you don't expect me to sit by your side for the rest of my days, passing you the Kleenex box and watching you vegetate and feel sorry for yourself.

"Now, look. I've arranged for a visitor to be there at seven-thirty tonight. He's a friend of mine and I ask, as a favor to me, that you get yourself cleaned up so that you won't scare him to death. You haven't been out of that bathrobe for weeks and you look like something the cat refused to drag in. Go get pretty and be nice to this man. And stop that crying. Do you understand?"

The only answer was a sniffle, a sob, and then a click. Goddammit. Dorothy Mary had hung up. She was a lost cause. Pat thought about calling Lee and canceling the comedian when her intercom buzzed and the secretary said that Mr. Shubert was on the phone.

"I got Jack at his farm in Bucks County," he said. "He's on his way and will be at Mrs. Liddell's at seven-thirty. It was hard to convince him on such short notice, but when I told him that he'd be doing it as a special favor to my banker, he agreed. Jack's a great guy. If anyone can cheer up your friend, he can. Now, let's get back to that loan…"

IV
New York City

When she slammed down the phone Dorothy Mary was hurt because Pat had spoken so sharply with her but, more than that, she was mad.

The *nerve* of Pat Roebling, inviting some complete stranger over to this apartment, without even bothering to ask!

Dorothy Mary strode up and down in her bedroom for at least half an hour, fuming at Pat, telling her where to go and how to get there. She considered telling Dora that she wasn't receiving any visitors tonight, but that wouldn't be fair to this poor man who was coming here at Pat's behest. It punished the wrong person and went against her sense of fairness. No, she'd see this man, but she did *not* like the whole thing. She suspected that this mysterious visitor of Pat's was a psychiatrist. She'd noticed that Pat had been watching her in a funny way lately, as if she thought that she was losing her marbles. Well, she'd show them both that she wasn't crazy. She'd be polite to him and she'd look presentable, but after he was gone, Pat Roebling was going to get a piece of her mind—a large piece.

Dorothy Mary bathed, arranged her hair, put on makeup for the first time in weeks and dressed in a soft gray wool skirt, matching cashmere sweater, and her best pearls. She made herself a drink and sat down in the living room to wait for this man that Pat thought was so important.

V

Jack had driven his red MG from Bucks County to the New Jersey approach to the Holland Tunnel before he heard about the snowstorm. The weather broadcasts predicted a major storm would blanket New York, New Jersey, and Pennsylvania with eight to twelve inches of snow. He'd have to start for home by ten to arrive before the snow got too deep. The road to the farm was a bitch in snow. It drifted over quickly and he'd been snowed in several times last winter. His main worry was the pair of puppies that he'd left in a cardboard box next to the furnace. They were only eight weeks old, and he didn't want anything to happen to them. That furnace wasn't too reliable. Like everything else at the farm, it was old and cranky. Those pups came from a line of field trial champs and he planned to hunt pheasant with them next season.

He bristled that Lee Shubert himself had asked him to give a one-night stand for some neurotic friend of his banker. Because it *had* been Lee himself who called, Jack couldn't refuse; but he wished he were back home. He tried to feel optimistic. With any luck at all, he'd be home before the farm road drifted over, the puppies would be fine, and he'd be five hundred dollars richer.

It would be a strange performance, that was for sure. Who ever heard of giving a whole show for only one woman? And some old Park Avenue bat who couldn't stop crying, at that. The whole thing was weird.

Just before he left the farmhouse, he'd taken a jar of jam from the cupboard. He'd made it last summer from strawberries that he picked himself. He wouldn't have time to get this old biddy any flowers and the jam would have to do.

As he emerged from the tunnel the first flakes of snow melted against his windshield, and Jack wished he'd taken the puppies to the neighboring farmhouse. Oh, well. No use regretting it now.

He didn't know exactly what he would do to make this old biddy laugh, but he wasn't worried about it. He remembered the shell-shocked vets in the VA hospital where he'd recovered after Guadalcanal. He'd been able to make them laugh, and they were guys with no arms or legs and worse—guys with wounds only in their minds. He'd discovered that once he got them to look at him, to really *see* him, they would always laugh. Getting them to come out of themselves and their pain long enough to focus on him was the key. Jack was sure that "Mrs. Gottrocks" would be the same way.

The address was in the high fifties off Park Avenue.

"Mrs. Liddell is expecting me," Jack told the doorman, who looked dubiously at Jack in his green rubber woodsman's galoshes and hunting clothes. But after speaking on the intercom, he led the way to the elevator.

Jack had been in plenty of ritzy apartment buildings before and knew immediately that only really rich people lived in this one. The lobby was nice enough, but it was a little shabby. It wasn't furnished in West Side Rococo or East Side Chintz. It didn't scream "expensive" at you.

When the elevator opened at the tenth floor, he was surprised to find a foyer that would have served as a living room in another apartment. Next to the door with its brass knocker stood a Sheraton side table, and on top of it a square celadon vase held a craggy bouquet of branches studded with a few delicate blossoms. From its crackled glaze Jack recognized the vase as the Real McCoy, and figured that the table was probably real, too. He thought about taking a drawer out to check the size of its dovetailing, but decided against it. Someone might be watching. If both pieces were real, they were worth a small fortune. And here they were, just sitting in a foyer where any delivery boy might steal them. He considered the worth of the vase and for a moment wondered if he could get out of the building with it under his coat. In order to do it without getting caught he'd need an accomplice to create a diversion. The vase was too large for him to just walk out with it.

He straightened his bow tie, knocked on the door and smoothed the back of his hair, feeling with a practiced hand to ensure that his crewcut toupee abutted what there was of his real hair. *Goddamn rug,* Jack thought. He hated to wear it but without it he looked at least ten years older. Not good for his image, and terrible for business. He was reaching up to knock again when the door opened and a gray-haired woman in a yellow uniform and a starched, white apron said, "Good evening," and asked his name.

When he said "Jack Goode—Mrs. Roebling sent me," she opened the door, took his overcoat and galoshes, and preceded him into a room to the left of the foyer. She stopped at the room's entrance, and announced in a brogue, "Mr. Goode to see you, Mum."

A faint voice inside the room said, "Thank you, Dora."

Jack strode into the room and tried to take everything in at a glance. He noticed that there was very little furniture in this big room, and what there was, was low and upholstered in blue or pale gray satin. Large, lighted portraits glowed on three walls, and contrasted with the muted decor. The fourth wall was mostly glass framed by curtains, and from floor to waist-height, a bank of white irises bloomed along its length. At first Jack thought the flowers were plastic, but then he noticed the variation in size and fullness of the blossoms and smelled their faint perfume. *Jesus Christ, they're real. And in the middle of winter.* Behind the flowers was a terrace with evergreens in tubs, and beyond that was a beautiful vision of snow falling on a twilight cityscape. At the far end of the room near the fireplace, a thin young woman in gray sat on one of those low blue and gray couches, flicking cigarette ashes into a large crystal ashtray on an otherwise empty plate glass and chrome coffee table. She didn't smile. He wasn't sure if she knew he was there.

Suddenly Jack knew what to do. In a raucous Brooklynese busybody's voice, as if he were selling slicing machines on late night television, he announced: "I heard you was sick, and I didn't know what to bring you, so I brung you this." He started across the pale blue carpet toward her and took the jar of strawberry jam from his pocket. He flipped it high into the air and caught it as easily and surely as if he were tossing and catching a coin.

She frowned at his voice and brushed the brown-blonde hair from her forehead. Now that she was watching, Jack pasted a sloppy, simple-minded grin across his face. But then something went wrong.

He stumbled in the thick carpet. The jar of jam flew out of his hands and arced toward her, threatening to crash on the glass-topped table.

Miraculously, Jack regained his balance and dashed after it, snatching the jar just as it was about to smash into the table in front of her.

Jack caught himself when his face was inches from hers. He looked straight into her bright blue, bloodshot eyes and added sheepishly, and a bit shyly, "I made it myself." He handed her the jar and watched her start to smile, watched her smile become a grin, and then she giggled.

Dorothy Mary kept seeing him trip and then regain his balance and dash across the room to hand her the jar. And that rubber-faced grin.

He's a very funny man, for a shrink, she thought. *More like a live cartoon character.*

She didn't want him to think she was crazy and tried to keep a straight face while he was introducing himself, but she kept breaking out in fresh waves of giggles.

Dora brought in a tray of canapes, and Dorothy offered him a drink. He had held it in his hand for about thirty seconds, and before her eyes, he degenerated into a drunken rubber man who kept sliding to the floor. He clowned and tried to tell stories. She knew now that he was no shrink. She also noted that, except for his black bow tie, which seemed to have been added to his costume as an afterthought, he looked like he belonged to the North Woods. He wore a pair of reinforced canvas hunting pants with pockets for shotgun shells, a soft red flannel shirt, and a patched tweed jacket. He had a dark crewcut and twinkly blue eyes set in elastic. When he wasn't mugging, he was very handsome. She had never met an entertainer like him. He was too good. He had to be a professional.

She thought of the comedians she had interviewed and decided that this Jack Goode was funnier than Red Skelton, funnier than Bert Lahr, funnier than Milton Berle, and certainly funnier than Jerry Lewis. Of course he was a bit of a show-off, but unlike most comedians she'd met, this man knew when to quit. She had the distinct impression that even as he did his drunk bit, he was watching her and guiding his performance by her reactions. God bless Pat Roebling. What a delightful surprise. It was the first time in weeks that Dorothy Mary's drink tasted good. Suddenly she was hungry.

"Would you stay for dinner?" she asked him. "I'm not sure what Dora can put together on such short notice, but it would be wonderful if you could stay."

Slipping into his Tall Texan routine, Jack replied, "I'd be pleased to stay, ma'am, but I can't linger too long. I have to get back to the south forty and to the little ones."

Dorothy Mary noted only the words "little ones." She excused herself and went to the kitchen to ask Dora to serve dinner as soon as she could—steaks if there were any. She stepped into her bathroom to comb her hair and put on fresh lipstick. She pinched her cheeks to make them glow and realized that she wanted very much for Jack Goode to think she was pretty. It mattered very much. But damn, he was married. Well, she'd have to deal with that later.

When she returned to the living room, she asked, "How many children do you have?"

"Just two."

"Boys or girls?"

"They're both girls," said Jack and then added, "and only eight weeks old."

"That must be quite a handful for you and your wife—twins, and so little. You must be very proud."

"Oh yes. I'm proud of them, but the only thing wrong with them is the way they take after their mother."

"What do you mean?"

"It's just their tails…"

"Tails?" Dorothy Mary was incredulous. "Your wife has a tail?"

"Oh no, not my wife. I've been divorced for years now."

"But the twins…" faltered Dorothy Mary.

"They're not twins. They're just from the same litter."

Dorothy Mary finally got the idea and felt the joke was on her. "But you made it sound like they were real children," she objected.

"Well, they're the closest thing to them that Father has, right now."

Jack was telling animated, exaggerated show business stories when Dora announced dinner. He watched Dorothy Mary react to his gags, and saw her improve on some of them. He thought, *I could love this woman. She looks like a Tiffany necklace. She's the Real Thing.* Jack was overjoyed that she seemed to like him. They seemed to be hitting it off. He thanked his lucky stars for Lee Shubert and wished that he didn't have to get back to the farm so soon.

During dinner Dorothy Mary found herself holding Jack's eyes just a little too long, and she suddenly had a pang of guilt about Joe. Then it occurred to her that Joe had nothing to do with her anymore. The shithead left her without even saying goodbye in person. To hell with him. Did he expect her to sit around and cry for the rest of her life?

And here was this adorable funnyman who made her laugh and feel sexy and pretty all at once. *And* he seemed to be available. Who needed Ambassador Padrosche and his precious Castilian pesos? They finished dinner with Jack pretending to conduct an orchestra using a piece of broccoli, while Dorothy Mary convulsed with laughter.

After dessert Jack said that he was sorry, but he'd have to be heading for home soon. He had to get back to the girls. He explained about how the road to the farm quickly became impassable in a bad snow. Dorothy Mary looked so wistful when he said that he had to leave, that he suggested that maybe some time she would return the compliment and be his guest at the farm. It wasn't grand like her place, but he did have some wonderful pheasants that he'd smoked last year and if she liked venison…

"When does that offer go into effect?" she asked.

Jack looked at his wristwatch and said, "Anytime. Anytime at all. Come now. And, if you've got skis, or snowshoes, bring them, too."

The Dressing Drink

"I couldn't," said Dorothy Mary, hoping that he would urge her once more.

"Of course you could, Mrs. Liddell. You can do anything you want to. Now, go get packed. We've got to drive to Pennsylvania, and it looks like the snow's starting to stick out there."

Dorothy got up from her chair, planted a kiss on his cheek and said she'd be ready in fifteen minutes.

On the way to her room she called quietly for Dora, trying not to betray her giddiness. "Please pack some steak and wine and cheese into the picnic hamper," she said, and rushed off, only to stop again. "And Dora, do give Mr. Goode some more coffee and dessert."

She hurried into her room and tossed her sweaters, woolen socks, and ski pants into a Vuitton bag. She pulled out her warmest coat. As an afterthought she threw in the lacy black negligee she'd never worn for Joe, just in case. "What the hell," she said to herself, and giggled.

Years later, when asked how she and Jack came to be married, Dorothy Mary would smile at Jack, nuzzle his cheek and say that she came to visit his Brittany spaniel pups for a weekend and just stayed.

Dorothy Mary in her New York Apartments.

22

Pretty picture, isn't it?

Mother snuggling up to Father the way a cat twines around your ankles when it wants something. Very cozy.

They married just two days after they met. Since neither had very much ready cash on hand and since this was a decade when hard liquor was much more glamorous than it is today, they bribed the judge who married them with a case of Johnny Walker Red Label Scotch. Apparently, the judge was an old friend of Father's and was delighted to waive the usual blood tests and waiting period for a marriage license and whatever other nuptial legalities the State of Pennsylvania required at the time.

When he got to Father's vows, he said, "Do you, uh…" and couldn't remember Father's name. In a small and rather apologetic voice, Father said, "Irwin Thomas Whittridge."

Mother turned to him and in an incredulous voice, thick with a Philadelphia accent, crowed "ERR-Win? I'm marrying an ERR-Win?" He hadn't bothered to tell her his real name. They laughed all the way through the ceremony and got the judge, his wife, and also two strangers who were their witnesses into the act with them. Too bad that bubble of iridescent, infectious laughter had to burst.

They started projects together, refurbishing the farmhouse and the barn when they weren't renovating Father's career. I suppose Mother tried to use her show business and social connections to help him. She knew he was a great comic and since he was only a second-rater, he must have had poor handling. So, she started to guide his career.

That's where their trouble began.

The Dressing Drink

Father had always taken care of his own business, and had resigned himself to being a second banana on the straw-hat circuit. Who did he have to impress anyway? He made a lot of money and always had work. One thing that other performers said about him was, "Jack was always working. Whenever the rest of us were flat broke, Jack always had work." When he married Mother, he was making a good living in the tent circus route and he had free time to hunt and to refinish antiques. But Mother wanted more for him. She wanted him to be recognized as a comic genius. She wanted people to know she had married a STAR.

So, she pushed him, fostering his career by introducing him to people she knew who had connections. Father didn't fit in with those fancy folk. I imagine he could sense their disdain. After all, in the '50s, show business people were still pariahs in high society. Grace Kelly hadn't happened yet. So, Father hadn't much to say to any of Mother's terribly civilized friends who had all known each other for ages. Behind her back they whispered that Dorothy Mary Liddell had married beneath herself.

Father's friends were no better. All those old troupers had nothing in common with her and thought she was a stuck-up, conceited bitch. They were jealous of her money and called her "the Snow Queen."

So, Mother and Father were left to themselves at the farm. When their relationship was new, this was fine. The real trouble didn't come 'til about a year after I was born.

Father had been offered a fat part in the musical Pajama Game, *that would tour Australia, New Zealand and South Africa. He saw this as a way to get rich quick since he wouldn't have to pay income tax on any of his salary.*

Mother saw the offer in a different light. He'd left her alone at the farm the preceding winter when she'd been pregnant. She'd found that the life of a pioneer woman wasn't for her. Having wood for the fireplace and breaking the ice in the toilet bowls weren't her favorite pastimes, and she'd be damned if she'd spend another winter stuck at the farm alone with a small child, while he waltzed off to South Africa to entertain a bunch of savages. She told him that if he left her, she wouldn't be waiting for him when he arrived home.

I was first told this story by my Mother when I asked what happened to their marriage. The answer always puzzled me. After all, Mother was a very rich woman. If Father were going away and winter was coming, she could have gone almost anywhere in the world. She didn't have to stay at the farm if she didn't want to. Until a short while ago I never understood why her reaction had been so violent.

On my twenty-fifth birthday, an old friend of Father's told me he thought I was old enough to know the truth. That my Father and Mother really separated because she found out about the affairs he was having with faggy antique dealers in New Hope.

Then this whole episode began to make more sense.

What Mother was really doing was using the Pajama Game *tour as a way out. She couldn't come right out and accuse him of being bisexual, even if she understood what that was. Remember, this was the '50s. People were still being put into prison and mental institutions for homosexuality. So, Mother couldn't confront him with her horror of his sexual proclivities, but she could charge him with desertion.*

And that's what she did.

I was present at the breakfast table when their quarrel reached its highest pitch. Only a year old, I was begging from my highchair in the most winning way, for a piece of bacon from Father's plate. I'd just returned from a stay with Grandmother Flagg, who made sure I got anything and everything I wanted at all times. Father thought I was acting spoiled, and at the height of their argument, slapped me across the face. Mother always said he sent me flying across the room. She was shocked that he could slap a child, especially her child, but before she could react, Mary Gillespie, our cook-maid, grabbed an ornamental copper skillet that hung alongside the fireplace, and conked Father on his bald skull with all her might.

Mary was a tiny Irish woman with a nasty temper. I'm sure she put all of her strength into that blow because it knocked Father unconscious. Mary had never liked him anyway. She once told me that he was "no gentleman."

Mother didn't waste any time on reconciliation. She swept up the dogs and me and Mary, and drove to New York where we started all over again.

Eventually they were divorced. The next time I saw my father I was nearly grown up.

Dorothy Mary with her beloved dogs in New York City.

23

Dogs.

Dogs have always been a part of my life. The Flagg family had dogs when Mother was a child. The Brittany spaniels had played a part in bringing my parents together, and thus in my existence. Poodles were my pals when I was a young child, though sadly, they were not there to console me after I'd been orphaned. Still, I think of them fondly.

Although I'd been an only child, I had, in fact, been part of a pack—a pack of poodles. Moppy and Inky were Standards. Tinsel and Josephine were Minis. "Yum Yum," also called Cupcake, my closest pal, was a Toy. One of my fondest childhood memories is of traveling in the back seat of Chryssie, our 1959 black-and-white pushbutton-transmission Chrysler—the poodles and me. And we were back there quite often because Mother thrived upon the freedom of being behind the wheel, controlling that behemoth of an automobile, traveling from Manhattan to Philadelphia and the Main Line, or to the farm in Bucks County.

Our journeys always began the same—Mother herded the poodles into the back seat. Once she and I were in the front, Mother would palm my bum and unceremoniously dump me over the front seat into the pile of poodles in the back. Of course, the poodles protested, grumbling and panting, until my squirming (and theirs), settled.

Poodles are known to be diggers, and Tinsel was the diggingest of our dogs. She did an admirable job of pawing through the seat fabric to the stuffing below, leaving the back seat smelling of pungent foam rubber and dog breath. In the winter this was my nest. I would curl up into the pawed-out indentation, surrounded by the warm furry pack, and feeling secure, I would sleep. In the back seat of that car, surrounded by the pack, is—to this day—my memory of the safest, most loved I've ever felt.

The Dressing Drink

Thomas relaxing with his pack.

Mother took as much care to ensure that the poodles were as impressively coiffed as she was herself. In New York City, up Madison Avenue, turning onto 71st between Park and Lex, was where the poodle parlor was located. It was run by an eccentric, formidable French spinster known only as "Madame"—Mother's most worthy adversary. Madame would pour on her most Parisian French when Mother arrived at the salon to have the poodles groomed. In many ways the two were equal—Mother and Madame—French superiority trumps all cards. Mother spoke perfect French like a Parisian born and bred, including perfect French poodle French. Mother insisted on having all the poodles groomed together, ending with red bows and blood red nails, and Madame would launch into a tirade in French, complaining that coiffing our five poodles would take her all day. Mother would dismiss Madame's outburst as though she were casually flicking ash from her cigarette.

I vividly remember the time when I was five or six years old, when the five poodles and I were relegated to a room on the eighth floor of the Barclay hotel. This small hotel room was part of my grandmother's apartments, which occupied half the floor—twelve rooms in all, a huge space.

Mother had dolled up in her daytime cocktail and luncheon attire: a confection of a black Hattie Carnegie with matching veil. Everyone at that time wore hats, veils, and, of course, gloves, hiding long red fingernails. It was a ritual perfection. I could feel the heady, bubbling excitement of the party that raged just off the hotel's lobby—and instead here I was, stuck in this too-small bedroom. There I sat, dressed in my finery, itching to go out later in the day as Mother had promised.

I sat with the anesthetized poodles strewn everywhere, watching Philadelphia's version of children's daytime television. Thank God for Gene London. Whatever his guise, playing Tinker Tom or hosting Cartoon Corners, he was the best diversion around. I loved television and sat way too close. Captain Kangaroo had been disappointing, especially when my class at school visited the set. The Captain wasn't shooting that day, and the set was dark. It was eerie seeing Bunny Rabbit limp and lifeless. Traumatic. I trusted Gene London. He could do it all—act, draw amazing pictures, and take everyone on flights of fancy. He was a lovely, non-condescending genius for kids. Later in my life, Gene became my friend, confidant, coach, and Gay Father.

As I rose out of boredom, so did the pack of poodles. The black Standard matrons, Moppy and Inky, and the others—Minis, silver Tinsel, and black Josephine—were constantly embattled in competitions. The endless Tong war only subsided when Mother would raise her voice. The sole Toy—silver Yum Yum—vied for Mother's attention and paid the price from me. I wasn't a kind kid, and more often than not, I terrorized the little darling until she took refuge under a couch or bed to find sanctuary.

Impatient because of the confinement and boredom, it seemed only fitting to leash the poodle mob and visit Mother below in the Barclay Bar or dining room or take them for a walk, as I routinely did in New York. After all, it made good sense to show Mother how well I handled the dogs. It also served my deep inner showbiz to make a surprise entrance. A singular chaos was set to ensue.

The poodles, for a time, had experienced the countrified freedom to romp and explore at will. Squirrel chasing was all the rage. More recently the poodles became citified, having moved with us to our New York apartment. Mother had dolled 'em up. The black poodles had their nails painted blood red, which matched the dual bows behind their ears, and the long red leather collars and leashes. Mother knew her authority was enhanced by expanding her physical power base to include a pack o' poodles and a decked-out child. This was our traveling show, always.

The moment had arrived. I leashed the pups, held all five leads in my diminutive hand, opened the door and broke free. I rang for the elevator and waited. The poodles looked up to me as if to ask, "Where we goin'?" They were excited, and heck, so was I. The elevator arrived, the door opened, and there was William, the tiny elevator man, eyes a-poppin'. After all these years, I now consider William a collaborator, a conspirator. The poodles and I simply walked right into the elevator... too many poodles, not enough room. William must have assumed that a five-year-old Flagg knew what he was doing. Mother had taught me to always look in charge.

William paused, closed the doors and we descended the eight floors in silence as if a young boy with a herd of poodles was an everyday occurrence on the Barclay Hotel's elevator. Even though the poodles were excited, they were sophisticated enough to understand that an elevator ride was a journey to freedom in the city. They behaved admirably. I still had the audacity to believe I had the whole situation under control.

The moment the elevator door opened all hell broke loose. They tore free from my grubby mitt and burst forth into the crowded lobby. Moppy and Inky lurched forward, but ultimately held their ground, becoming more supervisors than participants. Josie and Tinsel, however, bolted in search of lunch, Mother, or squirrels, and headed straight for the big brass revolving doors onto Rittenhouse Square. Yum Yum just ran in circles until fear and anxiety overtook her and she slinked under the skirt of the nearest couch.

Shrieks and exclamations of shock ensued. Anyone seated was now bolt upright, swiveling their heads to view the chaos. Gentlemen and dowagers arose from their calm. George, the ever-present liveried doorman, blocked the revolving doors and attempted to restore order.

The far end of the lobby was capped by the intimate Barclay Bar. Jimmy the bartender, in his brass-buttoned white mess jacket, was hard at work pumping out Manhattans with maraschino cherries, not muddled fruit. He immediately spied the gravity of the situation from behind the bar and shot Mother an unmistakable look. They were pals.

I can still see Mother's face when Jimmy's message resonated with her. She went vertical. She rounded her corner table, planted her heels, and in a booming voice, commanded, "Help!"

Christine, the very Irish coatroom angel in her black uniform and white apron, sprang into action. The poodles and I were outflanked. Mother and Christine continued clapping and calling, fixed on the pandemonium, with Mother controlling the space, dignity deferred, moving forward with apologies to the breathless audience. Mrs. Russell, Mrs. Cavanaugh, and assorted posed characters spouted off exasperations such as "Well!" and "Shocking!"

Moppy and Inky were easy to wrangle, but Josie and Tinsel were determined to conquer that revolving door to freedom. George would have none of it and scooped up Tinsel into his arms. Grateful, Mother, in shock and horror, finally released her infectious laugh, and the fear subsided. She was again in command of her pack. She found Yum Yum under Mrs. Russell's chair, and order—for the moment— was restored. Tightening her grip on the leashes, Mother looked me in the eye, and hissed, "Tommy, upstairs now."

William's head was bowed as we ascended in the elevator.

Some of those times with the poodles were wonderfully comical. But, as Mother became increasingly ill with cancer, there began a subtle loss of the ironclad discipline in our regimented household. Canine chaos ensued when the poodles' schedule for outdoor activities began to wane. We began finding "presents" on the antique Queen Anne dining table. We had a part-time maid who would come in a couple of afternoons a week, but certainly, we did not have a staff of six, the kind of help to which Mother had been accustomed at Denbigh. The dogs would have to go.

And, go they did—one by one.

Each time we returned from a trip, Mother was increasingly frail, then eventually bedridden. Moppy died on her own of cancer. Mother was inconsolable. If she were not well enough to care for the dogs, how could she care for me? Misery, alcoholism, and chaos enveloped Mother as her mental health began a downward spiral.

Cupcake was the last to go. I was on my way out to my weekly meeting of the Knickerbocker Greys—400 uniformed young men, practicing military drills at the Park Avenue Armory. Mother had airily dropped the bomb that Cupcake was going to stay with our Hungarian seamstress, Alma, who lived in Queens. But, Mother told me, that was okay, because I could visit Cupcake any time. As far as I was concerned, Queens just might as well have been Hungary.

Because I was an only child, Cupcake had been my constant companion, my confidante, my best friend. I was angry, desperate, and defeated. I cooked up a scheme to kidnap Cupcake and bring her to the armory with me. But who would watch her while I was performing my drills? And what would we do afterward?

It was then that I had the realization I was just a powerless kid living a real-life tragedy. I hated Mother and all the adults involved in this cabal.

I visited Cupcake only once, taking an interminable subway ride out to Queens. When I was finally reunited with my best friend, she no longer recognized me.

Thomas and Yum Yum.

24

I want to tell you about Mother's death, but I hesitate. I'm afraid that you'll be just like the others. After all, you're not the first visitor to my tent and the Strange Tale of Mother's Death is one of the main attractions of my Side Show. I've discovered that like all Side Show freaks, like the Half-Woman/Half-Serpent, like the Rubber-Faced Man, or the Frog Boy, this story repels and fascinates the audience.

People usually treat me differently when they learn how I rejoiced at Mother's death. Well-meaning people are often shocked into silence. They gather their belongings and hurry off, glad to be away from me. Some pretend to be sympathetic, but only in the most patronizing way. They advise me to go into analysis, to meditate, or to eat only brown rice. I recognize them for the fools they are, and I loathe them. A few listeners get angry. They chastise me as if it were still possible to change things. I think of them as the Sunday School teachers I never had, and they make me want to laugh out loud.

I pretend that nothing bothers me. If the audience hurries away, I watch them go; if they go cold, I listen. I can usually maintain this unruffled facade in the daytime.

But things are different at night.

Then I am haunted by the memories of gaping mouths, staring eyes, painted accusing fingers, medicinal cocktails. These visions sit on my eyelids and infest my ears like moths clustering to feed on mucus. The darkness is filled with the whirr and clatter of their scaly wings. It happens over and over again. I can't make it stop.

So, if I tell you the story, you must promise that you'll be different from all the others. It's important. Remember, you promised.

Thomas getting his first haircut with his mother and grandmother.

25

New York City, 1968

If Mother had known how little time there was she might have done things differently. I often wonder what the doctors told her. Did they give her hope that she could overcome cancer and live a normal life again? I do know that pain was her constant companion in the last three years of her life. Like two familiar black dogs, pain and her fear of death always nipped at her heels, replacements for those beloved poodles she'd had to put down.

I remember her in the hospital after the first mastectomy. "Uncle Grover," her last confidant and sometime lover, suggested that a surprise visit might cheer her up, but it didn't work that way at all. I was nine and had been dressed in my short pants, long socks, shined shoes, clean shirt and tie, and new blazer. I'd bought her a pink carnation with my own money. The florist wrapped it in special paper for me.

I entered the room, she turned to the *click-clack* sound of my shining shoes, and she saw me. She was propped up in bed, wearing one of those skimpy hospital gowns. Uncle Grover sat beside her. I expected her to return my smile, but she started to cry. The sobs got louder and louder, and in her hysteria she sounded like an animal vomiting. I had never seen anyone, especially my mother, cry so violently. I wanted to comfort her, but she covered herself with the sheet and turned her face to the wall. Between sobs she begged Grover to take me away.

Mother didn't want my carnation and she didn't want me, either. We must have both reminded her of death.

She convalesced at home, and for a while she was better. And then it began again. This time a different sort of pain and bleeding. I remember the blood stains on her sheets when I would help her to the bathroom. She had a second operation and the

The Dressing Drink

doctors removed tumors from her uterus. A year later there was a final operation that took her other breast and her lymph nodes. Did the doctors tell her that she only had a finite amount of time? Did they know?

I'd just turned eleven when she had the final operation. I remember it clearly because I wasn't given the usual big birthday party and felt neglected. My nanny, Mrs. Pitz, had a small cake and one present for me. She said it was from my mother, but Mother would never have bought that second-rate copy of a Steiff stuffed animal. I knew Mrs. Pitz felt sorry for me, but she was no replacement for Mother. I said thank you, and never played with that toy dachshund. It made me sad.

It seems incredible now. Mother healed from the last mastectomy and decided we would take a trip to Europe. She should have known she was too sick, but she must have felt the weight of all the unresolved plans for my future. Would I go to secondary school in Switzerland, or somewhere in the U.S.? Who would be my guardian? There seemed to be plenty of candidates. Uncle Grover, a career army officer was the best choice, but he was a confirmed bachelor and usually stationed overseas. I would only tie him down. There was also "Uncle George," a stodgy, fastidious Wall Street lawyer and Mother's lifelong friend. In addition, there were people I'd never met: English relatives who could supply a foster family; Mother's French friends who could give me continental social advantages; and "Cousin Katy," Mother's dear friend in San Remo who was my rich godmother, although I had never met her. All the decisions that Mother had thought were years off became pressing, and had to be made soon. So, we took a Pan American flight to London on the first leg of a journey that would end in Monte Carlo.

Pan American was the only airline Mother ever considered. It had comforts she thought essential. For one thing, there were stewards who kept a respectful, but attentive distance. Other airlines allowed stewardesses to manage the first-class cabin. Mother thought they were corn-fed gold diggers who had learned to flirt, but had never been taught to serve. Pan's first-class cabin also had a front seat with extra leg room, and Mother demanded this seat. She was tall, and constantly complained about cramped accommodations. Her idea of purgatory was a ten-minute ride in a Volkswagen Beetle.

London calmed us. Its streets had the same grayness as New York's, but there were none of those awful irritations like blacks, riots, Puerto Ricans, Jews, or a young Democratic President whom Mother knew and despised. In London there were only the stolid British, who seemed to understand all the things that Mother needed to make her happy. At home she was always so on edge: fighting with the servants, upset by the news, screaming at me for little things. It was a great relief to have two or three days when she wasn't mad at me. But, in retrospect, it wasn't that she liked me any better. On the contrary, I irritated her constantly. However, in London she wasn't so mad at *other* people, and consequently, when she was angry at me, she had the energy to do it justice.

Mother did a great job of flaring up and screaming. Then it would all be over like a sudden storm at sea.

We stayed at the Ritz with its high ceilings and brass beds, freshly made with pink satin quilts. Ice always came in a silver bowl, and the room service glasses and crockery were small and light. It was as if Mother and I were playing house.

The bathroom adjoining our suite had an unfamiliar fixture which intrigued me. Mother told me it was a bidet—an appliance that no proper Englishwoman would *think* of using, and which most Americans had never heard of but which ladies from the Continent considered essential. They used it to wash their private parts after making love. It kept them from having babies. I guess this new information and all the gleaming white and gold plumbing made me bold, because I remember asking her how a man and a woman did it. I think I used those words. I asked, "Are they side by side?"

She was flustered, but answered, "Well, er um… they can be, but, er, um—no, they are usually on top of each other. That is, the man is usually on top and the woman is on the bottom."

I had other questions, but I was too shy to ask. I should have. I didn't know it at the time, but the Ritz bathroom would be my last opportunity to learn such things from Mother.

London was not filled with wonderful things to do for an eleven-year-old traveling with a sick woman. Much of what occurred during what turned out to be Mother's final desperate trip to Europe with me was my ability to supplant boredom with action and investigation. Mother was desperate to do so many more things than entertain me. She was intent upon introducing me to Europe, as I know she hoped for a more continental upbringing and life for me; she despised the provincial. And she was half in panic of finding me appropriate guardians, as well as trying to relive a life she missed, as well as finding an English cure for cancer, and in her own way attempting to bring closure to a person I had no idea existed at the time. That was a lot for anyone—even the force of nature known as Mother.

During this trip, I was constantly commanded to be on my best behavior. How else could she sell to anyone the possibility of taking care of Tommy?

But what could Mother seriously do if I didn't listen? She was ninety percent bedridden and had been reduced to peeing into a glass etched with the word "RITZ" so she didn't have to walk to the bathroom. This was the indicator of impending death. I knew it. She knew it. She and I were now locked in an unspoken pact of sharing our foxtrot of her death and my survival.

My personality wasn't up to the challenge of behaving. I was bored and amazed myself with my manufactured creative options. Often I just walked out of the Ritz, chatted with Victor the concierge, and explored right outside the side entrance. After New York, I was comfortable in any city. Intrigued with flower sellers, arcades of shops,

The Dressing Drink

and a different hustle and bustle that was decidedly not New York, it all seemed totally digestible to a ten-year-old boy properly dressed and on the loose in London. I *so* wanted to be dressed in the latest fashion from Carnaby Street, but that wouldn't happen for many years to come.

One afternoon, Mother pulled herself together as only she could. Never have I known a stronger-willed woman. We took a cab to a part of London that was certainly not Mayfair. Squat houses were clustered together in a post-World War II postcard. We arrived at the door and Mother took a deep breath. The red wooden door swung open, Mother beamed, and in her formal but happy voice said, "Tommy, say hello to your Aunt Allie."

This was all news to me—but everything seemed to be different on this trip. I knew the drill. I stood at attention, bowed from the waist, put forth my hand, and said, "Hello, I'm Tommy."

The drinks came out and so did Uncle Teddy—very tall, curly-headed—and stayed. At no time could he rein in Aunt Allie, who after one drink, was off to the races. There was a black-and-white TV in the back room, broadcasting the Irish Derby. I so missed my American television of Batman, Donna Reed, Daniel Boone, and Mingo, but the quality of this broadcasting provided no escape for me.

We were seated for dinner, which was no thrill. Allie flew around the room delivering dishes of unpleasant English food. Mother was as happy as I had seen her in a long time; however, there was a pervasive sense of concern in the air. And it wasn't about me this time.

Halfway through the meal, a quiet, poorly-dressed teenager descended the stairs and stood at the head of the table. He was introduced simply as Derrick. The room went silent. It was all pretty strange. Clearly he was detached, uncomfortable, not seated... But what did I care, what did I know? The rest of the visit was a blur. I was tired and bored and retired to my friend the television. With nothing there to excite me, I dozed off.

"Nevertheless, what's done is done," said Teddy. "Thank goodness your mother financed Derrick's upbringing, and that you have continued to do so since she suffered that debilitating stroke. While you rest tomorrow morning, Allie will take young Thomas to Madame Tussauds house of wax figures or some such nonsense."

I must have been semi-conscious when I heard Teddy say this, and it snapped me right out of my drowsiness. I was wide awake at the exciting thought of seeing the blood and gore of Jack the Ripper in living wax.

The next morning Mother dolled me up in my crisp seersucker suit, telling me in no uncertain term that she expected me to behave as a gentleman when I was with Aunt Allie at Madame Tussauds. She then dropped the bombshell that Aunt Allie and I would be meeting her, Uncle Teddy, and Derrick at Simpson's—in the Strand—not the Tavern. I could have hugged my Mother. But naturally, I didn't.

"Is Derrick Aunt Allie and Uncle Teddy's son?" I chirped.

"Well, no. But he is rather like a cousin to you. Now, I want you to behave—"

"I know," I cut in. "Tomorrow, you want me to be polite and on my best behavior. Act like a gentleman. You don't have to keep reminding me, Mother."

"Tommy. Do *not* cut-off my words! *That is not behaving like a gentleman!*" Mother shouted.

"Yes, Mother. I apologize."

"And do not ask Derrick a lot of questions. We don't want to make him feel uncomfortable."

"Yes, Mother," I responded sheepishly.

Madame Tussauds was better than I could have expected. And although I was put in Aunt Allie's care, she allowed me to behave like the overzealous child I was. She scuttled behind as I practically ran to the exhibit in the basement. I can still recall the cool, dark, and hushed Chamber of Horrors. It smelled like mildew—a result of the dry ice smoke they pumped in to give the illusion of that sinister London fog. In addition to Jack the Ripper's victims, there were the many atrocities from the French Revolution—the beheaded Madame du Barry; Marat, stabbed dead in his bathtub; Robespierre, gaping at me, his bloody jaw garishly hanging askew; the guillotine, which appeared to have just been used, the basket full of severed heads still in position. I silently thanked Mother for telling me about French history. The figures were so real. I especially remember the eyes. They all looked stunned and in disbelief as their lifeblood drained away.

Soon the fun was over, and Aunt Allie insisted we visit Her Royal Highness, Queen Elizabeth II, before we left the waxworks. That reminded me that I was going to meet Derrick at lunch, and I wanted to get going immediately.

But Aunt Allie stood her ground. "Tommy. I never leave this museum without paying my respects to our beloved Queen. You've had your enjoyment for the morning. It is now time to settle down and behave like a gentleman," she said, sounding strangely like Mother.

The Queen looked out at us with her serene smile. Aunt Allie curtsied and commanded me to bow. Mother had taught me to bow, but not how to bow to royalty. "A slight tip of the head is the correct way a gentleman greets the Queen. Now, do it the correct way, Tommy."

When Aunt Allie and I arrived at Simpson's in the Strand, Mother, Uncle Teddy, and Derrick were already seated at the table.

"You're late, Allie," scolded Teddy.

"No doubt my son had a hand in that. Tommy, did you dawdle at some silly exhibit?" Mother asked sternly.

"No, Dorothy Mary. It's my fault we are a quarter-of-an-hour late. Tommy behaved like the perfect gentleman," responded Aunt Allie, giving me a wink. Good old

Aunt Allie.

I was more awake than I had been the previous night at dinner, finally having the opportunity to get a good look at Derrick. There was something familiar about his face, but I couldn't put my finger on it. Plus, he was much older than I had originally thought. Derrick looked to be ten years older than me. His clothing was no better than what he'd been wearing at Aunt Allie and Uncle Teddy's house—olive green weathered corduroy slacks, navy blue moth-eaten vee-neck vest, and a yellowed-white long sleeve shirt.

Derrick was very quiet. Unless he was being spoken to or answering one of the adults' questions, he kept his eyes cast down. After an uncomfortable lunch during which I regaled the table with stories about the grotesquely killed victims the wax figures depicted, Mother took Derrick aside and spoke quietly to him. I saw her handing him a few pounds, saying something about the tube and making his way back home with the Waggs. He nodded. We said our goodbyes for the afternoon as Derrick, Aunt Allie, and Uncle Teddy turned and walked to the subway, just as our taxi arrived at the curb.

We were to stay another few days to visit with Aunt Allie and Uncle Teddy, but that night, Mother and Aunt Allie had a huge row. I was dozing in bed when I heard Mother's voice raised several decibels above the volume she used when she yelled at me. I ran to the door of my room in our suite and quietly cracked it open. I could see Mother on the phone.

"It's not like you raised that boy with no help. My mother, and now I, have ensured that you and Teddy received your stipend every year to keep Derrick clothed, fed, and taken care of. But Tommy is well-behaved and would be no bother to you or Teddy if you were to become his guardians. His *true* guardians, not to be treated like some bastard cast-off like Derrick. I believed I could count on you. I guess I was wrong."

I quickly jumped into bed and under the covers as Mother slammed down the phone. She rang for the maid and pulled out our suitcases while she waited.

"Begin packing our bags, Antoinette," Mother commanded the half-asleep, wide-eyed girl. As Antoinette rushed about, Mother called the train station, booking the earliest available from London. We never saw Aunt Allie or Uncle Teddy again. But Derrick—who turned out to be Mother's illegitimate nephew through one of David's early trysts—paid us a visit in Manhattan about a year later.

Derrick was eighteen when he arrived at our apartment in New York. He stayed for about a week, but much of his trip was forgettable to me with the exception of our day at the zoo. Early that morning, I woke up my cousin by nudging him.

"Derrick, we're going to the zoo today. The weather is perfect."

And it was. I enjoyed the feeling of the warm sun on my face, as I marched ahead of him down Madison Avenue toward the small zoo at 65th and 5th.

Derrick and I smelled the zoo before we saw it, but that did little to quell my excitement. That was the reason why Mother never wanted to take me to the zoo—the smell. Not to mention, Mother always thought seeing the animals in such small cages was sad, but that was revolutionary thinking for the time. I enjoyed dragging Derrick around the exhibits, especially the monkeys and the big cats. But my favorite activity was spin art, something that had nothing to do with animals at all. Spin art is a painting activity meant for children around my age, but Derrick seemed to enjoy it, too. We strapped a small canvas to a spinning board and squeezed every color of paint we could get our hands on. I even got a little dizzy watching each new paint splatter spin round and round.

When the sun was setting and the chill air raised goosebumps on our arms, Derrick and I headed back to the apartment. We dumped our canvases into a trash can on the way. I knew Mother wouldn't want them cluttering the place.

Derrick left a few days later. I never saw him again, nor gave him much thought. But decades after, when I was in my thirties, I was summoned to visit my cousin, "Mrs. Geyelin," who must have been in her eighties, living on the Main Line. Her house was particularly well-appointed, but filthy. She couldn't see the dust or the dirt because of her advanced years. I remember her sitting across from me at her dining room table and just pushing this stack of letters at me. At first I didn't understand what they could possibly be about, but after skimming a few, I understood.

The Flagg family had paid off Derrick's mother to disappear. The family had sent Derrick far away to London and paid a yearly stipend to the Church of England to care for him. Grandmother sent the checks. When she could no longer take care of that task, Mother took on the job. The money stopped with Mother's death. I later learned that Derrick had died in his mid-forties, a ward of the Church.

Despite her falling out with Aunt Allie and Uncle Teddy, the high point of Mother's visit to London was to have been her day at Ascot. But it was a fiasco like so many other things that summer. She hadn't been back to Europe since her schooling in Italy, and even though she was invited into the Royal Enclosure, she wasn't pleased with her reception. She may have been snubbed or treated too casually.

I don't know exactly what happened because I was left outside with the chauffeur. All I know for sure is that she'd dressed beautifully and was excited when we arrived, and she was crabby and touchy when it was all over. We left the racetrack as quickly as possible. Somehow, it seemed to be all my fault.

After Ascot, Mother got sick again and was too exhausted to get up. I would walk around the block outside the hotel and buy freesias, jonquils, or narcissus for her.

As we continued on our catastrophic tour of Europe, Mother and I left London and headed to Paris, where we stayed for about two weeks. Most of that time I was sick with stomach cramps that made me double up in pain, whether from nerves or the food, or just something I caught in our travels. Mother made me swallow paregoric and I threw it up immediately, all over her new Chanel suit. She was feeling better and saw friends and went shopping and to wonderful restaurants. I was too sick to go; I stayed in our hotel and read French comic books.

Everyone always raves about Paris, but for me it was just all right. I suppose it's hard for a child to appreciate that city. At the time I loved to collect stamps and the only thing I remember fondly were the stamp vendors in the park on Sunday.

Our next stop was San Remo and "Cousin Katy." I guess by now Mother had also eliminated her French friends as possible custodians, and no doubt she had high hopes that Cousin Katy would take me. The two women had been friends for years and Mother was happy at the prospect of seeing her.

We arrived at Villa Aloha, which overlooked San Remo. Villa Aloha was a lush wonderland of extraordinary gardens and greenhouses. Exotic trees, jungle foliage, and flowers were everywhere, blanketing every surface and towering over our heads in a canopy.

Our hostess was away, but her steward helped us to our quarters: a ten-room guest cottage. Cousin Katy arrived later and there were lots of hugs, kisses, and apologies. She was terribly sorry, but her old cook had just quit, and she wasn't sure how things would be. She was sincerely worried. We sat down to lunch not really knowing what to expect. I had never had an Italian lunch before, and believed each course to be the last, but they kept coming. Cousin Katy encouraged me to be a healthy eater and since I was feeling hungry for the first time since my attack of stomach cramps in Paris, I ate and ate.

First there was an antipasto, then pasta, then the meat course, then salad, and then fish. Last was a superb bread pudding. I asked for seconds and told Cousin Katy over and over how much I enjoyed it. That bread pudding was the all-time best dessert I'd ever had. It was better than a Sno Ball. I liked my godmother and wished I could stay with her. It was nice to have someone saying pleasant things to me instead of threatening me all the time the way Mother did.

That evening we had cocktails at KATY'S BAR. It flashed those words in blue neon, in a cave carved into a rock formation near her pool. It was all so gay. So extravagant. So Cousin Katy. Friends of hers joined us, and I'm sure they all watched Mother surreptitiously, saw how cadaverous she looked.

During cocktails I was again seized with stomach cramps and had to make an unpleasant scene to get Mother to pay attention. She had to leave the party and tend to me instead of mingling with the guests.

I guess Cousin Katy found my behavior distasteful, because when Mother asked her if she'd be my guardian, Cousin Katy apologized once more and declined. She said I would be too much of a strain for her and for Villa Aloha.

We drove to Monte Carlo where we met "Uncle George," who would become my guardian by default. He'd been to Russia on business and gotten sick there, sick enough to nearly die. That frightened me.

We stayed in Monte Carlo for about a week, both adults in bed. I shuttled back and forth between their rooms, bringing tissues to Uncle George and grape juice to Mother. All this time she was upset and anxious. I remember the deep crease between her eyebrows. The world tour to find my guardian had backfired. She should have known it would be a disaster. It's tough enough to find homes for orphaned dogs or kittens, much less a half-grown child.

On the voyage home aboard the *Queen Elizabeth*, Mother got sick again—but it was a different kind of illness. During dinner at the Captain's table she went pale, clutched at her chest, gagged and shrieked. Her face had that inward total concentration on pain that I'd seen before. But there had never been anything like this. They took her to the infirmary, and when Uncle George returned to the table, he told me she'd had a heart attack. The adults wouldn't let me see her and there was nothing else to do, so I went to the ship's movie, *Thoroughly Modern Millie*. I don't remember much of it.

Thomas and his Uncle George aboard the Chant Ester IV.

Back in our cabin, I expected to be alone, and was amazed to see Mother in the bunk across from mine. Where were the stewards or the doctors or the nurses? No one was around to explain, so I got undressed and into my bunk. The light above her head was on and she raved incoherently all night, calling out names of friends and relatives. Nothing she said made any sense, but I knew she was angry and in pain. I can still hear her, feel the movement of the ship, and see that contorted face in the dim overhead light. She remained in her bunk 'til we docked in New York.

It was scary to see her so close to death but somehow, once again, she rallied. I kept expecting her to die, but she survived, time and again. One thing that made her condition worse was having to deal with the Customs people in New York. The inspector doggedly went about his job without any regard for Mother's illness. She often told me how other family members, Grizzy for example, would be whisked away, luggage and all, upon their return from Europe. Yet she had to answer all the man's annoying questions from her wheelchair. It took forever. He opened and pried into everything. She was so furious but there was nothing she could do.

When we got to the apartment, the elevator was broken and the attendants had to carry her up the five flights of stairs. Once she finally made it into her own bed and her door was closed, she must have known that she was close to the end.

I was sent away that weekend to stay with a school friend in Madison, Connecticut. Mother probably called his mother and asked her to take me. Before I left she gave me a hundred dollar bill. I remember thinking that this was strange because she never doled out more than seventy-five cents or a dollar at a time. I called her that night. We chatted and had one of those *heartwarming* mother-son conversations that were more like business conference calls.

"What time did your train get there?"

"Three-thirty."

"Was it late?"

"Only a little."

"Did you speak to any strangers?"

"No, Mother."

"Make sure you thank Mrs. Helsel."

"Yes, Mother."

"Are your fingernails clean?"

"*Mother!*"

"And don't drink too much Coke. I don't want you making a pig of yourself and getting sick again."

"All right, Mother."

26

After the weekend I returned home alone. I rang the doorbell and when no one answered, I let myself in. It made me feel grownup and important to use my own keys. I announced myself and put my suitcase down. The apartment was hot and humid, and the late morning sun in the living room was filled with an unwavering gray dust. I was surprised not to hear any of the familiar sounds of our apartment. Mother had destroyed the dogs a year ago, so there hadn't been any of the yapping of toy poodles for a long time. But where were the servants? There should have been the scurrying of the maid; the fat, padding feet of my German nanny; or the steady, quiet movements of Mother's nurse. The silence didn't bother me at first. I thought everyone was busy or hiding. I took off my jacket and called again, "Mother, I'm home. " I knew she couldn't answer easily, but I expected some sound. But none came. None at all.

All of a sudden I was seized by the silence. The only noises were from traffic on Madison Avenue.

I went through the living room and turned the corner to look into Mother's bedroom. I was astonished to see that her bed was made. Its delicate, blue silk and lace bedspread blended with the gray dust in the air. Her room was empty.

Something was terribly wrong. Because of her illness, Mother was always at home. On those rare occasions when she did go out, she always took me along. I'd never been alone in our apartment before and I didn't like it.

I raced through the apartment, checking every room. I called for Mother, Mrs. Pitz, Annie, Martha, but no one answered. I was alone. No one was there. The only thing I could think of was to phone Uncle George at work.

He said that Mother was in the hospital and that she was very bad off. He made a lunch date with me at the Yale Club and hurried me off the phone.

The Dressing Drink

Well, I would not be had. I'd be damned if I would not see my mother. Uncle George mentioned that she was in Lenox Hill. It hadn't been suggested that I go to the hospital to find her, but I needed to. Now I understood why she'd given me that hundred dollar bill. She never told me what she had in mind. No doubt she hoped it was an unnecessary precaution.

I found a cab and rushed to the hospital, ready for the worst. I knew that children under the age of fifteen were not allowed into the hospital. Period. No exceptions. Yet, because of the special ways in which Mother had always arranged my life, I assumed this was just another rule on the way to the slaughter.

I approached the big desk, prepared for the nurse to check through all her Rolodexes to find the room number, only to stop and say, "I'm sorry, but you can't go up. You're underage." Then another nurse, older and wiser, would butt in and explain that this was Mrs. Liddell's child and that the room number was thus and so.

But the nurse behind the desk never even glanced at the Rolodexes. She just smiled that icy, middle-aged nurse's smile and said, "No."

I asked for the doctor then, trying to go over her head, but she ignored me and answered someone else's question.

I never bothered to say thank you. Instead I turned and walked out the double glass doors. After the proper wait outside, I followed the first big man back in and then peeled off, unseen.

Once inside the corridors of the first floor, those awful colors started to get to me. It seemed that instead of being chosen to comfort patients, they'd been picked to confuse young boys in search of their dying mothers. Arrows and lines and numbers were painted on the walls. The further along I went, the more confused I got. It felt as though I were entering the bowels of the hospital. I knew the kinds of specimens that they keep in those catacombs and I was petrified. I felt helpless, lost, and had no information to go on as I traversed the maze of corridors and rooms full of sick strangers with needles and tubes stuck into them.

I changed my mind. Maybe I couldn't see Mother right now, but surely Uncle George would bring me back later. Everything was going to be all right. There really wasn't anything to worry about. So I gave up the search for Mother, found my way out of the hospital and got a taxi to the Yale Club and Uncle George.

I must have been really flustered, because I couldn't remember where the Yale Club was. The driver was no help because he spoke almost no English, and was obviously not a member. We eventually arrived, but where was Uncle George? He'd never seemed to be the collegiate type, especially the American collegiate type. He came from a strong German background. His parents had made a fortune in the beer business, which had been sold a long time ago.

A young studious Thomas with his Uncle Grover.

Mother and Uncle Grover were always joking about Uncle George's siblings, Virginia and Louis. They were seriously nuts. Virginia was actually locked up for a while. She was always nice to me, but I'd overheard that men were often slipping into her bedroom at parties to comfort her. She had a vacant blonde expression, and seemed like a woman who would keep live electric wires next to her tub. Louis was another winner. He always wore a Homburg and light yellow gloves, carried a stick and had terribly blond hair for a man in his late sixties. The sad thing about both of them was that they were broke now and neither knew how to work. They lived in apartments adjacent to Uncle George's, and he took care of them. Behind his back Mother and Uncle Grover called him "Mother George."

I finally found him and was immediately angry because he'd brought along Mother's friend, "Aunt Marie." I imagine that he thought she might bring a feminine touch to an awkward luncheon, but I never forgave him for this mistake. I needed a response from a man I had never respected. He had his chance, but he lost it because Aunt Marie ruined everything.

The Dressing Drink

The only thing I ever felt for her was lust. All I had wanted to do since I was nine was sleep with her. I would chase her round and round at parties in hopes that she would trip and fall so I might have a chance. She would drink vodka after vodka until she got looped and loose. More than anything, her slurred language excited me. Otherwise she was a classic dumb blonde. If she were going to help in this crisis, I knew I was in for a struggle.

I realized that Mother was ill, but how close she was to death was impossible to learn. Perhaps Uncle George didn't know but I'd expected more from him. Moreover, it was difficult to grasp what death was. It was never anything real—just a word. Mother had been ill for three years, yet she kept surviving, moving from one kind of pain to another. I had the impression that her pain would continue but in different forms. She'd always been able to scream at me, or at least communicate on a fierce, instinctive level, no matter how sick she was. Now, I began to get the impression that even this was about to end.

Uncle George was caught in the middle, translating the wishes of all of Mother's friends and relatives. A doomed job for a man whose biggest fault was that he was never able to make his own decisions. It was doubly unfortunate that he would start our relationship by stuttering now.

It was decreed that Mother was too ill to take care of me, and that Uncle George was too busy and unsure to do anything right away. So I was to be sent to camp. In retrospect, although it wasn't a bad decision, it certainly wasn't a sensitive way to handle a mother's impending death. I didn't realize it then, but they were going to shuttle me back and forth like a poisoned hot potato. It was the beginning of the years when institutions would care for me instead of people. Being sent to camp didn't bother me then because I thought I'd see my mother again. But I never did.

I'd spent the previous summer at Camp Adirondack and knew there would be lots of schoolmates there. I looked forward to that even though I was a loner and unpopular. They always called me Fatty Flagg or Fat Flagg. As a child I didn't have a best friend and teachers always sent home poor reports in the "works and plays well with others" department. But don't feel too sorry for me; I was an unpleasant little wisenheimer and gave a lot of pain to anyone I didn't like.

Uncle George told me that my things were being packed and would be waiting at the station in the morning. I would stay in Louis' empty apartment that night instead of going home. Then we were off to Abercrombie's to outfit me for camp. This was fun, and was the start of a lifetime string of spending sprees. After all, it could be argued, it was no time to deny this poor little kid anything. And I knew it.

So, Uncle George purchased just about everything I wanted as long as I said it was for camp. I knew I was rich and there were so many things Mother had never allowed me to have. I especially enjoyed getting my own bow and arrows. Archery was one camp sport in which I excelled, and with this new bow I'd be better than ever. When we got to Uncle George's apartment, I discovered that in the confusion I'd left my bow in the cab. I had a tantrum and blamed Uncle George. I was more upset about losing that bow than by any fear that my mother would die. Even today, it still irritates me that I lost that bow.

As a twelve-year-old I wanted freedom more than anything else. Mother had been overly restrictive, supervising my every move. Any chance I got to be alone was pure joy. That evening I was locked into Louis' apartment, supposedly to rest for the morrow's journey, but I saw it as my opportunity to guzzle unlimited Coke and watch as much television as I wanted. No one would reprimand me. No one would watch me or check on me, so I stayed up all night.

A favorite pastime then was to investigate other people's personal property. Since Louis' bathroom was papered with jokes cut from dirty magazines, I reasoned that there had to be a mother lode somewhere. I searched the entire bedroom, replacing every piece of clothing and underwear so that nothing looked suspicious, until I finally found the magazines in a bottom drawer. Wow! Magazines that showed nudist colonies!

But something was wrong. These magazines showed nude boys reclining on rocks, and nude men with very blond hair and strangely misshapen faces lying on the beach. I remembered how excited I'd become when Uncle Grover let me look at *Playboy*, but this stuff of Louis' was so strange. I paged through the magazines looking for breasts, but there were mostly crotch and ass shots of men. Mother had told me these kinds of guys existed, but it was hard to believe that anyone would get excited over these reclining blondies. Thank *God* there were some women, albeit pregnant, in the nude beach scenes.

I stayed awake all night looking at the nudist magazines, drinking Coke, and watching the *Chartreuse Caboose* on TV. I might have dozed on Louis' couch, but I didn't want to sleep in his bed.

In the morning I was taken to Grand Central and boarded the train for Glens Falls, New York. Uncle George gave the porter a tip and instructions to look after me. Later, the porter served warm milk and pound cake as I sat in the club car. It was the same comforting snack that Mother used to allow me to have on the train to Philadelphia. It made me feel innocent after my night of debauchery and I fell asleep with pound cake crumbs on my shirt. I didn't wake till the porter shook me.

There was no platform where the train stopped in Glens Falls and, since I never traveled lightly, I disembarked with some difficulty. I was as encumbered with possessions as I could have been. Maybe they took the place of the other things I didn't have. I often traveled with a record player, all my records, a radio, and a portable TV: all the things I thought essential to survival in the woods.

Colonel Warwick, the owner and director of the camp and the head of the Knickerbocker Greys, seemed happy to see me. He put out his hand as usual and I could tell that he knew about Mother because he was especially kind to me. Whenever he shook hands he'd always say, "Shake the hand that shook the hand," and the recipient would smile. I always wondered who the other hand had belonged to. It seemed like it should have been some President, maybe Ike. I never asked the Colonel about it but thought it was a good question.

After we did some errands in town we arrived at the dirt road with the inconspicuous sign, "Camp Adirondack." The road climbed and twisted through a hardwood forest and then broke into a clearing edged by a swamp. I never understood how all those mosquitoes knew exactly how to fly all the way to my cabin and attack me. Then we climbed higher into a pine woodland and to the camp itself. On the left were the Indian Meeting Grounds, where the whole camp, in their handmade Indian regalia, would gather every Saturday night. The beginning of each season was very moving. All campers would line the lake shore at twilight, chanting, "Hey Um Da," over and over to the beat of a drum. Then, out on the middle of the lake would appear a canoe with a chief in headdress and two braves. The brave in the bow held a torch that reflected onto the still water. It was corny but the camp was very big on what were then called "Indian" rituals, and we were all true believers.

The Colonel's house was at the bottom of the hill, overlooking Lake George. His office was there as well as the living quarters he shared with his wife, daughter and "She," the inevitable gray toy poodle. Mrs. Warrick's room was incongruous in that rough and woodsy setting. Right out of a Park Avenue apartment, it included an animal fur bedspread and that soft, sexy, I'm Taken-Care-Of look. The Colonel himself was a very genuine man who felt strongly about children. He let me out at the bottom of the hill, saying, "You're in Senior Camp this year, Tom."

I thought that was strange and connected to Mother's illness, because the previous year I'd only been in Junior Camp. Somehow, I'd skipped Intermediate altogether. Perhaps that was the only space left on such short notice or perhaps the Colonel wanted to improve my self-esteem by making me seem older than I was. As it turned out, it caused me nothing but trouble with my cabin mates.

The first days were awful. Two tough Irish types, appropriately named Stone and McGrath, were the kings of my cabin. They were two years older than me and awfully good at inducing fear. I was intimidated, unhappy, and under their thumbs. I probably deserved the treatment I got, but I hated being tormented and teased. Since I was the outsider and continual scapegoat, I found out that Stone and McGrath's taunts hurt. It didn't make me a more compassionate boy, though, it merely honed my already well-developed talent for tormenting others.

There were many sports and activities at camp, and I enjoyed myself, despite being rotten at most. I detested sailing and would only rarely swim, but the worst was baseball with all that waiting around in right field. It made me think that Mother was dead.

I loved every aspect of wrestling, though. The old canvas mat was stored under a lean-to next to the wrestling platform. Each day when we unrolled that mat it was filled with ants the size of raisins with pincers as big as tweezers. Once we got rid of the ants we worked on easy, basic moves. My back, knees, and shoulders were always covered with mat burns, but I didn't care. I was proud of them. The coach was usually some prep school hopeful and hardly expert, but as long as I was wrestling, it didn't matter.

Mail came every day after lunch. After a week went by with no mail for me and no news, I relaxed and settled into the camp routine. Mother and her illness faded to the back of my mind.

At the end of each day the bugle would call all campers to assemble. One night as the flag was lowered and we were dismissed to dinner, I noticed the Colonel was absent. This was strange because he had never missed the flag-lowering ceremony. He was also absent at Mess Hall. A senior counselor said grace and the night's gorging began. There was the buzz of talk, slap of fly swatters, and dinner was brought to each table. Before we were finished, song sheets were handed out. These had the words to the popular tunes that we'd sing after dinner. The song sheet distributor said something to our counselor and he quickly excused himself. When he returned, he said to me, "The Colonel wants to see you at his house."

"Now?"

"Yes, I think you should go now."

Oh, I thought, *Mother may really be ill*. Then it hit me.

Maybe Mother had died.

My first reaction was not sadness or fear; I was thrilled. I was *free*. I was rich. Now I could have everything I wanted.

Mother and I didn't get along. Fighting was the rule. Mother always did as she thought best, but her decisions were seldom pleasant. She was not warm or demonstrative. Had I been older, I would no doubt have developed an ulcer from her yelling. She was a difficult woman and the continuous stream of maids and nurses that we had didn't help any, either. My childhood had not been a carefree, happy time. But now things would be better. I would start to have fun.

I walked toward the Colonel's house, thinking that I was free, that I would have everything I'd always wanted. Behind me the boys' voices sang a Beatles song. The melody floated across the baseball diamond and followed me to the Colonel's house.

The Colonel walked me past his leather chair, past his bookshelves with big volumes on World War II, past his military engravings, and onto his screened porch. We were not good friends, but Mother had respect for what the Colonel did. He provided a male figure for boys like me who didn't have their own homegrown variety, and Mother approved of him. Mainly because of Mother's opinion, I liked and respected this man as he sat me down in a rattan rocker to say, "Tommy your Mother is dead."

There was a long pause. We sat there on that screened porch, looking through the pine branches onto the lake. The campers were singing, and the lightning bugs signaled to each other. In the distance someone laughed and banged a paddle on the hull of a metal canoe. And I kept thinking, *I'm free. I'm free.* There were no tears for Mother.

The Colonel didn't say anything, but I knew he expected some response.

I often think that things would be all right for me now if I could somehow just be twelve years old again and go back to the Colonel's screened-in porch, back to that rattan rocker beside Lake George, and cry as the Colonel expected me to.

II

In the morning I was driven to the airport and a Mohawk Airliner flew me to La Guardia. Uncle George was supposed to meet me, but I was surprised to see Uncle Grover there, too. He'd just returned from a tour of duty in Vietnam. I found out later that he'd been handed the message that Mother died as soon as he reached the States. It was almost as if she had chosen to die knowing that Grover would be coming home.

He stood there in his officer's uniform, his face masked with the fatigue of endless flying. It sounds terribly sappy, but I wondered if he had passed Mother on her way up to Heaven. Grover had always done things for Mother that no one else did. He helped her through recovery after recovery, and was always there when she needed him. Years later he told me that Mother had once asked him if it would be all right if she said they were engaged, in case anyone asked. They had been lovers, but more than that, they were friends.

I made a big fuss over Uncle Grover and I'm sure that it rankled Uncle George.

When we arrived at the apartment, I realized with a thrill that everything there was now *mine:* all the paintings, the furniture, Mother's jewelry. Everything except the mink coat she would be buried in. The servants were in tears—but only crocodile tears. As they wept, they filled their pockets with leftover Chanel No. 5 and our best silver. Mrs. Pitz was honest, but honesty was only relevant to clothing that was several sizes too small.

I was dressed and sent to the Westbury Hotel where the whole Flagg contingent was staying: Grizzy, Grandmother, and all. It was really the Addams family, only a little better dressed.

Grandmother was there in her wheelchair, and lots of cousins milled about. They snatched me away from Uncle George. The Flaggs were upset because none of them had been chosen as guardian. Grizzy was especially annoyed. He never forgave Mother or me for telling him this final time where to go and exactly how to get there. But he got even.

When I returned to the apartment a few days later, I found that the day after the funeral he had taken Mother's only Holbein. He sold it and I'm still trying to get it back. It's queer, but Grizzy actually thought that he was a normal, well-adjusted fellow.

Grandmother was brokenhearted, and to make things worse she could only communicate with her eyes. She had now outlived her husband and her eldest son, David, as well as Dorothy Mary, and she'd done a lot of that as a stroke victim in a wheelchair. She took my hand and looked hard into my eyes. I wonder what she saw there because she tried to speak, but ended up weeping. All that came out of her mouth were strangled vowels.

Later we went down to the Polo Bar for lunch. As you can imagine, it wasn't a pleasant meal and I've hated that place ever since. The cheerful green-and-white latticework decor was meant to be fun. Instead, I found it oppressive.

After lunch we went back upstairs to prepare for the service at St. James. Everyone was crammed into a two-room suite, trying to be calm, when out of the back room came Aunt Kay, supposedly Mother's best girlfriend. The room got quiet when she said to me, "Your Father is on the phone, Tommy. Come and speak to him."

Well, that was the last straw. Here was this stupid woman telling me that the man I was brought up to hate wanted to talk to me on the day of my mother's funeral. I let her have it. "What the hell do you think you're doing? Here's a guy who's never sent me a penny postcard on my birthday and now you've gone and gotten him on the phone the day of my mother's funeral. Real good, Aunt Kay. Real good."

"Stop being the rude little bastard that you are," Grizzy snapped.

But Aunt Kay had already left the room. For once she had no rebuttal. She always had her nose in it. She and Mother had been through a lot together, but she was never genuine with me. She never offered me any special sympathy, never tried to make sure I knew she cared about me. It wasn't until I was a grown man that "Uncle John," Mother's financial advisor, told me the truth about Aunt Kay. She had made the mistake of asking him exactly what Mother's assets were. That was her second unforgivable blunder. The first was calling my father.

We walked the three blocks to St. James, Uncle Grover on one side of me and Uncle George on the other. Most of the mourners had gathered by the time we arrived. We were ushered into the front pew where all I could see was the closed casket on the altar. I kept saying to myself, *That's Mother in there. That's Mother in there.* I tried to imagine her lying there in her black mink coat with the collar turned up. She'd always wanted to be buried in that mink so that she wouldn't be cold when she went under. She was terrified of the cold, of the dark, and of dying. The terrible thing that I came to find out was that she had been all alone when she died.

Still, I really wasn't upset at all; I just sat there wondering why I had to be there.

Uncle Grover put his arm around me and said, "Cry. Let it out. Go ahead." I tried to be sad, tried to cry, but I simply did not know how, even with encouragement or permission. I did manage to produce a few tears for Uncle Grover's sake. I did it by thinking of how Mother had gotten rid of my dog Cupcake without asking me. The tears seemed to please Uncle Grover.

The funeral service was dramatic and personal, with the minister pointing frequently at the freshly made orphan. I felt unique and very important.

As the service ended, I was the first to leave. Just as Mother would have wanted, I stationed myself at the church door and thanked all the guests for coming. Mother's funeral may well have been one of the big social events of that death season. But there was none of the usual cocktail party banter. All those people were quiet and sad as they paid their respects to the family and to the little boy in the shadowed arch of the church door. Flanked by Grover in his uniform and Uncle George in his best dark suit, I shook hands and bowed and said, "Thank you for coming," to each of the over 300 people that filed by. Mother's life was passing in front of me, person by person.

III

When I think about my childhood, I realize that happiness, joy, and magic were at a premium. But looking back upon it, I was by no means an unhappy child. As Mother became increasingly ill, there was underlying stress. Or, in those days, the word *neurotic* would have been used to describe Mother's mental health. I knew that I was to be kept out of the fray, but inevitably I became angry as I became the direct object of Mother's inconsolable anger and resentment. It became natural.

As a young child, I was in awe of Mother. I remember being in the first grade at the Browning School for Boys. It was an exciting time to be six years old in New York City in the '60s. I remember sitting quietly with my classmates on the second floor, waiting eagerly to be dismissed at the end of the school day, hands folded atop my desk. I knew Mother was waiting for me half a floor below, sitting on the ornate Jacobean wooden bench. Her gold charm bracelets, four on each wrist, made a music of their own each time she moved. Not only could I hear her, I could smell her Chanel perfume as it wafted up the staircase into my first-grade classroom. I knew she was waiting for me. I couldn't reach her quickly enough as I eagerly bounded down the staircase. I understood why Mother always insisted that I not slouch when I saw her waiting, sitting ram-rod straight, all six feet of her. Seeing Mother impeccably dressed as always, I was damned proud to be her son, something other little boys most likely could not comprehend. Her regal presence was a force to be reckoned with, even by glamorous New York City standards.

Mother showed up again at the school for my first Christmas pageant. There she was towering over me in her mink stole and matching mink hat. Mother had come to see her child, me, in the pageant. Mother was *there*. She was present, not just some nanny or hired help. I remember how exceptional I felt. I believed we were happy at that point, each of us in our own different ways.

But another Christmas performance was not so grand. This one was homemade. It was after Mother had been diagnosed with cancer. She had already begun cobalt treatments "to get well." I don't believe Mother understood at that point that she was terminal. This was before the doctors began the first of the slow dissection of tortuous inhumane treatments, literally whittling away at Mother. I remember being in our living room, just the two of us. The room was lit only by the silver Christmas tree turning in its stand, lights twinkling in time to "Jingle Bells." I performed my reading of *The Night Before Christmas* to cheer up Mother. I lined up all the stuffed animals as part of the show while Mother sat drinking her Seagram Seven and ginger ale. When I ended my performance, Mother could no longer contain herself and she broke down. Her eyes were like two poached eggs.

Mother rarely, if ever, broke down, at least that I saw. There were no hugs, no kisses, and no overt panic from her. She willed strength into me as best she could. Do as I do—stand up straight, look straight ahead, look into the future, the unknown. She had a will of steel and imparted that in me. Pure will. Strength.

That same winter Mother took me to see Angela Lansbury in *Mame*. The nature of Mame's relationship with Patrick Dennis mirrored Mother and me, little Tommy. Again, Mother's eyes were like two poached eggs. It was the show of the year, a grand magical production, but I remember something more remarkable from that night on our walk home from the theater. As devastated as Mother may have been, the evening was capped off under a streetlight at 66th and Madison as the snow fell. I spontaneously broke into a catchy song from the musical. There, Mother lit up. She glowed. She laughed. She threw her head back and laughed some more. I was still of an age when I could discern one snowflake from another. I examined each crystalline structure. Mother was enraptured with joy with her own Patrick Dennis. It was a miracle for us *both* to have been so jubilant that night.

Dorothy Mary (left) with Thomas and the poodles.

27

After the funeral I moved in with Uncle George, my newly appointed guardian. It was a hot summer in New York and there wasn't anything for me to do. Mother's friends with country houses and all my relatives seemed to evaporate after her death. If they thought of me, I never knew it. It is incredible that none of those friends ever called to see if I were all right. Perhaps they thought it was enough to come to the funeral. I felt sorry for myself and gleefully took it out on Uncle George and his household.

I never fit in there. He was a lifetime bachelor, accustomed to his solitude, and I was accustomed to a lot of attention as well as always getting my own way. I'd always been polite to him when Mother was alive, so I'm sure he never expected that having me around would be as taxing as it turned out to be.

I got into a lot of trouble that summer. There wasn't much excitement around the apartment, so I generated some by turning on fire alarms. Uncle George must have suspected me, but he chose to ignore it. Mother would have yelled right away. Perhaps it was the incident with Delilah that triggered his decision to send me away.

Delilah was Uncle George's elderly maid and cook. She was Haitian, and always reminded me of a wrinkled spider. I had absorbed Mother's prejudice—her opinions were my opinions at that age—and didn't want Delilah touching my food. I refused to eat her cooking. I didn't want her snooping through my things and never let her in my room, not even to clean it. Then I remembered the trick that I'd used to get rid of one of Mother's servants whom I didn't like. Since it had worked with Mother, I reasoned that it was foolproof.

Whenever Delilah went home after a day's work, I would run to the elevator and scream obscenities at her down the shaft. This went on for about a week until the old snitch complained to Uncle George. I knew she'd do that sooner or later and wasn't at

The Dressing Drink

all afraid of punishment. I'd denied doing the same thing to Mother's maid and Mother had fired her immediately. When Uncle George called me into his study and confronted me with Delilah's charges, I stoutly denied everything. But Uncle George didn't fire her. Instead, he sent me to my room.

A week later he deposited me and my nine pieces of Vuitton luggage at The Fay School in Southboro, Massachusetts, the ordained repository for boys of a certain circumstance.

Fay would be my home for the next two years. Oh, I would be invited to spend Christmas and Easter vacations with either Uncle George or Uncle Grover. I looked forward to those times and behaved myself. But I knew there was no place for me with either man. I spent summer vacations at wrestling camps, determined to become the best middleweight in the nation.

I suppose I was lonely and scared at Fay, but that wasn't my focus. One thing was sure… I was pleased to be independent. Just as Mother would have wished, I began to learn to take care of myself.

Fay was full of fussy rules and punishments. There were specific times for everything. Bells rang to wake us up, to send us to chapel and meals, to begin and end classes, to terminate study hall and sports. There was almost no free time. When classes were over for the day we were herded into a huge study hall and made to do our homework at rows of desks—bolted to the floor. I always hated those unmovable desks.

I'd arrived at the school as a sixth grader and was never really accepted by the other boys in my class. I made few friends and was alone most of the time. The teachers knew I was without family or friends and some tried to be kind to me, but it was cold comfort. Their names or faces never stuck. The only teachers I really remember were those who terrified me.

There was Mr. Moran, who of course we called Moron. His favorite trick was to snap inattentive students to attention by zinging them with flying bits of chalk. Fay was an ingrown little community. I'm sure the teachers were ill-paid and overworked, and men who loved boys could flourish there in safety. Mr. Fogarty was one such creature. His high voice, rouged cheeks and buffed nails made the already-small French classroom even more claustrophobic. I had spoken French fluently for years and was always thankful that Fogarty never thought it necessary for me to receive *special help* after class.

The school was unflinching in its dress code, which demanded that a jacket and tie be worn at all school functions except sports. I hadn't realized how passé my wardrobe was. So I wrote to Stephan, Mother's designer in New York, and begged him to send me new clothing. I wanted something hip and cool for the school dance. If I couldn't have friends, at least I could have a wonderful wardrobe. And Stephan, bless his little homosexual heart, did not disappoint me. He sent up boxes of bellbottoms, Day-Glo ties, loud shirts and double-breasted blazers that were the height of fashion and more. The headmaster was livid when he saw my mod display, but I was within the dress code and he couldn't do anything about it.

Thomas K. Flagg, Knickerbocker Greys.

Those clothes were the not-so-humble start of my rebellion. I can see now that Fay's chief effect on me was to transform the twelve-year-old pudgy brat into the fourteen-year-old, militant, pot-smoking, acid-dropping, self-proclaimed Black Panther. When I entered the school, I carried the legacy of Mother's conservative political views. For a child who'd been made an educated world traveler, I was isolated and without the human interaction that allowed me to develop my own thoughts and morals. After two years at Fay and all its rules, my politics had swung from a second-hand, unopposed version of Mother's to a position a little to the left of Malcolm X. From the safety of the back row of my Current Events class, I agitated for social change. I became the class bleeding heart, arguing for the oppressed. I identified with the black people burning and looting the ghettos, with the Puerto Ricans starving in Spanish Harlem, with the militant American Indians, with the Mexican itinerant workers on strike against the lettuce growers. In my flawed judgment, we were all brothers. I guess we did have a common bond: oppression. But theirs was real, while mine was only temporary. As I embraced

The Dressing Drink

their rhetoric, I overlooked the fact that I had no more in common with them than I did with Mother's staff. I would eventually learn this lesson but as an eighth grader I was sullen, idealistic, voluble, cynical, and ready to fight the world. You've known a thousand kids like me. It makes me sick to think about it now.

When graduation came, I agonized over my next move. Where should I go to secondary school? Uncle George wanted me to attend a conservative school—but he had chosen Fay and I was leery of a four-year replay. My grades weren't good enough to get into Lawrenceville, Groton, or St. Mark's, but I had been accepted by The Hill and The Gunnery.

I didn't want to go to school in Pottstown, Pennsylvania. Mother had hated that town because the family factory was the main industry there and the Flaggs practically owned it. So, I rejected The Hill and its town of toadies. The Gunnery appealed to me because it was supposed to be a very, very liberal place, and without a dress code. It sounded relaxed and right for me. I accepted The Gunnery's offer, and even though their wrestling team was only third-rate, I sent away for a blazer with the school's crest on the pocket.

The last day of classes at Fay was over and I had just returned to the room I shared with Charles Durning, a boy from Charleston. The nicest thing about Charles was the continuous supply of chocolate pecan fudge that one of his maids sent north. He kept it in his bureau drawer and whenever he was out of the room, I would snitch some. He would probably have given me the whole box if I'd asked but I didn't want to ask. I helped myself to a big piece of fudge and threw my sweat clothes down onto my bunk. There was to be an eighth-grade dance with girls imported from Dana Hall that evening. I was gobbling Charles' fudge and thinking about girls when I saw the letter on my bed.

Mail was a rare treat and I wondered who had written to me. It was probably a graduation card from Uncle Grover or Aunt Kay. Then I saw the name in the corner of the envelope and sat down in shock.

It was from Jack Goode, my father.

It was as if I had been given a present, something precious that had belonged to me a long time ago that I'd lost. A part of me wanted to run out the door and shout to the other boys that I had a father, too. But then I heard Mother's hard-edged voice ringing clearly: "That son of a bitch never sent you a penny postcard on your birthday."

Why had it taken him so long to find me? Was he really as dangerous and crazy as Mother said? She'd always been afraid that he'd kidnap me. The maids would report to her that he would sometimes loiter across the street from Browning, trying to get a glimpse of me after school. I'd never seen him, but I'd spent a lot of mental effort protecting Mother from this madman. Now he had written to me.

I opened the letter. It was on Lambs Club stationery, an exclusive club for actors and showbusiness elites, and didn't sound like something a mental patient would write.

It told that he was married again and was in *Hello, Dolly!* on Broadway. He hoped very much to hear from me soon and included addresses and phone numbers. It was signed, "Your father, Jack Goode."

I sat on the edge of my bunk. The floor around my feet was littered with dirty clothes, discarded ties, half-filled Pepsi cans and bubble gum wrappers. Charles Durning's fudge was forgotten on the Shetland blanket beside me.

I didn't know what to do. I reread the letter and then called Uncle Grover who was stationed in Washington.

I had sort of forgotten about Father. Now that he'd reappeared in my life, I wanted to know whether Uncle Grover thought it would be a mistake to see him. We decided that the best thing would be for me to meet him. I couldn't talk to Grover long because yet another bell rang, so I dressed by reflex and hurried down to dinner. I had fished my jockstrap from beneath a mound of dirty underwear. It was of little use to me on the playing field but was invaluable at dances. The dance and graduation the next day passed in a blur.

I was going to meet my father.

II

Mother had taught me that there was safety in numbers, so I asked my second cousin Jane to go with me to meet my father. I figured he was probably harmless, but another person would provide additional protection. We taxied to the St. James Theatre and stood there on the street, waiting for him. Jane looked spectacular in a black evening dress studded with rhinestones. She'd also worn her mother's diamond necklace. I was in my best double-breasted blue blazer and bellbottoms. Jane wasn't much taller than me, but she wore heels that made me look short. I stood as straight as I could, wished I were taller, and braced myself. He would appear at any moment.

Jane kept a lookout in one direction as I watched in the other, but we stood there for fifteen minutes before he made his entrance. I spotted him first. He didn't appear at the corner of the block as I had expected, but instead stepped out from behind a strolling couple.

I had never seen my father before but recognized him immediately. He wore a pink seersucker jacket and golf hat. I could tell from his walk that he had seen us. He didn't speed up or slow down, but his manner subtly changed. He knew I was watching him. I realized that he must be at least as afraid to meet me as I was to meet him, and that made me feel better. And then there he was right in front of us, smiling and shaking hands. I felt comfortable but was glad I had brought Jane along. He hadn't expected her, and it gave me a chance to observe him.

As I stood there and watched him talking to Jane, he seemed to grow and exude around us, like a genie escaping from a bottle, projecting his personality, working his new audience. He was very much in charge and was cool, although overtly happy. I don't remember what we said, but I can still see his bald head and mustached face smiling down at me. I kept saying to myself, *This is my father,* my *father.* Other than to shake hands, he didn't touch me; but then, he didn't have to. Just being there was enough.

He invited us to his dressing room and we followed him through the winding tunnels and corridors backstage at the St. James. We ascended the spiral metal stairs that led to his dressing room. On the way up I could tell that the cast and crew of the show knew that he was meeting me for the first time. Father introduced me to everyone.

This was a big deal for him.

Cassie, his seventh and youngest wife, greeted us at the dressing room. She was only nineteen, a blonde chorus girl who worshipped Father. Cassie, from Australia, had met Father there when he played Cap'n Andy in *Show Boat.* She was spectacular in her hoop earrings and mini skirt. The four of us—Father, Cassie, cousin Jane, and I—chatted in Father's crammed-full tiny dressing room. A delivery boy knocked and handed Cassie a fifty-pound Hershey's kiss. The president of Hershey's, a golfing partner of Father's, had heard that he was meeting his son for the first time.

Was there anyone that night who didn't know that Jack Goode was meeting his son for the first time?

The dressing room got even more crowded once Father's very effete dresser entered and was barely introduced. Father must have considered him fair game because he worked over the poor fellow for at least ten minutes. I was embarrassed. Father's humor was quick, sarcastic, and vicious, but the dresser seemed oblivious to it. The blithe energy then shifted to serious business—the donning of his costume and the application of Father's makeup for the first act.

Before our very eyes, Father transformed into Horace P. Vandergelder—head-to-toe purple silk, from his top hat to his trousers. A scene stealer if there ever was one. Even in his sixties Father was a spectacular dancer, magic maker, Mr. Rubber Face. He was ready to take his gruff character on a rollercoaster of audience delight. A seasoned professional, he undertook all the intricacies of comic arts, mugging and gagging his way through the show, which he carried.

Once Father was fully costumed, the man slipped from the room. He must have been glad to go. I now wonder how many other sets of ten minutes there had been for that man before the one I witnessed. Jane and I watched in silence while this preparation transpired. We then said goodbye and found our orchestra seats.

It was a wonderful show. Father filled the entire stage and he danced spectacularly. I especially remember some high kicks he did over chairs. In another nice routine, he spun round and round across the stage while bandying a broom overhead. Chorus boys darting in front of him became his props. He did a lot of shaking of fists and growling. It was marvelous to hear him make the audience laugh. Both he and Ethel Merman got ovations that night, deafening cheers and whistles. I wondered if he were always this good, or if he were trying especially hard for me.

Shortly after I met my Father, we experienced an unsettling (but after-the-fact, poignant) experience while driving to New York City from his New Jersey farm in his MG TD canvas top during a storm. The car was not built for treacherous weather, but Father had to get to the theater for the Sunday matinee of *Hello Dolly!* And, as everyone knows, the show must go on. We were driving at sixty miles per hour during a turbulent thunderstorm on the New Jersey Turnpike when a stray dog crossed the highway. Father slammed on the brakes, avoided the dog, and the MG spun out of control. Only God knows what could have happened. We didn't hit the guard rail or other cars, and we were back on our merry way to Broadway. Father's comment was telling. "My God, you and I just met, and it was almost over." He was right; it was a petrifying incident. But Father was far more astute, realizing we really should have both died then and there.

Unbeknownst to Father and me, he had only six months to live.

During the various times I saw him perform, one particular matinee really stood out in my memory. Into the second act, Merman had a customized scene, "a special," made just for her in which she was seated downstage at the ice cream parlor table, enjoying an intimate exchange with the audience. But this particular performance took an ugly turn. As she kibbitzed and laughed with the audience, a man stood and began calling her every name in the book, most notably, a communist bitch. Yep, right in the middle of the monologue. It was not a joke. And the only thing separating her from that raving man was the pit of musicians. America, being what it was in the 1960s, another audience member suggested that the heckler sit his fat ass down or that someone throw him out of there.

As tension mounted, out of the wings came Father. He took stage left and let out, "Stop the show!" He came down the lip of the stage, descended the abbreviated steps to the audience, worked his way past patrons, spun the fat ass around, grabbed him by both the collar and belt, pulled him out of his row, and ran him up the aisle, building steam as he ran. After giving this guy the bum's rush, Father deposited him with the ushers who were waiting on the red carpet to escort the jerk out. Father calmly turned around, headed back toward the stage, looked out to the audience, and called out, "Start the show." The audience went crazy with gratitude and enthusiasm as Father exited, and the show went on. Merman continued her monologue without missing a beat.

But not all was amiable between Father and "La Merman," as she was hailed. The hatred between them mounted throughout their time together, finally culminating in a remarkably unprofessional—but hilarious—event. One evening, as Merman began her special solo at the ice cream table, she garnered the usual laughs, but then the laughter increased exponentially, uproariously, beyond anything she had experienced. The timing was off—the laughs were coming at the wrong points—an irregular interlude of laughs. Merman then realized that it was Father in his purple, first-act costume, standing upstage, twirling a baton, and inducing audience convulsions as only he could. Once Merman caught on, she played along, but as soon as she was off stage, Merman did everything she could to have Father fired. Producer David Merrick would have none of it. Father was brought up on equity charges. This, Father and Merman's mutual hatred, the stress of keeping his young wife satisfied, and the prospect of becoming a new father—yes, Cassie was expecting—eventually killed Father. He was found unresponsive from a bleeding ulcer in his bathtub on Christmas Eve.

It was the first show Father ever missed in his career.

Jack Goode and Ethel Merman on Broadway.

28

If I must be honest, I have to tell you—you've been a diversion. Although I've seen them a thousand times I've enjoyed trotting out the various performers in my Side Show and watching them go through their paces. But the curtain is about to rise, and although Mother would do nip-ups in her grave if she heard me speaking so rudely to guests, I can't help wishing that you'd go away. Soon. All this talk has made me tired.

I've saved one tableau for last. I usually don't show it to people because it scares me. It's about the last of the old Flaggs. I'll try to make the story as brief as possible and then you really must be on your way.

Grandmother lived well into her eighties. She was one of those anomalous dowagers who seem to go on forever, growing stronger instead of weaker as the years passed. The paralysis retreated to her left side and she regained most of her wits. On good days she could drink a martini with her right hand, lifting the glass with a concerted effort. Only the clinking ice cubes betrayed how her hand shook. Of course, she was too feeble to walk, but she could speak after a fashion, out of the right side of her mouth. If you listened very carefully you could understand her. If she got excited or upset, however, she couldn't even bring a Kleenex to her mouth, and she was reduced to pointing and unintelligible grunts. I could never stand to hear her struggle to speak, It was too painful. Too embarrassing.

And so, in the center ring, our last act—Grandmother and Grizzy in their Leap to Death.

Grandmother Flagg holding Thomas on her lap.

29

When she knew she was no longer an embarrassment to herself, Mrs. Flagg re-entered the social whirl and once again became a power in Philadelphia society. Only now, it wasn't her children, estate, or volunteer efforts that earned her a reputation—it was her money. She adopted the Philadelphia Orchestra as her pet charity and Mrs. Flagg and her rattan wheelchair became a familiar sight to concertgoers. She never missed a performance and made sure that her nurses, Parker and Stevens, dressed her immaculately. She always insisted on her tiara, ropes of pearls, and the oversize emerald and diamond rings that would have been more suitable for a Maharaja. This plethora of jewelry had been out of fashion for years but Mrs. Flagg couldn't have cared less. To her, a concert meant formal dress, and formal dress meant jewelry.

She always sat up front surrounded by her guests. Parker and Stevens trailed behind in their starched white uniforms and blue capes, keeping watchful eyes on their charge. In spite of all her infirmities, Mrs. Flagg wasn't ready to let go of Philadelphia yet. She'd become something of an institution there and continued to cultivate the younger generations. She didn't know many of the younger set intimately, and often confused them with their fathers, or in some cases, grandfathers. But still, dinner parties for forty at her Barclay Apartments in Rittenhouse Square were not unusual, and it seemed that she would just go on forever. Everyone commented on her fortitude.

Perhaps that's what set Grizzy in motion.

The $10,000 inheritance from his Father's will had been spent long ago, and Grizzy needed cash, mainly because of Dorothy Mary. Before she died, she had found out that he was planning to divorce his wife of twenty years and marry a younger woman. Dorothy didn't like his wife but thought this plan was monstrously cruel, even for Grizzy. She hired the shrewdest law firm in Philadelphia to see to it that Libby got

The Dressing Drink

everything the law would allow. The divorce left Grizzy financially crippled, and Dorothy Mary felt that her money had been well spent.

As children, Grizzy and Dorothy Mary had been competitive, and after his divorce they seemed to be trying to out-hate one another. Animosity, recriminations, slander—anything was fair. Stab, twist the knife and rip the blade slowly upward, were their versions of polite cocktail chatter. Grizzy started rumors that Dorothy Mary had an illegitimate, "retarded" daughter in New York City. Dorothy Mary discreetly announced to the entire Main Line that Grizzy beat his wife. She knew that she'd scored a decisive victory in their private little war when she learned that Grizzy was so broke that he was selling off the furnishings of Tiptonbrook. *Serves the bastard right*, she thought. She relished the idea of his living in an empty house.

(Left to Right) Grizzy, Great Grandfather and Mrs. Flagg,
Dorothy King Flagg, David Flagg, Stanley Griswold Flagg.

About a year after Dorothy Mary died, Grizzy realized that he had been ignoring an unexplored treasure that belonged to him. His financial problems would be over if he could get hold of just a few of the things in Mamma's house that were really his. After all, he was the only heir, and if Mamma realized how much he needed the money, she would surely have given it to him. She was so sick and he didn't want to bother her so he decided to help himself to just a few things from her house in Ardmore.

One night while she was at The Barclay he went to Ardmore and helped himself to anything of value that he could carry. He stole the Holbein paintings, crystal, silver, and small antiques. His Mercedes was *crammed* with plunder. Mamma would be at the apartments until summer. Even when she returned, she probably wouldn't miss the things. She had so much.

But Grizzy had underestimated his mother. When she returned to Ardmore she immediately noted everything that was missing. The police told her that it looked like an inside job. At first, she suspected the servants. Since Rodgers had retired, the staff was so unreliable. But over the ensuing months it became evident to her that Grizzy was the culprit. He dropped sly hints, almost daring her to do something about it. Though Mrs. Flagg was furious, she felt helpless. Whenever she tried to speak about it she lost control of her voice and her words wouldn't come out right. By the time Parker and Stevens, those two idiots, finally understood what she was trying to tell them, she was exhausted with the effort. If only she could write down what she wanted to say, but that was also impossible. But, even if she could communicate immediately with Parker and Stevens, what could they do? Grizzy was uncontrollable when he was drunk—and he was nearly always drunk. There was no telling what he would do next.

Mrs. Flagg decided to cut Grizzy off. She had everything of value moved to Barclay Apartments and closed the house in Ardmore. She would never see Grizzy again.

Grizzy went from bad to worse. He'd tried to marry again but that had been a fiasco. This time he chose a woman who had what he called Real Money. However, when she learned about his drinking and discovered his temper she canned him.

Now Grizzy was desperate for money again and it occurred to him that, even though Denbigh had been out of the family for years, certain things there still belonged to him. The Episcopal Diocese had turned it into a private school.

One day Grizzy arrived there with a pickup truck full of workmen and ordered them to dig up the rhododendron bushes that lined the drive. The headmaster of the school appeared, and after he lost a shouting and shoving match with Grizzy, he called the State Police. They escorted Grizzy home and warned him to stay away from the school—but Grizzy meant to have those rhododendron bushes. When the school was closed for spring vacation he went back and dug up sixty of them by moonlight. He sold them to a landscaper. That kept him afloat for a few months. When Grizzy was sober he was truculent; when he was drunk he could be dangerous.

II
Barclay Apartments
Philadelphia, Pennsylvania

The Dressing Drink

Grizzy sat at the steering wheel of his Mercedes watching the lights in his mother's apartment on Rittenhouse Square. She'd had a big party that evening for all her swell new friends. She hadn't invited him but he'd decided to join her party anyway. He wanted to pay her a special visit.

The guests had started to leave an hour before. He watched them descend the front stairs and marveled at how banal, how trite, how predictable their conversations were. From where he sat he could hear everything they said on this snowy January night. Most of them mentioned his mother. "Old Mrs. Flagg is really something, isn't she?" was the most usual comment; followed by "just can't believe how well she looks." "Bright as a button," and "Hope I look that good when I'm her age."

They're just sucking up to her because of her money, Grizzy thought. *Who are they kidding? The Old Bag is a vegetable.* He took a sip from the leather-covered flask of Old Crow that he carried in his coat pocket. It was getting cold in the car.

Grizzy looked at his watch as the lights in the windows went out. It was eleven-thirty. Parker and Stevens would be wheeling Mamma into her bedroom. There. They'd just switched on the lights in her bedroom. They'd be undressing her and buttoning her into one of those long-sleeved flannel nightdresses she wore. The flannel always smelled musty, as if it had lain in a drawer too long. Now they'd be getting her out of the chair and sitting her up on the side of the bed. Now they'd be laying her down and covering her up. Now Parker would be tucking the hot water bottle beneath her feet. Poor Mamma. She always got cold at night. Poor circulation. Now Stevens would be efficiently covering her with the blue wool blanket and blue satin quilt and tucking the sides of the covers beneath the mattress. Now Parker would be plumping the down pillow and giving her the strong sleeping medicine. Grizzy started counting backwards from one hundred. By the time he got to seventy-three...

There... There... The bedroom light was out.

A check of his watch told him it was eleven-fifty. Parker and Stevens had it down to a science. They didn't waste a minute putting her to sleep. Real efficiency experts.

Grizzy had another swallow from his bottle and watched the door. There. It was opening, and Stevens came out. She closed the door behind her, locked it and then pulled her cape around her more tightly. The wind had picked up, but it wasn't snowing yet. She walked down the stairs and off toward the bus station. Grizzy watched the wind whip at the hem of her cape and thought, *Good. It's Parker's night.* Parker was a little Englishwoman. If there were any trouble, he could easily overpower her.

Grizzy exhaled slowly and carefully, as if he were blowing smoke rings. He watched his breath steam on the windshield. Thick clots of snow began to fall, accumulating until they completely covered the windshield and blocked his view of the building.

Mamma had been so unfair and mean. She never included him in her parties, never invited him to dinner anymore. Why hadn't she kept any of the promises she'd made him? She didn't seem to know he was alive. If he didn't get some money soon, he'd lose Tiptonbrook, the only thing he had left. Then what would he do? Libby and the kids wouldn't let him live with them. He couldn't live on the *Herreschauff* because he'd run it aground and sunk it last summer. Rotten luck—the insurance had lapsed. He *had* to get money from somewhere.

Mamma'd just have to help him.

Grizzy decided that he'd given Parker long enough to fall asleep. He screwed the silver cap onto the flask and slid it into his pocket. There was one shot left. He got out of the car, listened to the lock click metallically as he shut the door, strolled across the street and up the front stairs of Mamma's building.

Both street and square were empty. Only his trail of footsteps through the snow testified to his visit. He unlocked the front door without making a sound and slid into his mother's apartments.

In the front hall he waited until his eyes adjusted to the darkness. Then he released the doorknob. He listened for sounds but there were none. It was dead quiet. No one stirred. He proceeded. Past Parker's room, he paused. No sound. No strip of light beneath the door. *Good girl, Parker*, he thought. *Stay asleep. You've had a long, hard day.* Everything was going according to schedule.

He kept close to the wall to avoid squeaky floorboards, taking his weight on the balls of his feet. Then he got there.

He found the knob and opened Mamma's door. Through the dark room, he could hear her faint, regular breathing. Sound asleep. He closed the door behind him, grateful for the carpet that muffled his footfalls.

Mamma's bedside nightlight threw his shadow onto the ceiling in exaggerated relief as he bent over her and slowly removed her quilt. He did everything in slow motion because he didn't want her to wake and call Parker. Then it would all be ruined and she'd never be able to help him.

Grizzy placed one of the woolen blankets from her bed over the back and seat of her wheelchair. He wanted her to be comfy. Then he pushed the chair nearer to the bed and put on its brakes. There. Everything was ready for Mamma.

Inch by inch, he removed her last cover. Mamma was sleeping on her back, the hot water bottle beneath her feet. She had that musty old person smell. Her mouth was shut firmly. Except for her breathing, she was so still that she almost looked dead. Grizzy warmed his fingers with his breath in case he touched her bare skin. Starting at the neckline he unbuttoned her flannel nightdress, and then holding his breath, hoping that she wouldn't wake, he lifted her shoulders, freed her arms from the sleeves and pulled the nightdress down to her ankles. She wore a pair of cotton underpants, sparing him the sight of her completely nude body. He tried not to look at her as he lifted her to the wheelchair, but had the satisfaction of watching goose bumps rise on her shriveled shoulders. He sat her up in the wheelchair, supported her head against its high back and fastened the lap belt. There. She was finally in the chair and everything was going just as he'd planned.

Now to finish.

Grizzy opened each bedroom window as high as it would go, turned his mother's wheelchair around and pushed it in front of one of them. He stood behind her for a moment looking down at the pale, withered body strapped into the chair. There was nothing left to do now except to turn off the radiator at her feet. He left the apartment as silently as he had entered.

Outside, incredibly detailed, six-sided snowflakes were silently falling. Each one was different. But even as a kid, Grizzy hadn't marveled at snowflakes, and he didn't notice them now. Just before he got into his car he looked up at the second-floor window. He thought he could see the outline of his mother's pale head and shoulders against the darkness of the window. He took the flask from his pocket, drained it, and slid it back into his jacket. He smiled, waved at the window and in a soft voice he said, "Good night, dear Mamma. Pleasant dreams." Then he got into the car and drove away.

The weather forecast played on the radio, and by the time he was on the turnpike, the record cold snap had arrived. The snow stopped, the wind picked up, and it was already well below freezing.

Parker found Mrs. Flagg there the next morning, still sitting in the wheelchair in front of that open window. She was stiff and cold, and quite dead. Snow had blown in onto her knees. The coroner said she had died of exposure.

Although Parker and Stevens knew she was incapable of so much movement, the police dismissed it as suicide without investigation.

III

Nothing worked out the way Grizzy had planned.

When Mamma's will was read, he found that she had given him all the things he had already stolen from her and a measly thousand bucks. It was as if she had given him a final slap in the face. Everything else went to Dorothy Mary's little boy, Tommy. The will was ironclad, and his lawyers told him that it would be years before any legal action could be taken. Even then, it was doubtful that he could win.

Grizzy spent what money he had left on two cases of the finest champagne he could buy. He thought it was a fitting gesture, and went on a binge. Into his second case, the hallucinations about Mamma began. At least he *thought* they were hallucinations, but they seemed so real.

It was almost as if he were becoming Mamma.

He began to imagine her as she sat in front of the open window. He saw her struggle to get away from the cold. Saw how violently she shook, how her lips turned blue. She tried to call Parker, but all that came out was, "Aaakah... Aaahkah." After a while she stopped struggling. He knew that she no longer was so cold. He felt better when he realized how sleepy she became.

He imagined that he could see through her eyes into the snow-filled square. For the first time he noticed how the snow beneath each streetlamp caught the light and glittered as if someone had spread a blanket of diamonds. Then he knew she would have seen someone outside waving up at her window, trying to get her attention. She recognized her son Grizzy, saw him turn up his coat collar and get into his car. It was as if Grizzy had said goodbye. He must be going to a party but why hadn't he taken her with him? She watched Grizzy's car drive away and heard him laugh as if the sound came from inside her head.

Faintly and far away, she heard dogs barking. The sound got louder and louder and then all the dogs that she'd ever loved came bounding across the square. There were Mother's poodles, Moppy and Inky; Fritz the wire-haired terrier; and Mitzi the Airedale that she'd had as a little girl. She knew it wasn't possible. All the dogs had been dead for years, but she saw them, nevertheless. They fawned and chased and tumbled like puppies in the snow, sending spumes of white high against the night sky. The snow settled back beneath the streetlamps, lime lighting the frolicking dogs. They were having such fun that Grizzy laughed. He knew his mother would want to run and join them, but that she'd never be able to get out of her wheelchair. A part of him felt sorry for Mamma and wanted to help her, wishing he hadn't left her in front of that window; but that part of Grizzy was submerged as his hallucination continued.

He saw his mother try to undo the lap buckle of her wheelchair—but her fingers weren't strong enough, and her hands fell uselessly at her sides. The lap belt was forgotten. She had seen something else out in the square, something unbelievable. As she watched the dogs, she saw that long leashes snaked after them. Long, blood-red leashes against the snow.

There was the commotion of voices and laughter. Familiar laughter. Three people ran into the square as Mrs. Flagg looked on—her husband Stanley Griswold Flagg, and Dorothy Mary in her debutante's dress. And, behind them, puffing to keep up, ran her own father in his waistcoat, side whiskers, and top hat. Mrs. Flagg knew this couldn't be possible. They were all dead. How could they be running after a pack of dogs outside

The Dressing Drink

her bedroom window? But Grizzy saw them, too, as they scurried through the snow, stooping to grab at those elusive leashes and laughing as the dogs whisked them out of their fingers. It was some kind of joke—maybe a charade. But those long-lost loved ones saw her and waved. She wanted them to stop, to explain, to wait for her; but the dogs ran on, and the people ran after them.

Just as quickly as it had been filled with sound and movement, the square was empty. Grizzy saw his mother's lips tremble, and she started to cry. He looked out at the square through her eyes and saw that there were no tracks in the snow beneath the streetlights; she imagined all of it. The cold took her over again, and the only sound came from the snow that drifted onto her knees.

But then one last figure ran into the square. He wore his Army uniform and his medals shone in the lamplight. It was David, and in one hand he had Dorothy Mary's picture hat that had blown off. He was calling to the others, too, asking them to wait. When he saw her in the window and noticed her crying, David stretched out his hand to her and said, "Come on, Mother. Come on, Old Girl. I'll wait for you."

IV

Grizzy sat in the front seat of his Mercedes. It was all that was left that belonged to him. Tiptonbrook had been sold. The new owners would move in the next day. He started the car's engine and listened with pleasure to its powerful roar in the enclosed space. There were two bottles of champagne left. He removed the lead foil and the wire cap of the next-to-last bottle and eased off the cork without popping it in that garish fashion that some people seemed to think signified gaiety.

He put the bottle to his lips and drank greedily. Some of the wine dribbled down his chin and splashed onto his shirt. He lost consciousness before he finished the bottle.

The gardener found Grizzy the next day. The Mercedes had run out of gas, and before he died, Grizzy had vomited all down the front of his evening clothes. The last bottle of champagne was on the seat beside him. He'd never opened it.

30

The performers have fled without taking their bows, the way they always do. Every night they hurry off into the darkness, as if eager to arrive at parties to which we haven't been invited. They've hung up their soiled costumes, washed off their makeup, and disappeared. I can't call them back. Not now. Even if I wanted to. It's too late.

I'm the only one that's left. I haven't been the ringmaster in this circus long enough to devise a clever way of getting offstage. The only thing I can do is hope you won't notice how I've bitten the cuticle surrounding each fingernail. Some are bleeding; all are painful. Perhaps you won't see. Maybe you won't realize that I'm afraid to be alone. After you're gone, I will busy myself with the maintenance that's necessary to keep the show going. Repair torn canvas and listen for footsteps outside. I'll be hoping for another visitor so I can tell my story again.

If I'd thought of it before, I could have hired a man in a silver suit to be shot from a cannon. Or, I could have gotten a troupe of Chinese fire-eaters and sword swallowers. If they'd rehearsed, the band could play an upbeat number, and the chorus girls could wiggle and bat their eyelashes in mock sadness. I'm sure that any of these tricks would satisfactorily provide your cue for departure.

But before you go there's just one more thing. Thank you for listening to my story. Not thank you in the perfunctory way that we acknowledge restroom attendants when they hand us a clean towel, but in the most sincere way I can manage. You've given me the chance to understand myself a little better. And I have the feeling that maybe my show will change because of it. Perhaps I won't be so cavalier about my parents' deaths in the future.

I used to think it was convenient to be an orphan. Not like my illegitimate cousin Derrick who was discarded like a piece of paper ripped into a million little pieces, never able to be reassembled. Instead I fancied the tragic image of the desolate child wielding absolute power. Now I know that not having parents makes the puzzle even more difficult to solve. When your parents die before you can appreciate them, you're forced to assume a burden of loneliness, wriggling like Grizzy's trout on a hook. You can never abandon that burden, or misplace it, or thrust it onto someone else's shoulders. It's yours for life. I've got to pick up that burden once again after you leave, and I'm not looking forward to it.

I hope you won't be upset that our goodbye has been so abrupt and impersonal, but I've got chores to do and I must get started. The tents need to be mended, the rigging's got to be tightened, the flaps have to be secured for the night.

Come back another day, some other time, when you're in the mood for amusement. I can't promise you much, but... I guarantee that you'll never find any gaudy bunting outside this tent.

There will never be a Barker,

or a Fat Lady,

or an oily, tawdry Midget.

But me, I'll always be here. After all, I have nothing better to do. No matter what happens, part of me will always be nursing the ghost of a dressing drink.

Thomas King Flagg with his companions.

www.ingramcontent.com/pod-product-compliance
Lightning Source LLC
Chambersburg PA
CBHW080452100526
44581CB00004B/113